Business Transfers, Family Firms and Entrepreneurship

T0334389

'Business transfer' refers to the transfer of ownership and leadership from one or more outgoing owner-manager(s) to one or more incoming owner-manager(s). Apart from all the company's material assets, it presupposes that information, relationships, know-how and social capital are also transmitted from one to the other.

While much of the research on entrepreneurship has focused on new business ventures, few studies have considered business transfers as an alternative way of embarking on entrepreneurial activities. *Business Transfers, Family Firms and Entrepreneurship* provides the international community with more comprehensive, state-of-the-art business transfer studies, which will enrich readers' understanding. The business transfer is examined through different prisms: family businesses, internal business transfers to employees, external business transfers and woman in business transfers.

This book deals with business transfer as a whole, following a logic of continuity and sustainability for the transferred firm. It offers a refreshing point of view on business transfers, in terms of both the process and the actors, and from both the seller's and the buyer's sides. It presents the research on all types of business transfer including internal and external transfers and will be of interest to researchers, academics and students in the fields of entrepreneurship, small business management, family business and strategic management. It can also be instructive for practitioners and stakeholders involved in a business transfer.

Bérangère Deschamps is Professor of Entrepreneurship at Grenoble Alps University and Researcher at the CERAG Laboratory, France.

Audrey Missonier is Professor at Montpellier Business School, France, and a member of MRM (Research in Management) and of the LabEx Entrepreneurship.

Catherine Thévenard-Puthod is Professor of Entrepreneurship and Strategic Management in the Savoie Mont-Blanc University and a member of IREGE Research Institute, France.

Paulette Robic works at the Département Gestion des Entreprises et des Administrations, LEMNA, University of Nantes, France.

Dominique Barbelivien is Researcher at IAE Nantes, University of Nantes, France.

Routledge Studies in Entrepreneurship and Small Business
Edited by Robert Blackburn
University of Liverpool, UK

13 Information Technology and Competitive Advantage in Small Firms
Brian Webb and Frank Schlemmer

14 Entrepreneurship and Small Business Development in Post-Socialist
Economies
David Smallbone and Friederike Welter

15 The Management of Small and Medium Enterprises
Matthias Fink and Sascha Kraus

16 Small Business and Effective ICT: Stories and Practical Insights
*Carmine Sellitto, Scott Bingley, David A. Banks,
and Stephen Burgess*

17 Motivating SMEs to Cooperate and Internationalize
A Dynamic Perspective
George Tesar and Zsuzsanna Vincze

18 How Small to Medium Enterprises Thrive and Survive in Turbulent
Times: From Deconstructing to Synthesizing Organizational
Resilience Capabilities
Yiu Hia Chu and Kosmas Smyrnios

19 Managing People in Small and Medium Enterprises in Turbulent
Contexts
Alexandros Psychogios and Rea Prouska

20 Business Transfers, Family Firms and Entrepreneurship
*Edited by Bérangère Deschamps, Audrey Missonier, Catherine
Thévenard-Puthod, Paulette Robic and Dominique Barbelivien*

For more information about this series, please visit: www.routledge.
com/Routledge-Studies-in-Entrepreneurship-and-Small-Business/
book-series/RSESB

Business Transfers, Family Firms and Entrepreneurship

Edited by Bérangère Deschamps,
Audrey Missonier,
Catherine Thévenard-Puthod,
Paulette Robic and
Dominique Barbelivien

Routledge
Taylor & Francis Group

NEW YORK AND LONDON

First published 2021
by Routledge
52 Vanderbilt Avenue, New York, NY 10017

and by Routledge
2 Park Square, Milton Park, Abingdon, Oxon, OX14 4RN

Routledge is an imprint of the Taylor & Francis Group, an informa business

© 2021 Taylor & Francis

The right of Bérangère Deschamps, Audrey Missonier, Catherine Thévenard-Puthod, Paulette Robic and Dominique Barbelivien to be identified as the authors of the editorial material, and of the authors for their individual chapters, has been asserted in accordance with sections 77 and 78 of the Copyright, Designs and Patents Act 1988.

Library of Congress Cataloging-in-Publication Data
Names: Deschamps, Bérangère, editor. | Missonier, Audrey, 1979– editor. | Thévenard-Puthod, Catherine, 1972– editor. | Robic, Paulette, 1958– editor. | Barbelivien, Dominique, 1970– editor.
Title: Business transfers, family firms and entrepreneurship / edited by Bérangère Deschamps, Audrey Missonier, Catherine Thévenard-Puthod, Paulette Robic and Dominique Barbelivien.
Description: New York, NY : Routledge, 2021. | Series: Routledge studies in entrepreneurship and small business | Includes bibliographical references and index.
Identifiers: LCCN 2020035766 (print) | LCCN 2020035767 (ebook) | ISBN 9780367900854 (hbk) | ISBN 9781003022527 (ebk)
Subjects: LCSH: Entrepreneurship. | Small business. | Family-owned business enterprises | Strategic planning.
Classification: LCC HB615 .B93 2021 (print) | LCC HB615 (ebook) | DDC 658.1/6—dc23
LC record available at https://lccn.loc.gov/2020035766
LC ebook record available at https://lccn.loc.gov/2020035767

ISBN: 978-0-367-90085-4 (hbk)
ISBN: 978-1-003-02252-7 (ebk)

Typeset in Sabon
by Apex CoVantage, LLC

Contents

Foreword   viii

Introduction   1

PART I
Definitions   5

1 Business Transfer: Historical Perspectives, Definitions
   and the Transfer Process   7
   BÉRANGÈRE DESCHAMPS

2 Revisiting the Entrepreneurial Exit Decision Process:
   A Decision-Making Model   22
   MARIE-JOSÉE DRAPEAU AND MARIPIER TREMBLAY

PART II
Family Business Transfers   37

3 Emotions in Family Business Succession   39
   SOUMAYA SFEIR

4 Family Business Transfer: A Stressful Event for Successors   52
   FLORENCE GUILIANI AND LUIS CISNEROS

5 The Making of Family Entrepreneurs: How Heirs
   Become Entrepreneurs and Take Over a Family Business   70
   PAULETTE ROBIC, DOMINIQUE BARBELIVIEN
   AND NICOLAS ANTHEAUME

6 Succession and Family Business in Between Emotional
  and Financial Issues: The Role of a Governance
  With a Two-Tier System   84
  CÉLINE BARRÉDY

7 Succession and Strategic Renewal in Family Firms:
  Insights From a French Family Firm   99
  DIDIER CHABAUD, MARIEM HANNACHI AND HEDI YEZZA

PART III
Internal Business Transfers to Employees   115

8 Towards a Better Understanding of SME Employee
  Buyouts   117
  CATHERINE THÉVENARD-PUTHOD AND CÉDRIC FAVRE

9 Is a Workers' Cooperative an Effective Means
  for Transferring SMEs?   132
  MARIE-CHRISTINE BARBOT-GRIZZO

PART IV
External Business Transfers   147

10 A Research Framework for External Business Transfers
   of SMEs   149
   BÉRANGÈRE DESCHAMPS AND SUSANNE DURST

11 The Legitimacy of the External Buyer: Issues
   and Means of Acquisitions   165
   LYÈS MAZARI, SANDRINE BERGER-DOUCE
   AND BÉRANGÈRE DESCHAMPS

12 From Outsider to Insider: Organisational Socialisation
   in Takeover Situations   179
   SONIA BOUSSAGUET

13 How to Effectively Support External Buyers
   in a Post-Business Transfer Situation   193
   CATHERINE THÉVENARD-PUTHOD

PART V
Women in Business Transfers 207

14 Family as an Institution to Investigate the Role
of Women in the Transfer of Family Businesses 209
PAULETTE ROBIC

15 Gender and Succession in the Family Business 222
CHRISTINA CONSTANTINIDIS

16 Daughters: Invisible Heroes of Family Businesses? 236
AUDREY MISSONIER, ANNABELLE JAOUEN
AND BÉATRICE ALBERT

17 Female External Successors: Difficulties During the
Business Transfer Process and Types of Support Required 251
BÉRANGÈRE DESCHAMPS AND CATHERINE
THÉVENARD-PUTHOD

Biographies 265
Index 268

Foreword

What are we talking about when we talk about business transfers? Why would business transfers, as a social and economic phenomenon, be of the first importance for entrepreneurs, policy-makers, entrepreneurship stakeholders and, more particularly, for entrepreneurship scholars? These issues came to mind when I started reading this edited book.

Making an attempt to throw some light on the latter question would be probably easier than answering the former. So, let start with the 'why' issue. Looking at the literature and taking stock of most papers focusing on the topic leads to the evidence that business transfers are mainly a concern for policy-makers and institutions like governments, EU, OECD, professional trade unions, chambers of commerce, etc. To give only one illustration, the European Commission is claiming that "Every year, around 450,000 firms and over two million employees are transferred to new owners. However, up to one-third of these transfers may not be successful".[1] Consequently, for the European Commission, supporting business transfers is equally important to the EU economy as supporting start-ups. It seems easy to understand that policy-makers and stakeholders need to deal with at least two main challenges. The first refers to the number of firms (mainly small and medium-sized enterprises) (SMEs) for which the business owner is nearing retirement or has the intention to transfer her/his company for a lot of reasons in relation to more or less unexpected events such as illness, death, sudden incapacity, career or entrepreneurial opportunities. To avoid any problem, and notably the risk of losing businesses and jobs, there is an urgent need, case by case, for SME owners and their stakeholders to identify the most suitable business successors and forms of transfer. The second challenge relates to the high SME failure rate after a business transfer, but also to the impact and effects of firm ownership and management transfer on employees, jobs, work conditions and firm performance. There is a need to get a better understanding, through research and good practices, on the success and failure factors at all analysis levels (individual, organisational, environmental) of business transfers whatever the form of transfer.

Let's now examine the 'what' issue. What are we talking about when we talk about business transfers? There is no consensus at all about the meaning of business transfer between policy-makers and practitioners on the one hand, and researchers on the other. Moreover, the meaning of business transfer differs from one researcher to another depending on disciplines, interests in research or contextual/institutional factors. Policy-makers and practitioners (notably, SMEs owners) have a broad view of business transfer, generally focused on SMEs, and including all types of situations such as family business succession, transfers to employees, sales to external individuals or other enterprises, and initial public offerings. Researchers have a narrower view based on a fragmentation of the whole picture into a set of research areas such as, among others, family business (FB), management buyout (MBO), management buy-in (MBI), mergers and acquisitions (M&As), initial public offerings (IPOs) and firm takeovers. Research in these fields focuses not only on SMEs, but on larger-scale companies in a number of cases. Finally, apart from family business research, a well-established field of research in management with a strong relationship with entrepreneurship, there is very little research on these areas, based on international publication stocktaking, that attract a high-level of interest by entrepreneurship and management scholars, despite the fact that for the European Commission, "buying an existing company is an alternative way of starting a business. It is often more advantageous than starting from scratch".[2]

However, the definition of business transfer in this book seems very close to that proposed by policy-makers and international institutions. The European Union, for example, defines business transfer as "*the process of handing over a business to new owners and usually new management*".[3] From a general point of view, business transfer, in the world of business, relates to the transfer of ownership of a firm (or a business unit) to another enterprise or individual. This transfer notably aims at assuring the business continuity and economic activity of the concerned firm. In this book,

> Business transfer refers to the transition from one or more outgoing owner-managers to one or more incoming owner-managers. It presupposes that information, relationships, know-how and social capital are transmitted from one to the other, following a logic of continuity and sustainability for the transferred firm.[4]

The focus is much more on individuals rather than organisations. Moreover, there is a clear willingness of the book editors to distinguish business transfers to individual buyers from mergers and acquisitions. Together with the francophone culture, the French touch gives the book a specific flavour. It is very unusual to read a book that is the outcome of a collective work including 24 researchers belonging to the same research community founded three years ago around the topic of business transfer and entrepreneurship. The research group has a clear objective, notably with this book, to share with the international community the originality and the specificities of its particular approach (i.e., adopting an individual level of analysis, combining business transfer and entrepreneurship, and focusing on external business transfer to a physical person). Such an approach differs from what we can read in the international literature in which business transfers are mainly examined through the theoretical lenses of family business research and a focus on intergenerational business transfers within the same family (intra-family transfers). Even though, out of 17 chapters, eight address research issues in the family business context, the book also examines research questions in relation to internal transfers to employees, external business transfers and the place and role of women in business transfer.

The book offers interesting and contextualised knowledge looking at understudied research issues. Knowledge comes from the in-depth examination of process dynamics, difficulties and challenges of SME business transfers from an entrepreneurial point of view in the context of French-speaking countries. The book is opening new research avenues and inviting international scholars for a discussion around them. I hope this call will be heard and lead to international research collaboration. Among the number of research issues that remain underexplored that I would personally be interested in gaining knowledge about, there are three that appear important to move the business transfer research area further. The first would be to conceptually define the research object, such it has been outlined in this collective work, particularly in discussing its relationships, similarities and differences with other concepts and research areas, like MBO, MBI, IPO, and M&A. A second issue would be to examine the role and impact of institutions (formal and informal) and contexts on business transfer processes and outcomes. Finally, the third issue is much more a paradox: why do entrepreneurship and management scholars (apart from those engaged in family business research) pay very little attention to research on business transfers while policy-makers, entrepreneurs, SME owners and other stakeholders regularly express economic and social worries and needs about the phenomenon?

Anyway, I strongly encourage my French-speaking colleagues to go further in this stream of research and to succeed in building up a more-than-needed international research community.

Professor Alain Fayolle
Past President Academy of Management,
Entrepreneurship Division
Past Distinguished Professor and Entrepreneurship
Research Director—EM-Lyon Business School

Notes

1. https://ec.europa.eu/growth/smes/promoting-entrepreneurship/advice-oppor
tunities/transfer-business_en
2. https://ec.europa.eu/growth/smes/promoting-entrepreneurship/advice-oppor
tunities/transfer-business_en
3. European Union (2011): Business Dynamics: Start-ups, Business Transfers
and Bankruptcy; https://ec.europa.eu/growth/content/start-ups business trans
fers-and-bankruptcy-0_en
4. Introductory chapter

Introduction

This monograph is the achievement of a goal set by BeT (for Business Transfer and Entrepreneurship), a research group dedicated to communicating francophone knowledge on business transfers. Our objective was to provide the international community with a richer and more comprehensive view—indeed, a state-of-the-art view—on business transfer studies. The business transfer is a process, and the scope of this process is expected to greatly increase in the years to come. According to a 2013 European Commission report, a third of European Union business leaders will retire in the next ten years. It was estimated that 450,000 small and medium-sized enterprises (SMEs) and more than 2.8 million jobs would be affected each year. However, up to one in three transmissions fail, potentially threatening some 150,000 businesses and 600,000 jobs (European Commission, 2013). It is therefore essential to create the appropriate conditions for business transfers.

BeT was founded in January 2017 by Bérangère Deschamps (University of Grenoble Alps) and Didier Chabaud (University of Sorbonne Paris), both French experts in business transfer and entrepreneurship research. It is sponsored by two francophone research associations: the Academy of Entrepreneurship and Innovation (A.E.I.) and the International Association for Entrepreneurship and SME Research (A.I.R.E.PME).

The goal of this research group is to unite the francophone research community around the concept of business transfers, as between France and Québec alone, more than 20 years of research has been dedicated to this topic. BeT also intends to ensure the continuity of research in this field by encouraging and enhancing the smooth transmission of knowledge from senior researchers to younger ones, and by building an international community on business transfers within which researchers from the entrepreneurship and family businesses fields can dialogue.

Business transfer refers to the transition from one or more outgoing owner-managers to one or more incoming owner-managers. It presupposes that information, relationships, know-how and social capital are transmitted from one to the other, following a logic of continuity and sustainability for the transferred firm. The new entrant (natural or legal person) becomes the owner of the targeted firm and assumes leadership alone, as a part of a team or sheltered behind a legal structure. We distinguish business transfers to one or more individual buyers from mergers and acquisitions, in which a company is sold to another company or group. Mergers and acquisitions raise other issues, particularly related to the restructuring imposed by the merger of two companies whose businesses, cultures and structures may be very distant. In the international literature, business transfers are mainly examined within the field of family business research, where the focus remains on intergenerational business transfers (Sharma *et al.*, 2003; Le Breton-Miller *et al.*, 2004; Sharma, 2004; De Massis *et al.*, 2008; Salvato *et al.*, 2010). French-speaking researchers, on the other hand, have been conducting research on a wide variety of business transfers (intra-family transfers, of course, but especially to one or more external buyers and even employees) and related topics. In particular, one of the francophone community's specificities is its focus on the issue of the external business transfer to a physical person, and here researchers have acquired broad knowledge. While much of the research on entrepreneurship has focused on new business ventures (Delmar and Shane, 2004; Townsend *et al.*, 2010), a few studies have considered external business transfers as an alternative way of embarking on entrepreneurial activities (Durst and Gueldenberg, 2010; Parker and Van Praag, 2012).

Originally made up of well-regarded specialists, the BeT research group has been enriched by PhD students and assistant professors. In 2020, 36 researchers had become members and, unsurprisingly, its output is also growing. A book of case studies on business transfer was published in May 2020 (EMS Editions). Several tracks for international conferences have been organised and a special issue in the *International Journal of Entrepreneurship and Small Business* (IJESB) is also well underway. This monograph marks another achievement for the group, this time with the objective of sharing francophone knowledge on business transfers. To date, most of this research, which offers rich insights and major lessons for the entrepreneurship field, has been published in French-language journals and has thus had limited international readership.

It is within this context that this monograph was conceived. We here offer the international community a more comprehensive state-of-the-art of business transfer studies, which we hope will enrich and inspire our readers' thinking. The business transfer is thus examined through the prism of three themes: small and medium-sized enterprises (SMEs), family businesses and entrepreneurship. Twenty-four researchers have contributed, all writing at least one chapter on a topic about which they have been recognised for. They provide the fruits of their in-depth research on the business transfer process and the actors' behaviours. What has emerged is, in our opinion, a refreshing point of view on business transfers in terms of process and actors and from both the seller's and the buyer's perspectives. The book presents some of the abundant and complex thinking on business transfers, and it takes into account the semantic evolution of this term and its various definitions (e.g., succession, transmission, takeover and transfer), forms (e.g., internal, external, heritage and property), approaches (e.g., managerial, macroeconomic, historical and sociological) and processes (e.g., planning and learning), as well as the variety of actors (family members, board of directors, employees, coaches, external stakeholders, women, etc.) and the emotions it generates (grief, feelings attached to role change, etc.). In addition to presenting state-of-the-art research, we identify the key contributions of French-speaking research for the renewal and advancement of business transfer theory.

The essence of the book is the examination of the difficulties and challenges of SME business transfers from an entrepreneurial point of view. From this perspective, the book is organised around business transfer modes (family business transfers, internal business transfers to employees and external business transfers) and it is structured into five parts.

The first part is divided into two theoretical chapters that review the research literature on business transfers and discuss some of the most recent theoretical advances. Those chapters present a framework and agenda for research on business transfers and the entrepreneurial exit decision.

The second part contains five chapters dedicated to family business transfers. This part addresses the question of how can the inevitable emotions be managed and the heirs prepared for a successful transfer and the firm's sustainability? One focus is on how the psychological stress associated with the process of business transfer can affect the mental and psychological health of both the incumbent and successor. The authors also discuss how the choices relative to the succession are actually driven by emotions.

The third part focuses on a category of actors largely understudied in business transfer research: employees. This section explores the specific difficulties that employees face when they attempt to take over the company in which they are currently working. The authors also discuss the benefits of a peculiar type of employee buyout: workers' cooperatives.

The fourth part includes four chapters on external business transfers. This mode of transfer is specific because the new CEOs, as buyers, are external to the firm. They know neither the organisational culture and the employees nor the other stakeholders. One of the main challenges for external buyers is integration and socialisation within existing teams. Their needs for support are thus quite specific.

The last part is devoted to women buyers, a more recent topic. The following questions are addressed: Do women face specific difficulties? What might be the benefits of being a woman buyer? Why are daughters still not entirely considered as potential successors?

This monograph presents an overview of the knowledge acquired on business transfers with a view to promoting knowledge transfer. It contains theoretical thinking and cases studies and the themes of the chapters are various. In this regard, it is intended for a varied audience, ranging from researchers, teachers and postgraduate students to practitioners and business transfer stakeholders. As the monograph provides many examples of successors and buyers, we believe it would be helpful for the practitioners around the outgoing and incoming CEOs to be aware of the difficulties that arise during a business transfer so that they can guide them towards a successful and sustainable business transfer.

References

De Massis, A., Chua, J.H. and Chrisman, J.J. (2008). "Factors preventing intra-family succession", *Family Business Review*, *21*(2), 183–199.

Delmar, F. and Shane, S. (2004). "Legitimating first: organizing activities and the survival of new ventures", *Journal of Business Venturing*, *19*(3), 385–410.

Durst, S. and Gueldenberg, S. (2010). "What makes SMEs attractive to external successors?" *VINE: The Journal of Information and Knowledge Management Systems*, *40*(2), 108–135.

European Commission. (2013). *Programme for the competitiveness of enterprises and small and medium-sized enterprises (COSME) and repealing decision.* https://eur-lex.europa.eu/legal-content/EN/TXT/PDF/uri=CELEX:32013R1287&qid=1591197437662&from=FR.

Le Breton-Miller, I., Miller, D. and Steier, L.P. (2004). "Toward an integrative model of effective FOB succession", *Entrepreneurship Theory and Practice*, *28*(4), 305–328.

Parker, S.C. and Van Praag, C.M. (2012). "The entrepreneur's mode of entry: business takeover or new venture start?" *Journal of Business Venturing*, *27*(1), 31–46.

Salvato, C., Chirico, F. and Sharma, P. (2010). "Understanding exit from the founder's business in family firms", in A. Stewart, T. Lumpkin and J. Katz (Eds.), *Entrepreneurship and family business. Advances in entrepreneurship, firm emergence and growth*, 31–85, Greenwich, CT: Emerald Group Publishing, Chapter 12.

Sharma, P. (2004). "An overview of the field of family business studies: current status and directions for the future", *Family Business Review*, *17*(1), 1–36.

Sharma, P., Chrisman, J.J. and Chua, J.H. (2003). "Predictors of satisfaction with the succession process in family firms", *Journal of Business Venturing*, *18*, 667–687.

Townsend, D.M., Busenitz, L.W. and Arthurs, J.D. (2010). "To start or not to start: outcome and ability expectations in the decision to start a new venture", *Journal of Business Venturing*, *25*(2), 191–202.

Part I

Definitions

The two conceptual chapters that open this book provide us with two models to define and analyse the phenomenon of business transfers. The emphasis is put on transfer as a process. We are hence offered the opportunity to think about business transfers from two new angles.

Chapter 1, **Business Transfer: Historical Perspectives, Definitions and the Transfer Process**, reviews the history of the concept of business transfer. **Bérangère Deschamps** proposes a consensus definition to be used in this field, as well as a method for mapping business transfers. A breakdown of the transfer process into three steps of a recurrent cycle—entry, transfer and entrepreneurial exit—is introduced as a framework to analyse the entire process. The business transfer process is thus modelled in such a way as to propose a unified vision that cuts across the French and English-speaking worlds.

Chapter 2, **Revisiting the Entrepreneurial Exit Decision Process: A Decision-Making Model**, proposes to delve deeper into the question of the exit of the outgoing CEO by revisiting the decision-making process leading to the exit. **Marie-Josée Drapeau** and **Maripier Tremblay** build upon the model of strategic decision processes, which has been adapted and refined. They detail the decision-making process of the CEO about to leave the SME, which makes it of primary interest. They end by proposing a reviewed model that integrates the factors that can be used for further studies.

1 Business Transfer

Historical Perspectives, Definitions and the Transfer Process

Bérangère Deschamps

Over the last two decades, the topic of transferring a business has been of increasing interest to researchers. On one side are the francophone researchers. Since 2011, francophone researchers have seemed to agree on the term 'transmission-takeover process', which refers to the relationship between two main actors: the outgoing and incoming CEOs (Cadieux and Deschamps, 2011). Through transmission and takeover, ownership and management are transferred from one CEO to another (Cadieux and Brouard, 2009). On the other side, Anglophone academic literature has studied this issue almost exclusively in the context of family business succession (Le Breton-Miller *et al.*, 2004; Sharma, 2004 for instance).

The two research topics—business transmission-takeover and family business succession—appear distinct and specific; indeed, so far, they have not crossed over. However, Haddadj and d'Andria (1998) have questioned whether the differences between internal (i.e., family) and external transfers are significant enough for these topics to be separated to this degree. Barbot and Richomme-Huet (2007) also question the boundaries of these two academic fields. In this chapter, we aim to bring these two research communities together through entry and exit theories. Indeed, Parker and Van Praag (2012) and Block *et al.* (2010) include takeovers in their entrepreneurial entry mode, and Nordqvist *et al.* (2013) integrate the exit mode in their definition of the entrepreneurial process. In doing so, these authors cast a new light on the field: through their association of entry and exit, they recognise that the founder will one day be the outgoing CEO.

We have so far observed two different ways to study business transfers. Academic literature also demonstrates that there are many ways in which a business may be taken over, for example, internal vs external or the whole firm vs a part of it (Deschamps and Paturel, 2009). Indeed, from a closer look at the published papers, we have noted confusion in the vocabulary in both the francophone and Anglophone literature. For instance, Parker and Van Praag (2012), who compare new ventures and takeovers as entrepreneurial entry modes, do not specify the kinds of takeovers they include in their study. Meanwhile, francophone researchers use 'transmission', 'succession' and 'reprise' interchangeably, whereas we observe nuances between the terms: 'transmission' refers to the outgoing CEO's point of view; 'succession' concerns family business transfer and 'reprise' refers to the incoming CEO's point of view. Chapter 10 (Deschamps and Durst, this volume) also displays confusion in vocabulary, as the authors do not always specify which kinds of business transfers they are referring to. How can researchers work on papers in which the vocabulary does not precisely correspond to the business transfer modes they are studying? Words create meaning. Yet, if this meaning is not defined, they can obscure comprehension of the issue.

In this chapter, we pursue two aims: first, we analyse existing literature to demonstrate the evolution of the concept and opinions over time; second, we propose a conceptual framework on business transfers with the ambition of becoming the international reference for future research in entrepreneurship and family business. In doing so, this chapter proposes three contributions: (1) a unified concept of business transfers for the academic community; (2) a mapping of different transfer modes as a frame of reference; and (3) a processual model of the business transfer to unify the previously separated Anglophone and francophone visions.

The chapter is divided into three sections. The first provides a historical perspective of the existing research on business transfers. The second defines the issue. The third section explains the business transfer process in the context of entry and exit entrepreneurial theories.

Historical Issues Around Business Transfers

Until the end of the 1980s, entrepreneurship was associated with a new venture (Vesper, 1980; Shapero, 1984; Gartner, 1988; Davidson, 1989; Bygrave and Hofer, 1991; Bygrave, 1995). In 1988, Carland, Hoy and Carland asked the following questions: "Is buying a firm an entrepreneurial activity? Should people who take over a firm be excluded from entrepreneurship studies?" (p. 36). These questions went unanswered, but they became the basis for a broadening of the definition of entrepreneurship beyond new ventures as the only way to become an entrepreneur. For instance, Donckels (1995) has since studied the takeover as an entrepreneurial career, while Sharma and Chrisman (1999) recognise the person who takes over a business as an entrepreneur (albeit in the context of family business succession).

In France, research has mostly focused on external business transfers. The first PhD thesis on business takeovers, for example, studied strategic choices from the point of view of the incoming CEO (Siegel, 1989). Deschamps (2000) elucidated the takeover process (by an external individual, a previous employee or a previous commercial partner). After this work, francophone researchers agreed to include business takeovers within the academic field of entrepreneurship (Deschamps, 2003). Several studies have contributed to a deeper understanding of both the takeover process (Boussaguet, 2005; De Freyman, 2009; Saoudi, 2010) and actors' behaviours (Picard and Thévenard-Puthod, 2004; Deschamps and Geindre, 2011), all of which have focused on the perspective of the incoming CEO. Research on the previous owner-manager of the target firm has also increased (Cadieux and Lorrain, 2004; Cadieux, 2007; Bah, 2009).

Excluding Barbot and Richomme-Huet (2007) and Meiar (2015), exit and entry are considered as quite distinct in the literature. However, Cadieux and Deschamps (2011) explain that former and new CEOs cannot be considered as two separate and independent actors, but rather as partners who share a common project: transferring the firm from one to the other. According to Cadieux and Brouard (2009), the issue of transfer always applies to takeovers because the outgoing CEO is, it can be assumed, concerned with the continuity of the firm, while the incoming CEO aims to manage an existing activity. In a special issue of a scientific review, Cadieux and Deschamps (2009) invited researchers to think of takeovers as linked to transfer and to consider the relationships and the interconnected actions between the two CEOs.

Since then, the literature has been enriched by new scientific knowledge on the relationship between the two main stakeholders, for instance on transferring: networks (Geindre, 2009), social capital (Coeurderoy and Lwango, 2014), social representation (Bornard and Thévenard-Puthod, 2009), strategic orientation (Grazzini *et al.*, 2009) and corporate social responsibility (Mazari, 2018). Meiar (2015) compared previous and following outgoing and incoming CEOs' perceptions of the business model of the target firm. This duality has also inspired research in different business areas, such as the specifics of industry (Audet and St-Jean, 2009; Picard, 2009), the wealth of the firm (Geraudel Jaouen *et al.*, 2009) or advisors (Deschamps *et al.*, 2010; Thévenard-Puthod *et al.*, 2014). In parallel, some authors have studied the stakeholders in the business transfer: employees (Estève, 1997), characteristics of the outgoing CEO (Bah, 2009), incoming CEOs in the context of a team (Thévenard-Puthod, 2014), sibling successors (Cisneros and Deschamps, 2014), advisors (Deschamps *et al.*, 2014) and succession by a spouse following the CEO's death (Robic and Antheaume, 2014).

Chronologically speaking, the two actors' business transfer processes are separated, but francophone academic literature has tended to unify these points of view, placing them on a continuum from exit to entry. Researchers have thus understood takeovers within a global perspective that does not bring the outgoing and incoming CEOs into opposition. In this context, De Freyman and Richomme-Huet (2010) have suggested a unified vision for takeovers based on two criteria: the transmission mode (internal/external to the family or to the firm) and the recipient of what they call the 'succession' (inheritor, employee, physical person or legal person).

In parallel, entrepreneurial entry and exit theories in the Anglophone world also began to integrate the two actors in a business transfer. Business transfers are a good illustration of the entrepreneurial process because they are at once an exit mode (for the outgoing CEO) and an entry mode (for the incoming CEO) (Parker and Van Praag, 2012; Block *et al.*, 2010; Nordqvist *et al.*, 2013). Nordqvist *et al.* (2013) explain that "the entrepreneurial process does not end with new venture creation and that entrepreneurial exit should be acknowledged as a core part of the entrepreneurial process" (p. 1087). Indeed, with the entrepreneurial process the authors offer an integrated vision of entrepreneurship. This vision was ground-breaking: until then, Anglophone literature had never considered business transfer as a part of entrepreneurship; on the contrary, business transfer was reserved for family business (see Part IV, Chapter 10, this volume, for some explanations).

Finally, scientific communities do not cross over. We wonder why, because the characteristics of the process, the needs of the main actors or the emotions each one feels are not self-evident. Even if the family element is characteristic, it appears that such issues are relevant to all types of business transfers.

In summary, francophone researchers have consolidated knowledge on the subject of business transfers, specifically on external takeovers and from a dual perspective of the outgoing and incoming CEOs. The evolution of the literature from considering takeover to transmission-takeover shows the progress of the research. Academic research on this topic is now considered to be a legitimate part of the entrepreneurship field. However, as explained in the introduction, several terms are used to refer to the same phenomenon, which causes confusion. To increase academic spreading, we feel it is necessary to clarify the vocabulary. That is our aim in the next section.

What Is a Business Transfer?

As explained in the previous section, until now, research has been structured around three trends: (1) the term 'transmission', referring to the outgoing CEO (either a predecessor in the family firm or a seller) (Cadieux and Brouard, 2009); (2) the term 'takeover', which considers the perspective of the incoming CEO (Deschamps and Paturel, 2009); and (3) the term 'transmission-takeover', which brings together the two points of view and denotes the two boundaries (entry and exit) of the practice (Cadieux and Deschamps, 2011). Today, we think that research needs to go further to integrate and define these terms while, at the same time, simplifying them. The lack of consistency in the vocabulary puts into question the scientific validity of the research. Indeed, a field of research cannot develop without such a consensus; research needs to be clear and structured around an agreed word—crucially, a word that makes sense. We therefore propose the generic term 'business transfer' ('transfert d'entreprise' in French), as a basis from which the *type* of business transfer the researcher is studying can be specified (see the mapping later in this chapter, Mapping Business Transfer Modes). This term seems sufficiently inclusive to establish the vocabulary and to unify and clarify international research on the topic (see the next section).

Defining Business Transfer

'Transfer' implies both that there is something to transfer from an issuer (exit) to a receiver (entry) and the path from the one to the other. Different fields also use the term 'transfer', for example law, IT, photography, psychology, psychoanalysis and sport. Deschamps (2018) shows that, within those fields, the definitions of 'transfer' share common key words: change, acquisition, movement, activity modification and contact. Etymologically, the term is related to transport, which fits with the idea of a business transfer (the firm is transported from one CEO to another). These themes are present in all modes of business transfers, and they help to build a common basis for all transfer practices—in turn, reinforcing the structure of the literature on this topic. For instance, we can imagine a common interest in the new CEO's managing abilities or the outgoing CEO's ability to prepare the business transfer. We can also envisage a common interest in the different cycles of the transfer process (see later in this chapter, The Business Transfer Process) or the question of organising the knowledge held by the firm.

This understanding consists of business transfers, ownership and leadership transfers between two (or more) stakeholders, in a logical continuity from the one to the other, and with the aim of ensuring the sustainability of the target firm. The new entrant becomes the new owner-manager of a firm they will manage—alone, in a team or hidden behind a legal structure. However, this understanding excludes partial business transfers, which have different issues. As such, we refer to the following definition:

> business transfer represents the transition from one or more outgoing owner-managers to another, incoming owner-manager. It presupposes that information, relationships, know-how and social capital are transmitted from one to the other. Two aspects of the firm are transferred: leadership and ownership. Transfer aims to sustain the firm, the project and vision are different as soon as the leader has changed.
>
> (Deschamps, 2018, p. 202)

The word 'transfer' could lead researchers to write in general terms about types of transfers and their different actors. However, it is important that researchers specify which type of business transfer they are studying and that they qualify the studied mode of transfer (internal or external) as well as the studied point of view—outgoing CEO or new entrant—because the term also refers to actors. Using the word 'transfer' also helps to evolve the distinction between physical and legal persons: for example, in the case of an acquisition led by a small firm, the leader of the firm deals with the transfer directly. For this reason, the issues facing both small firms and physical persons are quite similar (Grazzini and Boissin, 2013); although a physical person usually creates a holding (which owns the target firm), behind this legal structure there is always a leader in the form of a physical person.

Mapping Business Transfer Modes

The word 'transfer' serves to unite researchers around the same topic. As the modes of business transfers are numerous and specific, researchers have to be precise about which transfer modes they refer to. Figure 1.1 maps different transfer modes.

This mapping can appear paradoxical because, on the one hand, we aim for a semantic reconciliation and, on the other, we propose a global representation of business transfer types that are necessarily quite different. The business transfer modes allow for multiple possibilities, and the semantic precision produces a non-ambiguous comprehension. For instance, external business transfer refers to takeovers led by people with no link to the acquired firm, while internal business transfer with a hybrid team corresponds to family business succession where the successors are not only family members but also include non-family members.

Even though each business transfer mode is unique, some issues concern all of them (evaluation, management of employees already working in the firm, knowledge transfer and, above all, emotion). Using a generic word like 'transfer' as an umbrella term for all the specificities of different modes is a way to integrate concepts, to consolidate knowledge, to open up new perspectives and to unite research fields that have until now existed only in parallel. Indeed, external takeover is related to entrepreneurship, but it can also be studied in the context of accumulated knowledge about internal hybrid transfers. Similarly, external business transfers by a team can be linked to research on entrepreneurial teams, internal family transfers to employees can be studied in the context of research on management buyouts (MBOs) or leveraged buyouts, and external business transfers led by a moral (legal) person can relate to mergers and acquisitions. Cross-fertilising research fields in this way contributes to increased knowledge on business transfers. The umbrella term

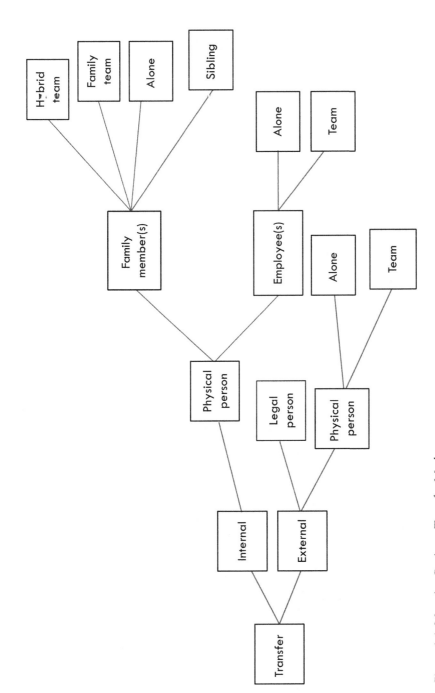

Figure 1.1 Mapping Business Transfer Modes

Source: Author created

'transfer' thus proposes a dialogue between entrepreneurship (external business transfer) and family business (internal family business transfer).

The entry and exit theories complete the definition of a business transfer.

The Business Transfer Process

We leverage the entrepreneurial entry and exit theories to revise the definition of the business transfer process, in which two main actors are associated.

Two Main Stakeholders

On one side, there is the owner-manager who intends to leave their firm. This entrepreneurial exit can take different forms: a sale to one or several family members, to an employee, to a firm, to an external buyer or by closing the firm (De Tienne, 2010). According to our mapping, this corresponds to internal family transfers alone or in a team, to internal employee transfer and to external transfers (i.e., towards a physical person or a firm). In the literature on ownership transfer, Wennberg *et al.* (2010) oppose inheritance and the selling of shares. Wiklund *et al.* (2013) disagree with literature that specifies that family transfers must remain in the family context. There are different reasons for exiting a firm, for example ending an entrepreneurial career (De Tienne, 2010) or due to age, education or experience. An exit may also be voluntary or involuntary, with the feeling of success or failure (Wennberg *et al.*, 2010); indeed, the money made through selling a firm corresponds to a life commitment (Wennberg *et al.*, 2011). Battisti and Okamuro (2010) demonstrate that the size of the firm has an impact on the exit mode: CEOs of big firms do not tend to close the firm or opt for external business transfers; CEOs of profitable firms tend to prefer internal transfers.

The CEO also has numerous ways to exit. Entrepreneurial exit is defined as "the process by which the founders of privately held firms leave the firm they helped to create; thereby removing themselves, in varying degrees, from the primary ownership and decision-making structure of the firm" (De Tienne, 2010, p. 204). Here, we observe the fact that business transfer is recurrent. That is to say, the founder of the firm is not the only actor that can transfer a business: the new owner, buyer or successor may themselves exit the business in the future. On the other side, there is the incoming CEO, who becomes an entrepreneur as a result of the business transfer. The literature outlines the different entry points of entrepreneurship: setting up a new venture from scratch, inheritance, buying a firm, MBO, management buy-in (MBI) and franchise (Ucbasaran *et al.*, 2001). Verstraete and Fayolle (2005) include takeovers within this paradigm of entrepreneurial opportunity, with the idea of 'impulsion'. For them, business transfer is seen as an opportunity for the new CEO to become an entrepreneur and to invest in a firm. Referring to Shane and Venkataraman (2000), Nordqvist *et al.* (2013) also consider taking over a firm and developing it as being a way to identify and exploit business opportunities. Parker and Van Praag (2012) focus on entry modes to an entrepreneurial career, distinguishing between new ventures and takeovers. Furthermore, they distinguish between new entrepreneurs coming from family businesses and those coming from non-family businesses. Westhead *et al.* (2005) compare those who are already entrepreneurs according to the same criteria. Cadieux *et al.* (2014) propose an exploratory model of the entrepreneurial career, one modality of which is a business takeover. For them, there is no doubt that founders and new entrants are different types of entrepreneurs in terms of their entrepreneurial behaviour and leadership.

A New Business Transfer Process

Based on these entrepreneurial entry and exit modes, Deschamps (2018) visualises the business transfer process as two 'faces' of the same practice (the entry and the exit), each face leading to the entrepreneurial transfer process. In this process, there may only be one person, or the seller and the buyer may work together. This is a new way to study the business transfer process. Deschamps (2018) also suggests a pre-transfer period, a transition step and a post-transfer phase. The business transfer process steps are as follows: (1) the entry of a CEO who, after some years, will exit the firm; (2) a transfer related to the transition between the outgoing and incoming CEOs; and (3) an entrepreneurial exit (the CEO is replaced again by a new entrant). These three sequences are juxtaposed and renewed at each new cycle of the transfer (cf. Figure 1.2).

This process is not simply a series of interrelated sequences, but more of a continuum of socialisation (Nordqvist *et al.*, 2013) between the cycle of the incoming CEO (who will exit further down the line) and that of the outgoing one. As the two cycles overlap, knowledge, competencies and social capital are transferred from the previous owner-manager to the new one. Within this representation, even if several stakeholders are concerned, the business transfer occurs in a close and trusting dyadic relationship between two (or more) owner-managers (Handler, 1990). As such, this representation should not be seen as the departure of one CEO and the arrival of the other, but rather a continuity. Both CEOs have a common project even if, in the end, only the new entrant stays and manages the target firm.

This process is built on a cycle. The first cycle usually concerns a founder, who becomes an entrepreneur via a new venture. As the

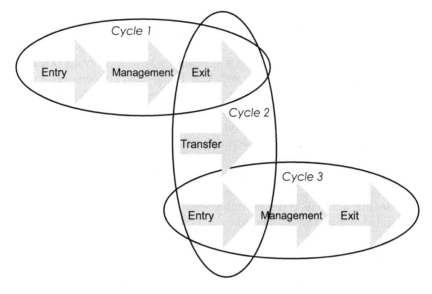

Figure 1.2 Business Transfer Process
Source: Author created

transfer is seen as a continuum, the business transfer becomes a strategic decision like many others: it is a part of the firm's life. Naturally, this founder will eventually exit, after transferring ownership to the new CEO; this is the second cycle. The third cycle starts with this new owner-manager (the second CEO), who has become an entrepreneur as a result of the business transfer and who will, after transferring, quit and be replaced by a new entrant, who will then pursue the firm's project. This cycle approach fits all the transfer modes and all new entrants. Exit represents an 'end phase' (Wennberg and Detienne, 2014). However, the exact timing of this ending requires further thought. We propose that the business transfer only really ends when each transfer is finished (from legal, economic, commercial and technical points of view) and when there is no more comparison with the previous owner-manager. As such, we posit that business transfer ends in the middle of cycle 3, when cycles 1 and 2 are over.

Conclusion

This chapter aimed to demonstrate the evolution of knowledge about business transfers and to suggest a consensus on definition and vocabulary in order to build an international research community around this topic.

The term 'transfer' includes both the actors in a business transfer and the different modes of transfer as a globality, while we describe each constituting parameter. The mapping of business transfer modes sheds light on the variety of different modes and leads to greater precision about what exactly researchers are studying. Finally, representing business transfers in cycles creates a global and integrated understanding of business transfers.

A consensus on this proposed definition, on the mapping of business transfer modes and on the business transfer process could open up many new avenues of inquiry, such as gender or knowledge transfer. Other research questions could include: how can we further distinguish the three cycles? In what ways can the backgrounds of the actors, their satisfaction, their difficulties, and their incentives for entry and exit be compared or considered together? Durst and Güldenberg (2010) observe information asymmetry in business transfers; in such conditions, how can technical and experiential knowledge (Zahra, 2007) and organisational knowledge be transferred? Is this knowledge transfer a way to reduce the risk for the new entrant?

References

Audet, J. and St-Jean, E. (2009). "Les enjeux de l'aspirant repreneur", *Revue Internationale PME*, 22(3–4), 31–57.

Bah, T. (2009). "La transition cédant-repreneur: une approche par la théorie du deuil", *Revue Française de Gestion*, 35(194), 123–148.

Barbot, M.C. and Richomme-Huet, K. (2007). "Pilotage de la reprise et de la succession dans le cas des entreprises artisanales", *Économies et Sociétés*, 16(1), 57–90.

Battisti, M. and Okamuro, H. (2010). "Selling, passing on or closing? Determinants of entrepreneurial intentions on exit modes", *Working paper*, Global COE Hi-Stat Discussion Paper Series, 151.

Block, J., Turik, R. and Van der Zwan, P. (2010, November). "Business takeover or new venture? Individual and environmental determinants from a cross-country study", *Entrepreneurship Theory and Practice (ERIM Report Series Research in Management)*, 37(5), 1099–1121.

Bornard, F. and Thévenard-Puthod, C. (2009). "Mieux comprendre les difficultés d'une reprise externe grâce à l'approche des représentations sociales", *Revue Internationale PME*, 22(3–4), 83–109.

Boussaguet, S. (2005). *L'entrée dans l'entreprise du repreneur: un processus de socialisation repreneuriale*, PhD Thesis, University Montpellier I, Montpellier.

Bygrave, W.D. (1995). "Theory building in the entrepreneurship paradigm", in I. Bull and H. Thomas (Eds.), *Entrepreneurship—perspectives on theory building*, 129–159, 182, Pergamon: G. Willard.

Bygrave, W.D. and Hofer, C.W. (1991). "Theorizing about entrepreneurship", *Entrepreneurship Theory and Practice*, 16(2), 13–22.

Cadieux, L. (2007). "Succession in small and medium-sized family businesses: toward a typology of predecessor roles during and after instatement of the successor", *Family Business Review*, 20(2), 95–109.

Cadieux, L. and Brouard, F. (2009). *La transmission des PME: perspectives et enjeux*, Québec: Presses de l'Université du Québec.

Cadieux, L. and Deschamps, B. (2009). "Une pratique entrepreneuriale de plus en plus reconnue!", Associate editor for the special issue on Business Transfers, *Revue Internationale PME*, 22(3, 4), 7–12.

Cadieux, L. and Deschamps, B. (2011). *Le duo cédant-repreneur, pour une compréhension intégrée de la transmission-reprise des PME*, Québec: Presses de l'Université du Québec. Ouvrage collectif.

Cadieux, L., Gratton, P. and St-Jean, E. (2014). "La carrière repreneuriale: proposition d'un cadre d'analyse exploratoire", *Revue de l'Entrepreneuriat*, 13(1), 35–50.

Cadieux, L. and Lorrain, J. (2004). "Et si assurer sa relève dépendait aussi de la manière dont les prédécesseurs réussissent à se désengager?" *Gestion*, 29(3), 120–129.

Carland, J.W., Hoy, F. and Carland, J.A.C. (1988). "Who is the entrepreneur it the question worth asking", *American Journal of Small Business*, 12(4), 33–39.

Cisneros, L. and Deschamps, B. (2014, hiver). "Comment transmettre l'entreprise familiale à plusieurs enfants?" *Gestion*, 38(4), 82–89.

Coeurderoy, R. and Lwango, A.B. (2014). "Capital social de l'entreprise familiale et succession entrepreneuriale: une approche théorique", *Management International*, 18(4), 164–174.

Davidson, P. (1989). *Continued entrepreneurship and small firm growth*, Stockholm: Stockholm School of Economics, The Economic Research Institute.

De Freyman, J. (2009). *La transition, phase essentielle de réussite d'une reprise*, PhD Thesis, University Bretagne, Bretagne.

De Freyman, J. and Richomme-Huet, K. (2010). "Entreprises familiales et phénomène successoral: Pour une approche intégrée des modes de transmission", *Revue Française de Gestion*, 37(200), 161–179.

De Tienne, D.R. (2010). "Entrepreneurial exit as a critical component of the entrepreneurial process: theoretical development", *Journal of Business Venturing*, 25, 203–215.

Deschamps, B. (2000). *Le processus de reprise d'entreprise par les entrepreneurs personnes physiques*, PhD Thesis, University Grenoble II, Grenoble.

Deschamps, B. (2003). "La reprise d'entreprise par les personnes physiques: premiers éléments de réponse à la question de son intégration dans le champ de l'entrepreneuriat", *Revue de l'Entrepreneuriat*, 2(1), 59–71.

Deschamps, B. (2018). "Evolution de la connaissance autour des pratiques de transmission—reprise réalisées par les personnes physiques: vers le concept de transfert d'entreprise", *Revue de l'Entrepreneuriat*, 17(3/4), 189–213.

Deschamps, B., Cisneros, L.F. and Barès, F. (2014). "PME familiales québécoises: impact des parties prenantes externes à la famille dans les co-successions en fratrie", *Management International*, Eté, 18(4), 151–163.

Deschamps, B. and Geindre, S. (2011). "Les effets perturbateurs des biais cognitifs et affectifs dans le processus de décision de reprendre une PME", *Management et Avenir*, 47, automne, 14–33.

Deschamps, B., Geindre, S. and Fatien, P. (2010, mai–juin). "Accompagner le repreneur d'entreprise: conduire, escorter mais aussi guider", *Gestion 2000*, 3, 77–88.

Deschamps, B. and Paturel, R. (2009). *Reprendre une entreprise, de l'intention à l'intégration*, 3ème éd., Paris: Dunod, Collection Entrepreneurs.

Donckels, R. (1995). "Taking over a company: an exciting carrier alternative . . . but not for adventurers", *Gestion 2000*, 6, 143–160.

Durst, S. and Güldenberg, S. (2010). "What makes SMEs attractive to external successors?" *VINE: The Journal of Information and Knowledge Management Systems*, 40(2), 108–135.

Estève, J.M. (1997). *La gestion des ressources intrapreneuriales et le succès du rachat de l'entreprise par ses salariés*, PhD Thesis, University Montpellier II, Montpellier.

Gartner, W.B. (1988). "Who is an entrepreneur? Is the wrong question", *Academic Journal of Small Business*, 12(4), 11–29.

Geindre, S. (2009). "Le transfert de la ressource réseau lors du processus repreneurial", *Revue Internationale PME*, 22(3–4), 109–137.

Geraudel, M., Jaouen, A., Missonier, A. and Salvetat, D. (2009). "Qui sont les repreneurs potentiels d'entreprises? Proposition de typologie en fonction de l'état de santé de la firme", *Revue Internationale PME*, 22(3–4), 13–31.

Grazzini, F. and Boissin, J.P. (2013). "Analyse des modèles mentaux développés par les dirigeants français en matière d'acquisition de PME ou de reprise d'entreprise", *M@n@gement*, 16(1), 49–85.

Grazzini, F., Boissin, J.P. and Malsch, B. (2009). "Le rôle du repreneur dans le processus de formation de la stratégie de l'entreprise acquise", *Revue Internationale PME*, 22(3–4), 109–139.

Haddadj, S. and D'Andria, A. (1998). "Transmissions internes et transmissions externes dans les PME françaises: existe-t-il des différences de changements et d'orientations stratégiques?" *Revue Internationale PME*, 11(4), 45–65.

Handler, W.C. (1990). "Succession in family firms: a mutual role adjustment between entrepreneur and next-generation family members", *Entrepreneurship Theory and Practice*, 15(1), 37–51.

Le Breton-Miller, I., Miller, D. and Steier, L.P. (2004). "Toward an integrative model of effective FOB succession", *Entrepreneurship Theory and Practice*, 28(4), 305–328.

Mazari, L. (2018). *Effets de la RSE sur le management de la reprise des PME: une analyse par la légitimité du repreneur externe vis-à-vis de ses salariés*, PhD Thesis, Universitéy Jean Monnet, Saint-Etienne.

Meiar, A. (2015). *Le Business Model de l'entreprise transmise: comparaison de la représentation du repreneur avec celle du cédant pour contribuer à réduire le risque de faux pas*, PhD Thesis, University Bordeaux, Bordeaux.

Nordqvist, M., Wennberg, K., Bau, M. and Hellerstedt, K. (2013). "Succession in private firms as an entrepreneurial process", *Small Business Economics*, 40, 1087–1122.

Parker, S.C. and Van Praag, C.M. (2012). "The entrepreneur's mode of entry: business takeover or new venture start?" *Journal of Business Venturing*, 27(1), 31–46.

Picard, C. (2009). "Continuité et rupture lors de la reprise dans l'artisanat: pour une lecture identitaire du processus", *Revue Internationale PME*, 22(3–4), 57–83.

Picard, C. and Thévenard-Puthod, C. (2004). "La reprise de l'entreprise artisanale: spécificités du processus et conditions de sa réussite", *Revue Internationale PME*, 17(2), 93–121.

Robic, P. and Antheaume, N. (2014). "La veuve: une partie prenante méconnue dans la transmission des entreprises familiales", *Management International*, 18(4), 175–186.

Saoudi, L. (2010). *Le management de Noyau dur humain en PME pour une transmission/reprise réussie*, PhD Thesis, University Montpellier I, Montpellier.

Shane, S. and Venkataraman, S. (2000). "The promise of entrepreneurship as a field of research", *Academy of Management Review*, 25(1), 217–226.

Shapero, A. (1984). "The entrepreneurial event", in C.A. Kent (Ed.), *The environment for entrepreneurship*, Lexington: Lexington Book.

Sharma, P. (2004). "An overview of the field of family business studies: current status and directions for the future", *Family Business Review*, 17(1), 1–36.

Sharma, P. and Chrisman, J.J. (1999). "Toward a reconciliation of the definitional issues in the field of corporate entrepreneurship", *Entrepreneurship: Theory & Practice*, 23(3), 11–27.

Siegel, D. (1989). *Contribution en vue d'une démarche stratégique de la reprise d'entreprise par des particuliers: le cas alsacien et franc comtois*, PhD Thesis, University Pierre Mendès-France, Grenoble II.

Thévenard-Puthod, C. (2014). "Formation et difficultés de fonctionnement des équipes successorales: une analyse fondée sur deux études de cas exploratoires et longitudinales", *Management International*, 18(4), 131–150.

Thévenard-Puthod, C., Picard, C. and Chollet, B. (2014). "Pertinence du tutorat comme dispositif d'accompagnement du repreneur individuel après la reprise. Une étude empirique à l'échelle européenne", *Management International*, 18(4), 80–96.

Ucbasaran, D., Westhead, P. and Wright, M. (2001). "The focus of entrepreneurial research: contextual and process issues", *Entrepreneurship Theory & Practice*, 25(4), 57–80.

Verstraete, T. and Fayolle, A. (2005). "Paradigmes et Entrepreneuriat", *Revue de l'Entrepreneuriat*, 4(1), 33–52.

Vesper, K.H. (1980). *New ventures strategies*, Englewood Cliffs, NJ: Prentice Hall.

Wennberg, K. and DeTienne, D.R. (2014). "The end is the beginning—or not: a critical review of research on entrepreneurial exit", *International Small Business Journal*, 32(1), 4–16.

Wennberg, K., Hellerstedt, K., Wiklund, J. and Nordqvist, M. (2011). "Implications of intra-family and external ownership transfer of family firms: short-term and long-term performance differences", *Strategic Entrepreneurship Journal*, 5, 352–373.

Wennberg, K., Wiklund, J., DeTienne, D.R. and Cardon, M.S. (2010). "Reconceptualizing entrepreneurial exit: divergent exit routes and their drivers", *Journal of Business Venturing*, 25(4), 361–375.

Westhead, P., Ucbasaran, D., Wright, M. and Binks, M. (2005). "Novice, serial and portfolio entrepreneur behaviour and contributions", *Small Business Economics*, 25, 109–132.

Wiklund, J., Nordqvist, M., Hellerstedt, K. and Bird, M. (2013). "Internal versus external ownership transition in family firms: an embeddedness perspective", *Entrepreneurship Theory and Practice*, 37(6), 1319–1340.

Zahra, S. (2007). "Contextualizing theory building in entrepreneurship research", *Journal of Business Venturing*, 22(3), 443–452.

2 Revisiting the Entrepreneurial Exit Decision Process

A Decision-Making Model

Marie-Josée Drapeau
and Maripier Tremblay

Entrepreneurial exit is an important subject for both scholars and communities, as many small and medium-sized enterprise (SME) owners[1]—more commonly called entrepreneurs—are about to make the decision to exit their business in several industrialised countries (Cruz, 2018; Koreen *et al.*, 2019). Yet, there is a significant gap in understanding this kind of decision: we know very little about how SME owners make the decision to exit their business. Research on entrepreneurial exit decisions is limited, compared to other entrepreneurial activities such as opportunity assessment, entrepreneurial entry, opportunity exploitation, etc. (see literature review by Shepherd *et al.*, 2014).

Even if we can find studies that focus on the decision-making aspects of the exit (Leroy *et al.*, 2007), work from this emerging field mainly concerns the result of that decision, that is, the choice of exit strategy (Wennberg *et al.*, 2010; DeTienne and Wennberg, 2013) or the factors associated with the different strategies (Battisti and Okamuro, 2010; Dehlen *et al.*, 2014). It does not address 'how' those decisions are made. While the exit phenomenon is relatively well documented with regards to large firms, we know very little about the exits of entrepreneurs from micro, small and medium-sized enterprises (DeTienne and Wennberg, 2016).

Furthermore, we know that the majority of those exiting entrepreneurs tend to prefer to transfer the firm to one or more individual(s) as an exit strategy (St-Jean and Duhamel, 2018). Business transfer is categorised in the entrepreneurial exit literature as a stewardship strategy (DeTienne *et al.*, 2015). It has been described in family business literature as a process of transferring management and ownership between two actors: the entrepreneur who is leaving the business and the new one who is taking over (LeBreton-Miller *et al.*, 2004; Cadieux and Brouard, 2010). However, this stream of literature does not address the decision process that led the entrepreneur to make the decision to leave, although this kind of decision can be a strategic one (DeTienne, 2010). The prevalence of entrepreneurs about to exit their business, combined with the lack of knowledge about how they make that strategic decision, has encouraged us to find an innovative axis to fill that gap.

In this chapter, we first propose to use a strategic decision-making model to examine the exit decision-making process. Strategic management researchers have participated actively in developing the concepts (Simon, 1965) and models of the decision-making process. Although their models were originally developed from an organisational management perspective, organisations are often characterised as being led by powerful, individual entrepreneurs. As such, Brunsson (1982, p. 30) states that "organisational decision processes are described in essentially the same terms as individual decision processes."

The rest of this chapter is structured as follows. First, we position business transfer within the context of studies that deal with entrepreneurial exit, as doing so provides an opportunity to highlight the links that bind these two literature streams, given that business transfer is also considered a stewardship strategy. Second, we introduce how the decision-making literature can contribute to a better understanding of the exit decision. We then propose a revisited framework with which to observe the phenomenon before concluding with the implications of our work and final remarks.

The Stewardship Exit Strategy

Entrepreneurial exit has recently emerged as a new body of research. This research stream addresses two different axes: (1) the exit of a business from the market and (2) the exit of an entrepreneur from his or her business. Our work fits into this second axis, which examines the strategies used by entrepreneurs when they leave their business, as we are interested in the entrepreneur's actual decision to exit.

The influential work of DeTienne and colleagues (e.g., DeTienne (2010), Wennberg *et al.* (2010), DeTienne and Cardon (2012), DeTienne and Chirico (2013) and DeTienne *et al.* (2015)) has contributed much to expanding this axis. On the one hand, DeTienne *et al.* (2015) have proposed a typology of exit strategies based on three categories: financial harvest (IPO and sale to another firm), stewardship (family succession, employee buyout and independent sale) and voluntary cessation (liquidation, closing).

Family succession, along with selling to employees (employee buyout) or to an external individual (independent sale), are therefore stewardship exit strategies. A stewardship exit strategy therefore involves the transfer of the business to another party; we refer to this as a 'business transfer'. Thus, a business transfer is one option for exiting a firm. This specific strategy presents multiple challenges, as it is often a long-term process that takes time and only begins once a decision to exit has been made—which makes it an important research subject.

Many business transfer studies focus on family succession and belong to the literature on family businesses. The field of entrepreneurial exit, however, is interested in all types of exit strategies, including business transfers to family or other parties. Studies on family businesses focus on the actual transfer process (LeBreton-Miller *et al.*, 2004; Cadieux and Brouard, 2010), on the changing role of the owner (Handler, 1990), and on resistance to (Handler and Kram, 1988; Fulford *et al.*, 2005) or obstacles influencing the transfer process (Bulloch, 1978; Ip and Jacobs, 2006). In contrast, entrepreneurial exit studies try to explain which factors affect the entrepreneur's choice of exit strategy by identifying different decision-making factors and relating them to an exit type. While entrepreneurial exit studies provide knowledge on the different factors involved in the final exit choice, they both fail to examine the decision-making process that leads up to that choice and do not focus on any one exit strategy in particular (though Wennberg *et al.*, 2011 looks at family transfer).

Some exits are more complex than others. Business transfers (a stewardship exit strategy) involve more than just a single transaction. They also involve ensuring that the business will continue to operate as an independent firm and contribute to a regional economy. Achieving this process is complicated (Cadieux and Brouard, 2010), as it involves varying degrees of emotions during both the decision-making process and the act of transferring the firm (Hytti *et al.*, 2011). The emotional state of the owners during the exit process influences their personal context (Hytti *et al.*, 2011) through either a grieving phase (Bah, 2009) or a disengagement phase (Cadieux and Lorrain, 2004). Thus, the process centres on the entrepreneur.

The Entrepreneur at the Heart of Entrepreneurial Exit

The entrepreneurial exit literature places the entrepreneur at the centre of the exit process. This stream has now acknowledged the exit of the entrepreneur as "the process by which the founders of privately held firms leave the firm they helped to create; thereby removing themselves, in varying degree, from the primary ownership and decision-making structure of the firm" (DeTienne, 2010, p. 204). From this perspective, SME-owner exit is viewed primarily in terms of the personal decision of the founder or owner of the company and, therefore, focuses on the decision-making aspects of the exit (e.g., whether or not to exit, transfer or sell the business) (Leroy *et al.*, 2007). Even though DeTienne's definition (2010) indicates that this is a process, no studies in the entrepreneurial exit literature, to our knowledge, have used a process perspective to examine the phenomenon of entrepreneurial exit. This insight reflects an important gap in this field.

The family business literature examines the transfer process itself, such as property and management transfers between the entrepreneur and the buyer (Handler, 1990; LeBreton-Miller *et al.*, 2004; Cadieux and Brouard, 2010). It provides abundant knowledge about family succession, but essentially focuses on the duality of the process: the transfer is considered a two-actor process in which the actors need to adjust their respective roles as the process advances (LeBreton-Miller *et al.*, 2004). The actor who initiates the entire exit process is not yet fully understood. The entrepreneurial exit literature focuses on entrepreneurs and the factors that influence their decision to exit. As such, individual factors such as prior experience in entrepreneurship (Van Teeffelen and Uhlaner, 2013; Leroy *et al.*, 2015), motivations or motives (DeTienne and Chandler, 2010; DeTienne and Chirico, 2013; Justo *et al.*, 2015), and age (DeTienne and Cardon, 2012) have been shown to influence an entrepreneur's choice of exit strategy. However, since entrepreneurs are part of an organic system, and since they mostly contribute to building the firm 'as they want it to be', organisational factors, such as family involvement (Battisti and Okamuro, 2010; Leroy *et al.*, 2015), performance (Wennberg *et al.*, 2011; Van Teeffelen and Uhlaner, 2013), business size (Ryan and Power, 2012; DeTienne *et al.*, 2015) and the independence of the firm from its owner (Van Teeffelen and Uhlaner, 2013) should also be considered. Finally, Ryan and Power (2012) mention that proximity to an urban centre is an environmental factor that can also affect the probability of transferring. All of these factors have shown their influence on the choice of exit strategy and thus influence the decision process of the entrepreneur. But when and how do they do so?

Although entrepreneurs are central to the exit process, actual studies examine the result of the decision to explain that decision, i.e., the exit strategy and the different factors related to a specific exit strategy. However, the entrepreneurs' decision to exit comes before their choice of exit strategy, which is actually the final step in the decision-making process. DeTienne *et al.* (2015) explain that this oversight is likely due to the fact that exit strategies are easier to observe and therefore easier to measure empirically. The entrepreneur's decision-making process nevertheless needs to be better understood. This would shed light on the decision-making process of entrepreneurial exits and highlight the impact of key factors that affect this process.

Decision-Making as a New Lens

The decision-making process can be defined as a process that consists of choosing a plan of action to solve a problem or seize an opportunity

(Schermerhorn *et al.*, 2010), a biased analytical approach (Huard, 1980), a set of actions and dynamic factors that begin with the identification of a stimulus for action and end with a specific commitment to action (Mintzberg *et al.*, 1976), or a cognitive process related to the pursuit of an opportunity (Messeghem and Sammut, 2011).

Many fields, such as politics, sociology, management and psychology, are interested in the decision-making process (Fayolle and Degeorge, 2012; Shepherd *et al.*, 2014). The management and political science literature that focuses on the organisational decision-making process provides a number of theoretical and conceptual frameworks (Mintzberg *et al.*, 1976; Nutt, 1984; Hickson *et al.*, 1986; Cray *et al.*, 1991; Hitt and Tyler, 1991; Allison and Zelikow, 1999). In this field, the decision maker is a (limited) rational actor within an organisational environment that includes the negotiation of power in any decision process (Mintzberg *et al.*, 1976). The literature looks at the organisation to explain how decisions are made.

Viewed through the lens of cognitive psychology, however, decision makers become the central input of decision-making, along with their imperfections and limitations (Corbett *et al.*, 2007). The decision process is mainly driven by the cognitive style of the individual, which is influenced by intuition (Kahneman and Klein, 2009) and emotion (DeTienne and Chirico, 2013). In entrepreneurship research, this is the mainstream stance used to investigate the entrepreneur (Douglas, 2009). These studies look at individuals through their behaviour or intentions to explain how they make decisions.

It is worth pointing out, however, that few researchers have used an entrepreneurial behaviour model, such as Ajzen's model of intention (Ajzen, 1991), to explain the decision to exit a business or the behaviour arising from that decision. Among them, Battisti and Okamuro (2010), as well as Leroy *et al.* (2015), demonstrate the importance of owners having control over their choices. Although interesting, the exit decision-making process is not explained, illustrated or understood, since these studies investigate the entrepreneurs' intentions, but not the actual decision-making process.

A decision is the conclusion of an act of intention as it is turned towards action (Fayolle and Degeorge, 2012). In entrepreneurship, making a decision is the central element to any entrepreneurial process (Fayolle and Degeorge, 2012), yet the exit decision still needs to be better understood. We therefore need to look beyond the exit intention to explain the exit decision.

Given that SMEs (the organisations) and their owner-managers (the individuals) are tightly interwoven in entrepreneurial organisations, "organisational decision processes are described in essentially the same terms as individual decision processes" (Brunsson, 1982, p. 30).

We therefore argue that organisational decision-making models are relevant to explain the individual decision-making process in SMEs. More specifically, as an entrepreneurial exit decision is a strategic decision (DeTienne, 2010; Wennberg and DeTienne, 2014), it could be described as a strategic decision-making process entrepreneurs might only make once in their lifetime. Moreover, the stewardship strategy adds to the strategic aspect of this decision, as the continuity of the organisation is an important component in this context. For these reasons, strategic decision-making models, which are a segment of the management field, could provide a new perspective from which to examine entrepreneurial exit decisions.

Using the Strategic Decision-Making Process to Explain Entrepreneurial Exit Decisions

In order to define an entrepreneurial exit decision-making process, the strategic management literature provides many conceptual models (Mintzberg *et al.*, 1976; Nutt, 1984; Hickson *et al.*, 1986; Cray *et al.*, 1991; Hitt and Tyler, 1991; Allison and Zelikow, 1999). The research by Mintzberg stands out in this field, as he includes entrepreneurial thinking into his studies. We have based our study of the entrepreneurial exit decision on his work.

Mintzberg and colleagues have been "researching the process of strategy formation based on the definition of strategy as 'a pattern in a stream of decisions'" (Mintzberg and Waters, 1985, p. 257). As such, Mintzberg claims that the process of strategy-making can be grouped according to three distinct courses of action (the entrepreneurial mode, the adaptive mode and the planning mode), which are not mutually exclusive: "the mode used must fit the situation" (Mintzberg, 1973, p. 52). This suggests that although planning may be necessary in order to identify both the means required to achieve a specific end and possible alternatives—in our case, the exit of the entrepreneur—flexibility in how the process is carried out is necessary. Likewise, "some situations require no planning, others only limited planning" (Mintzberg, 1973, p. 53). As such, an exit decision-making process could follow different courses of action. Some patterns could also emerge during the process.

Mintzberg and Waters (1985) also suggest that strategy formation can be deliberate or emergent through the decision-making process and thus propose eight strategy types: planned, entrepreneurial, ideological, umbrella, process, unconnected, consensus and imposed. However, we have noted from their work that "strategy formation walks on two feet, one deliberate, the other emergent" (p. 271). For us, 'emergent' strategy means that the process occurs mostly in an 'unintended order'—rather than in tandem—in which a willingness to learn must be present.

This, we believe, is in line with any exit decision process that can unfold in no particular order.

This work has contributed much to the understanding of organisational structures and their strategic counterparts (e.g., emergent or deliberate; see Mintzberg and Waters (1985)) and demonstrates that the analytical process used in the field of strategic decision-making needed to incorporate more flexibility. According to Mintzberg and Waters (1985),

> since strategy has almost inevitably been conceived in terms of what the leaders of an organisation 'plan' to do in the future, strategy formation has, not surprisingly, tended to be treated as an analytic process for establishing long-range goals and action plans for an organisation . . .
>
> (p. 257)

Foundational Framework

Although they recognised that rationality can be a part of the decision-making process, Mintzberg *et al.* (1976) were also able to capture the iterative character of the decision-making process and conceptualise it, thereby providing flexibility and emerging patterns. Their process model demonstrates that decision-making is not necessarily sequential, step-by-step or logical (DeTienne, 2010; Nutt and Wilson, 2010). Rather, it reflects both the main decision phases (identification-development-selection) and a series of sub-decision routines within each phase. Many loops are allowed between the steps, caused by dynamic factors (delays, interruptions, etc.) that can occur during the process or during any decision-making phase. The result "is that steps in a rational strategic decision process actually shift, branch, cycle and recycle" (Eisenhardt and Zbaracki, 1992, p. 21).

Their study "made a major contribution by identifying key phases of decision-making and external factors that influence the process" (Nutt, 1984, p. 414). It has become a classic model of the strategic decision-making process, and has been used both to study the decision-making process related to crises (Forgues, 1993) and to examine decision-making in organisations (McKinnon, 2003). It should be noted, however, that this model was developed to support a wide range of organisations with different strategic decision-making activities.

In applying this framework to a specific decision process (the entrepreneurial exit decision), in a particular context (the stewardship strategy) and in a restricted range of organisations (SMEs), we believe this model could provide new and captivating insights by making slight adaptations to SMEs as entrepreneurial organisations in which the entrepreneur is the central decision maker.

Revisited Framework

Mintzberg *et al.*'s (1976) general model of the strategic decision-making process is a dynamic model, which makes it possible to follow the main rationale of the decision maker and capture the real context of such a process (mainly exemplified by iterations). We slightly refine this framework by revising some phases and routines, and mostly by adding multilevel factors (such as individual, organisational and environmental) drawn from the entrepreneurial exit and entrepreneurial decision-making literature to reflect the influence they may have on the entrepreneur's decision to exit.

The revisited model maintains the basis of the original model: the three main phases (identification-development-selection), including subroutines and interruption caused by dynamic factors (see Figure 2.1), as they reflect the iterations and the structure behind the 'unstructured' decision that we usually find in entrepreneurs. We put forward the idea that entrepreneurs use their own decision-making process—one that is specifically adapted to their own context and structure. The decision to exit is no exception.

We thus remove the authorisation subroutine, which was the last step in the selection phase in the original model, because the entrepreneur is usually the only decision maker. He or she does not need any authorisation from a higher level to take action in his or her own organisation. This is the case for most SMEs. Instead, we incorporate a realisation routine into the model, as we consider this to be an important step towards concluding the decision-making process. It represents action.

Finally, our contribution to this revisited framework and the focus on stewardship exit strategy is the introduction of individual, organisational and environmental factors to highlight their importance in the exit decision-making process. Drawn from the entrepreneurial exit literature, these factors may influence specific steps, routines or subroutines of the exit decision-making process. This may contribute to opening the exit decision 'black box' which, for now, is only seen as a final choice rather than a process.

Based on what we presented in this chapter, Figure 2.1 proposes a revisited model.

Implications

This chapter proposes a conceptual model to better understand the decision-making process of entrepreneurs who are deciding to exit. We argue that the combined analysis of the exit decision-making process and the factors that influence the different steps of the process has potential contributions for studying the stewardship exit decision of an entrepreneur.

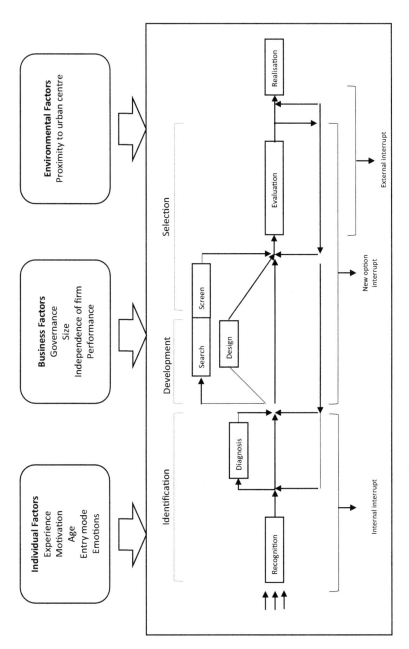

Figure 2.1 Revisiting Framework
Source: Author created

In fact, this chapter provides new insight into entrepreneurial exits and helps provide a better understanding of the critical steps involved in decision-making, as the entrepreneur is considered a central element in the decision-making process. The lack of theoretical knowledge on entrepreneurial exit processes and the looming prevalence of entrepreneurial exits in industrialised regions due to an aging population makes understanding these steps particularly important.

With this work, we expand on the entrepreneurial exit and decision-making literature. Until now, few studies have tried to understand entrepreneurial exit decisions based on Azjen's Theory of Planned Behaviour (TPB) and, to the best of our knowledge, none have drawn on the strategic decision process field, as this stream of management literature has traditionally explored larger bureaucratic firms. Wennberg and DeTienne (2014), however, have invited entrepreneurship researchers to examine the strategic management literature as, according to them, "[strategic decision models] could be a source of inspiration for researchers seeking to present in-depth studies of entrepreneurial exit" (p. 12). Researchers such as Mintzberg have explored strategic decision pathways, although their studies go back several decades. We have therefore brought back Mintzberg's original model, refined it and explained how it could be used to look into the decision to exit. Adding the strategic decision perspective to study the exit decision phenomenon also provides for the integration of two coexisting fields that are both interested in the stewardship exit: the emerging field of entrepreneurial exit and the field of business transfer.

We also contribute to filling the gap in knowledge on entrepreneurial exits in terms of how SME owners come to an initial decision to exit and subsequently choose an exit strategy. Our work complements that of DeTienne and others (DeTienne, 2010; DeTienne and Cardon, 2012; DeTienne and Chirico, 2013; DeTienne *et al.*, 2015; DeTienne and Wennberg, 2016), who explain exit decisions by exploring the factors that impact exit strategies. Different drivers (goals and motives) influence the decision patterns and, more specifically, the decision-making steps and routines.

For educators and consultants, our work has interesting implications. As the proposed framework considers the entrepreneur as the central focus of the process and illustrates the main steps that lead to the exit decision, as well as the factors that influence the process, it helps to understand why and how entrepreneurs makes their choices. It can therefore help explain non-rational choices and how the process is affected. Understanding the decision-making process of exiting entrepreneurs can also provide practitioners with more accurate knowledge to help them advise their clients more adequately.

Finally, from a broader economic perspective, considering that regional economies can be preserved through a prevalence of business transfers and that buying a business has a better chance of success than starting one (Commission of the European communities, 2006), political decision makers and leaders should be eager to learn more about entrepreneurial exit phenomena to help facilitate such transfers (Leroy *et al.*, 2010).

This model must be tested. It could be combined with individual theoretical models to add to the applicability of our proposed framework. For example, further research could reveal different patterns used by entrepreneurs specifically when they exit using a stewardship strategy. It could also be used to uncover specific behaviours to explain the exit decision process. Likewise, the effectuation perspective (Sarasvathy, 2001) could be a productive avenue to explore.

Furthermore, this model could be used to examine different exit strategies (IPOs and liquidation, for example) and to compare differences and similarities in the decision-making process. We have also only mentioned a few factors that could influence the decision process, but we have not linked them directly to the decision-making steps or phases. More work in this area could bring about further insights that would result in a better understanding of the entrepreneurial decision process.

On an empirical level, in order to fully understand the exit process, case studies should be prioritised (Gagnon, 2012) and put into context (Yin, 2011). This would contribute to the many quantitative studies in the field of entrepreneurial exits. For example, they could shed light on the nature of the relationship between dynamic factors and the decision process.

Final Remarks

An improved vision of the entrepreneurial exit decision must include the decision-making process itself, as well as the factors that influence this process. Decision-making models can help understand and explain the factors that affect this strategic decision in the life cycle of an SME. The stewardship exit strategy (transferring the business to another individual) is complex to adopt (Cadieux and Brouard, 2010), but nevertheless offers businesses the greatest chance of survival in terms of activity, jobs and value creation. As such, this chapter aims to enhance academic knowledge on entrepreneurship by proposing a process model that takes into account several variables (individual, business and environmental) and provides new insight into the question raised by Shepherd *et al.* (2014, p. 19): "What is the entrepreneurial decision-making process in exiting a successful venture?"

Note

1. We adhere to the definition put forward by Chevalier *et al.* (2013, p. 2): "the entrepreneur as someone who is self-employed and more precisely as someone who perceives an opportunity and creates an organisation to pursue it.

The entrepreneur can be a business founder, a purchaser, or a venture successor, but whatever the entrepreneurial mode chosen, all entrepreneurs can be simply defined as owner—managers". The terms 'entrepreneur' and 'owner-manager' are therefore alternately used without any distinction between them.

References

Ajzen, I. (1991). "The theory of planned behaviour", *Organizational Behaviour and Human Decision Processes*, 50, 179–211.

Allison, G.T. and Zelikow, P. (1999). *Essence of decision: explaining the cuban missile crisis*, New York: Longman.

Bah, T. (2009). "La transition cédant-repreneur: Une approche par la théorie du deuil", *Revue Française de Gestion*, 35(194), 123–148.

Battisti, M. and Okamuro, H. (2010). *Selling, passing on or closing? Determinants of entrepreneurial intentions on exit modes*, Massey U. College of Business Research Paper. SSRN: https://ssrn.com/abstract=1711336 or http://dx.doi.org/10.2139/ssrn.1711336.

Brunsson, N. (1982). "The irrationality of action and action rationality: decisions, ideologies and organisational actions", *Journal of Management Sudies*, 19(1), 29–44.

Bulloch, J.F. (1978). "Problems of succession in small business", *Human Resource Management*, 17(2), 1–6.

Cadieux, L. and Brouard, F. (2010). *La transmission des PME. Perspectives et enjeux*, Québec: Presse de l'Université du Québec.

Cadieux, L. and Lorrain, J. (2004). "Et si assurer sa relève dépendait aussi de la manière dont les prédécesseurs réussissent à se désengager?" *Gestion*, 29(3), 120–128.

Chevalier, S., Fouquereau, E., Gillet, N. and Demulier, V. (2013). "Development of the reasons for entrepreneurs' retirement decision inventory (rerdi) and preliminary evidence of its psychometric properties in a french sample", *Journal of Career Assessment*, 21(4), 572–586.

Commission of the European Communities. (2006). *Communication from the commission to the council, the european parliament, the european economic and social committee and the committee of the regions*, Brussels: Commission of the European Communities.

Corbett, A.C., Neck, H.M. and Detienne, D.R. (2007). "How corporate entrepreneurs learn from fledgling innovation initiatives: cognition and the development of a termination script", *Entrepreneurship Theory and Practice*, 31(6), 829–852.

Cray, D., Mallory, G.R., Butler, R.J., Hickson, D.J. and Wilson, D.C. (1991). "Explaining decision processes", *Journal of Management Studies*, 28(3), 227–251.

Cruz, M. (2018). *Réussir sa relève. Résultat du sondage sur la planification de la relève des PME*, Canada: C. F. o. I. B. (CFIB).

Dehlen, T., Zellweger, T., Kammerlander, N. and Halter, F. (2014). "The role of information asymmetry in the choice of entrepreneurial exit routes", *Journal of Business Venturing*, 29(2), 193–209.

DeTienne, D. (2010). "Entrepreneurial exit as a critical component of the entrepreneurial process: theoretical development", *Journal of Business Venturing*, 25(2), 203–215.

DeTienne, D. and Cardon, M. (2012). "Impact of founder experience on exit intentions", *Small Business Economics*, 38(4), 351–374.

DeTienne, D. and Chandler, G. (2010). "The impact of motivation and causation and effectuation approaches on exit strategies", *Frontiers of Entrepreneurship Research*, 30(1), 1–13.

DeTienne, D. and Chirico, F. (2013). "Exit strategies in family firms: how socioemotional wealth drives the threshold of performance", *Entrepreneurship Theory and Practice*, 37(6), 1297–1318.

DeTienne, D., Mckelvie, A. and Chandler, G. (2015). "Making sense of entrepreneurial exit strategies: a typology and test", *Journal of Business Venturing*, 30(2), 255–272.

DeTienne, D. and Wennberg, K. (2013). "Small business exit: review of past research, theoretical considerations and suggestions for future research, C. P. Forthcoming chapter", in *Small businesses in a global economy: creating and managing successful organisations*, Westport: S. Newbert.

DeTienne, D. and Wennberg, K. (2016). "Studying exit from entrepreneurship: new directions and insights", *International Small Business Journal*, 34(2), 151–156.

Douglas, D. (2009). "Entrepreneurial strategic decision-making: a cognitive perspective", *International Journal of Entrepreneurial Behaviour and Research*, 15(5), 521–524.

Eisenhardt, K.M. and Zbaracki, M.J. (1992). "Strategic decision making", *Strategic Management Journal*, 13(S2), 17–37.

Fayolle, A. and Degeorge, J.M. (2012). *Dynamique entrepreneuriale. Le comportement de l'entrepreneur*, Bruxelles, Belgique: de boeck.

Forgues, B. (1993). *Processus de décision en situation de crise*, Thesis, Université Paris-Dauphine, Paris.

Fulford, M.D., Breshears, R.G. and Breshears, R.C. (2005). "In it for the long haul? Succession planning within small entrepreneurial firms", *The Entrepreneurial Executive*, 10, 53–63.

Gagnon, Y.C. (2012). *L'étude de cas comme méthode de recherche*, Québec: Presses de l'Université du Québec.

Handler, W.C. (1990). "Succession in family firms: a mutual role adjustment between entrepreneur and next-generation family members", *Entrepreneurship: Theory and Practice*, 15(1), 37–51.

Handler, W.C. and Kram, K.E. (1988). "Succession in family firms: the problem of resistance", *Family Business Review*, 1(4), 361–381.

Hickson, D.J., Butler, R.J., Cray, D., Mallory, G.R. and Wilson, D.C. (1986). *Top decisions. Strategic decision-making in organisations*, San-Francisco, CA: Jossey-Bass Publishers.

Hitt, M.A. and Tyler, B.B. (1991). "Strategic decision models: integrating different perspectives", *Strategic Management Journal*, 12(5), 327–351.

Huard, P. (1980). "Rationalité et identité: Vers une alternative à la théorie de la décision dans les organisations", *Revue économique*, 31(3), 540–572.

Hytti, U., Stenholm, P. and Peura, K. (2011). "Transfers of business planning and bounded emotionality: a follow-up case study", *International Journal of Entrepreneurial Behaviour & Research*, 17(5), 561–580.

Ip, B. and Jacobs, G. (2006). "Business succession planning: a review of the evidence", *Journal of Small Business and Enterprise Development*, 13(3), 326–350.

Justo, R., DeTienne, D.R. and Sieger, P. (2015). "Failure or voluntary exit? Reassessing the female underperformance hypothesis", *Journal of Business Venturing*, *30*(6), 775–792.

Kahneman, D. and Klein, G. (2009). "Conditions for intuitive expertise: a failure to disagree", *American Psychologist*, *64*(6), 515.

Koreen, M., Schlepphorst, S. and Pissareva, L. (2019). Business transfer as an engine for sme growth, online, G. Japan, www.g20-insights.org/policy_briefs/business-transfer-as-an-engine-for-sme-growth/.

Lebreton-Miller, I., Miller, D. and Steier, L.P. (2004). "Towards an integrative model of effective fob succession", *Entrepreneurship Theory and Practice*, *28*(4), 305–328.

Leroy, H., Manigart, S. and Meuleman, M. (2010). "The planned decision to transfer an entrepreneurial company", *IUP Journal of Entrepreneurship Development*, *7*(1/2), 7–22.

Leroy, H., Manigart, S., Meuleman, M. and Collewaert, V. (2015). "Understanding the continuation of firm activities when entrepreneurs exit their firms: using theory of planned behaviour", *Journal of Small Business Management*, *53*(2), 400–415.

Leroy, H., Meuleman, M. and Manigart, S. (2007, November). "Drivers of exit processes: differentiating between intentions and actions", *RENT Conference Cardiff* (U.K.), Cardiff.

McKinnon, A. (2003). *Decision-making in organisations*, Research Paper. http://citeseerx.ist.psu.edu/viewdoc/versions?doi=10.1.1.516.915.

Messeghem, K. and Sammut, S. (2011). *L'entrepreneuriat*, Paris: Édition Management et société.

Mintzberg, H. (1973). "Strategy-making in three modes", *California Management Review*, *16*(2), 44–53.

Mintzberg, H., Raisinghani, D. and Théorêt, A. (1976). "The structure of 'unstructured' decision processes", *Administrative Science Quarterly*, *21*(2), 246–275.

Mintzberg, H. and Waters, J.A. (1985). "Of strategies, deliberate and emergent", *Strategic Management Journal*, *6*(3), 257–272.

Nutt, P.C. (1984). "Types of organisational decision processes", *Administrative Science Quarterly*, *29*(3), 414–450.

Nutt, P.C. and Wilson, D.C. (2010). "Crucial trends and issues in strategic decision making", in *Handbook of decision making*, 720, New York: John Wiley & Sons.

Ryan, G. and Power, B. (2012). "Small business transfer decisions: what really matters? Evidence from ireland and scotland", *Irish Journal of Management*, *31*(2), 99–125.

Sarasvathy, S. (2001). "Causation and effectuation: towards a theoretical shift from economic inevitability to entrepreneurial contingency", *The Academy of Management Review*, *26*(2), 243–263.

Schermerhorn, J.R.J., Hunt, J.G., Osborn, R.N. and De Billy, C. (2010). *Comportement humain et organisation*, Canada: Édition du renouveau pédagogique inc.

Shepherd, D.A., Williams, T.A. and Patzelt, H. (2014). "Thinking about entrepreneurial decision making: review and research agenda", *Journal of Management*, *41*(1), 11–46.

Simon, H.A. (1965). "Administrative decision making", *Public Administration Review*, 25(1), 31–37.

St-Jean, É. and Duhamel, M. (2018). *Situation de l'activité entrepreneuriale québécoise: Rapport 2017 du Global Entrepreneurship Monitor*, Canada: Institut de recherche sur les PME, Université du Québec à Trois-Rivières.

Van Teeffelen, L. and Uhlaner, L.M. (2013). "Firm resource characteristics and human capital as predictors of exit choice: an exploratory study of smes", *Entrepreneurship Research Journal*, 3(1), 84–108.

Wennberg, K. and DeTienne, D. (2014). "What do we really mean when we talk about 'exit'? A critical review of research on entrepreneurial exit", *International Small Business Journal*, 32(1), 4–16.

Wennberg, K., Wiklund, J., DeTienne, D. and Cardon, M. (2010). "Reconceptualizing entrepreneurial exit: divergent exit routes and their drivers", *Journal of Business Venturing*, 25(4), 361–375.

Wennberg, K., Wilkund, J., Hellerstedt, K. and Nordqvist, M. (2011). "Implications of intra-family and external ownership transfer of family firms: short-term and long-term performance differences", *Strategic Entrepreneurship Journal*, 5(4), 350–372.

Yin, R.K. (2011). *Qualitative research from start to finish*, New York: The Guilford Press.

Part II

Family Business Transfers

Historically, business transfer research has tended to focus on family successions, most likely in response to a clear preference on the part of predecessors to choose family members as successors, whatever their level of competence. Today, despite a trend in many countries towards a decline in this type of business transfer, particularly in favour of external transfer, succession is still a perilous operation that must be managed with the utmost care. This part of the handbook therefore brings together five contributions dealing specifically with family succession.

In the context of family business, succession is an emotion-influenced process that impacts many stakeholders. In order to ensure the success of the business transfer, it is therefore important to carefully manage a wide range of emotions. In Chapter 3, **Emotions in Family Business Succession, Soumaya Sfeir** shows how emotions influence the reasoning of the incumbents, including the selection of their successors. She describes how a keener awareness of this influence would help incumbents control their emotions and better prepare for succession planning. In Chapter 4, **Family Business Transfer: A Stressful Event for Successors, Florence Guiliani** and **Luis Cisneros** are more interested in the perspective of the successors. They focus on the stressors that emerge in the family business and the business family during the various succession phases and how the successors cope with them. They identify seven main categories of stressors, linked to either the family business or the business family, and then the strategies the successors employ to deal with them.

The preparation of successors is often considered a key success factor of family successions. Chapter 5, **The Making of Family Entrepreneurs: How Heirs Become Entrepreneurs and Take Over a Family Business,** examines how heirs turn into entrepreneurs and take over the reins of a family business. **Paulette Robic, Dominique Barbelivien** and **Nicolas Antheaume** suggest that becoming a family entrepreneur requires a long process of socialisation that is particularly complex. Based on a case study of a fifth-generation French family business, they identify a three-stage socialisation process (incubation, testing and selection, and choosing). They also show that sometimes a family's size and complexity can become an advantage: the larger the pool of potential successors, the higher the chances that a competent heir will emerge and take over the management of the family business.

Successful family succession also means finding the right mode of governance. In Chapter 6, **Succession and Family Business in Between Emotional and Financial Issues: The Role of Governance With a Two-Tier System, Céline Barrédy** demonstrates the usefulness for some companies of choosing a two-tier governance system (a public limited company structure with a management board and a supervisory board). Through the separation of management and control functions, and the collegiality of the bodies, this legal structure provides an answer to many family firm challenges: it strengthens family involvement, maintains the power of influential actors (incumbent and successor), and gives access to non-family resources and external expertise.

Finally, Chapter 7, **Succession and Strategic Renewal in Family Firms: Insights From a French Family Firm**, stresses the importance of strategic renewal for family businesses to ensure their sustainability. Based on a case study of a family SME, **Didier Chabaud, Mariem Hannachi** and **Hedi Yezza** show how succession can be a catalyst of this strategic renewal in family SMEs.

3 Emotions in Family Business Succession

Soumaya Sfeir

Succession—the transfer of leadership from one generation to the next—is an important challenge that family firms face (Daspit *et al.*, 2016). As the title denotes, we introduce a new approach to the study of family business succession, which we conceive as an emotion-influenced process, where feelings can affect the choice of a successor. We present the notion of viewing succession through emotions. This insight opens up a new understanding of family business succession. But why care about emotions? It turns out that they have not been studied extensively in family business succession literature (Radu-Lefebvre and Randerson, 2020). Yet, they bring into play what matters in our lives: emotions pass through us, they constitute our humanity, our relationship with ourselves, with others and with our environment. In fact, all human behaviour depends on the emotional experience. Hence, our everyday experiences leave little doubt that emotions influence the decisions we make (Schwarz, 2000). This concept also applies to organisations: emotions affect organisational processes, decisions and outcomes (Shepherd, 2016). Hence, one of the main reasons for the high failure rate among first- and second-generation family businesses is the inability to manage the emotional aspects of the succession process (Duh *et al.*, 2009; Van der Merwe *et al.*, 2009). The ability to take into account the feelings, decisions and behaviour of many actors at once creates potential for a significant breakthrough in the study of family business succession.

This chapter makes several contributions to theory and practice in family firms. The first is to think differently about family business succession by enhancing the influence of emotions on the succession planning process, which is a key challenge in family business research. The second is to point out that emotions have a different outcome regarding the succession planning process. The third is to explore succession through the emotions felt by the predecessor when choosing their successor. There are also implications for family firms' owners. In fact, emotions influence the reasoning of the incumbents. We aim to raise awareness of their emotions, which could help them control their emotions better and prepare for succession planning.

The remainder of this article is organised as follows. It begins by defining emotions and providing a literature review of emotions and decision-making in family firms, and of emotions and succession in the literature. Next, it empirically validates the influence of the predecessor's emotions when choosing a successor by using two short case studies. Finally, it concludes by discussing the results and their implications.

Emotions in the Literature

Emotions are defined by Cosnier (1994, translated) as "all the events or states of the affective field characterised by a set of experienced psychics accompanied in varying ways by the intensity and quality of physiological and behavioural manifestations" (p. 14).

Understanding the role of emotions in family succession means perceiving the nature of emotions and their role in the decisions and behaviour of the incumbent. This type of study poses many challenges because emotions are difficult to grasp: they can be hidden or simulated. According to Cahour and Lancry (2011),

> the emergence of an emotion is an eminently peculiar, subjective phenomenon, dependent on personal characteristics in interaction with the specific situation and the sense that this situation has for the subject. Affective states are generated by a process of evaluation of the situation by the subject according to the meaning that he attributes to it according to his interests, his goals and his motivations.
>
> (p. 101)

Therefore, it will be crucial to consider the particular situation surrounding each family succession, as we do in the case studies which follow, in order to understand the emotions experienced. But, in general, how do emotions intervene in a family firm's decision-making?

Emotions and Decision-Making in Family Firms

It has only been in recent years that emotions became a topic of interest for decision-making research. Until then, the decision maker was assumed to behave according to rational and distinctly formulated principles (Van Hoorebeke, 2008).

However, family firms are concerned with emotions. These businesses include a family system that is at least partially governed by emotional relationships, and a business system that is subject to the economic logic of the market (Stewart, 2003; Cohen and Sharma, 2016). Complexity emerges when these two systems are overlaid, resulting in substantial heterogeneity (Stewart, 2003; Cohen and Sharma, 2016). Given this complexity and heterogeneity, much remains to be studied about the causes and consequences of family firms' behaviour on succession planning (Whetten *et al.*, 2014; Gagné *et al.*, 2014).

Moreover, emotion is important for understanding the decisions and actions of family members in family-owned businesses (Harrell, 1997; Zellweger and Dehlen, 2012; Kellermanns *et al.*, 2012). The emotional aspect, omnipresent in a family business, dictates its mode of operation and its evolution over time. Indeed, when we speak of emotions, we refer to subjective affective reactions that have a clear cause or object, which are short-lived and focus on a specific target (adapted from Barsade, 2002). Emotions in family businesses emerge and evolve over time, especially during critical family and/or business events (Gersick *et al.*, 1997).

However, according to Shepherd (2016), there are substantial gaps in our understanding of emotions in family-owned businesses (see also Brundin and Härtel, 2014). Most of the research on family-owned businesses has been devoted to exploring the problems, challenges and solutions associated with the succession of family-owned businesses (e.g., Chrisman *et al.*, 2009). However, emotions in family succession have been scarcely studied empirically in the academic literature (Radu-Lefebvre and Randerson, 2020).

Research in the field of neuroscience has confirmed the physiological link between emotion and decision-making. Damasio (2003) has shown that individuals cannot make decisions when the areas of their brains associated with emotional processes have been damaged. Ledoux (1998) provided further neurobiological evidence of the link between emotion and decision-making. Many studies, often in experimental psychology, have more recently shown that emotions: (1) prepare for action and guide decision-making, and (2) influence creativity and reasoning, guiding judgements/evaluations, memory recall and perception, in the sense of a positive/negative congruence (Cahour, 2010).

However, according to Lazarus (1991), emotion depends on a combination of motivation, interest and environment, inducing the individualisation of the decision. He argues that the decision depends on human values, religion, politics, loyalty, righteousness, justice, compassion, trust and self-interest.

Emotions are thus not considered here as a marginal factor, intervening from time to time, but as constitutive of all activity, unfolding in a constant and moving flow of emotional states that direct and impact actions, relationships and reflections, and which are themselves modified by the activity that unfolds and the situation that is built (Lépine and Martin-Juchat, 2018).

Therefore, we aim to enhance our understanding of emotions and their influence on the succession planning process, which remains an under-explored research field (Brundin and Härtel, 2014; Shepherd, 2016), as the following section will demonstrate.

Emotions and Succession

Family businesses have long been considered by the literature to be strongly influenced by emotions from the family system (Labaki, 2019), because research has long recognised the importance of emotion in understanding actions (Harrell, 1997; Zellweger and Dehlen, 2012; Kellermanns *et al.*, 2012). However, one characteristic of a family business is that emotions exist within the two systems of both the family and the company, and that they pass from one system to the other, having repercussions on them both (Labaki *et al.*, 2013).

Much of this research has been carried out within the conceptual framework of socio-emotional wealth, which is based on the principle that family businesses have their own socio-emotional endowment, which represents "the stock of values related to the affect a family derives from its dominant position in a given enterprise" (Berrone *et al.*, 2012, p. 271). This socio-emotional endowment is essential to understanding the decisions and actions of family members, as well as family businesses making decisions and acting to preserve this endowment (Gómez-Mejía *et al.*, 2007; Cruz *et al.*, 2010). While its creators and supporters argue that the theory of social-emotional wealth is in its infancy (Berrone *et al.*, 2012), this work has had a major impact on research into family-owned businesses and lays the foundation for future contributions.

Succession planning is influenced by economic and non-economic considerations of the resigning owner-manager (e.g., Cardon *et al.*, 2005; DeTienne, 2010; DeTienne and Chirico, 2013; Wennberg and DeTienne, 2014), because owner-managers feel emotionally attached to their firm (DeTienne, 2010 and Dehlen *et al.*, 2014), strongly identify with their business (Zahra, 2003) and even care about its post-exit prosperity (Graebner and Eisenhardt, 2004).

Therefore, it would be relevant to empirically validate how emotions affect one particular type of decision-making in family firms: the choice of the successor.

In this context, the emotional influence of the family on the family business is considered inevitable and permanent (Carrau, 2019). The importance of emotions can be seen in the various stages in the life of the company and of the family members, including during family succession. "The family prints to the family business the specific emotional intensity" (Carrau, 2019, p. 236). Within this type of company, the influence of the emotions that are created and developed does not stop at the threshold of the family or the threshold of the family business. In this sense, Nordqvist *et al.* (2013) explain that "managing a transfer is like managing emotions" (p. 1112).

Deschamps (2014) emphasises the importance of emotions in business transfers and justifies the existence of emotions as the paradox between continuity and change on the one hand, and rupture on the other, and by fear, for each of the actors of the transfer, of what will follow. She points out the changes caused by this transfer, which constitute sources of anxiety and worries: "that of failing for the purchaser; that of another life for the salesman; that of the future for the employees of the transferred company" (p. 77).

Taking into account the psychological stakes that the succession provokes, it would be relevant to study family succession through emotions. The three actors (the incumbent, successors and employees) are concerned and affected. Employees feel fear. They must get used to the idea of what they are losing, while asking themselves the question of what comes next and facing the unknown of what will happen. The issue for the successor is taking the place of the incumbent and truly being up to the challenge. As for the incumbent, their final departure will be experienced as a rupture. In these conditions, how can stakeholders ensure the sustainability of a family business when everyone's emotions come into play?

To our knowledge, the literature on family business transfers has not yet shed light on succession through the emotions felt by the predecessor when choosing their successor. According to our reading, research on succession in the family business focuses on the emotions felt by those involved in the transfer of business, but does not concern itself with the emotions of the incumbent at decision-making time.

Empirical Study

The American psychologist Paul Ekman *et al.* (1972), a pioneer in the study of emotions, counted six fundamental emotions: joy, anger, fear, sadness, surprise and disgust. Let us therefore provide some details on the specific messages of each of the six basic emotions very often experienced.

1. **Anger** tells us that the current situation is unacceptable for three possible reasons:

   - One of our important values is being flouted;
   - Our limits have been crossed; or
   - Our needs are neither heard nor fed, and it is time to take action to change the situation.

2. **Fear** tells us that there is danger in our environment and it is time for us to identify security points so that we can continue to move forward.

3. **Disgust** tells us that something is toxic in the environment and it is time to get away.

4. **Sadness** tells us that the ideal situation hoped for cannot take place, and we will have to accept it in order to move on. Clearly, we will have to mourn the expected ideal situation.
5. **Joy** is directly associated with pleasure and happiness. It appears in response to the resolution of any personal goal or the alleviation of a state of ill-being.
6. **Surprise** is a reaction caused by something unexpected, new or strange. In fact, it appears when a stimulus that the subject does not expect in their predictions or schemas is presented.

To better understand the role that emotions can play in planning family firm succession, we chose two examples to examine and interpret this phenomenon. Through the following two cases, we wish to shed light on the emotions felt by the predecessor when making decisions about the choice of their successor and to examine the influence of these emotions on the predecessor's own behaviour and decisions.

Case 1: Joy, Fear and Sadness

PEB is the CEO of 'S'. This group, whose headquarters are located in the north-east of France, specialises in waterproofing, thermal insulation and roofing. 'S' was founded in 1908 by PEB's grandfather. Today, more than 110 years after its creation, the company employs nearly 7,000 people in 90 countries. PEB's family owns 100% of the company.

PEB expresses his concern about the succession and, in particular, the choice of a successor. " 'S' is certainly a family business, but I did not inherit it, I got into debt to buy it back". In 1992, he became the CEO of the family business group that then made 230 million euro in turnover.

PEB began his career in auditing before his grandfather asked him to join 'S' in 1989 as CFO. He was barely 30 years old. His mission was to improve the difficult situation of the company, which had unstable management. The young man never planned to stay long and yet, when his grandmother died, shareholder conflicts broke out. PEB started running a race against his grandfather to buy all the shares.

Since then, the businessman has learned lessons from the past.

> I do not want to make the same mistakes as my grandfather who didn't want to let go of the family business. We must know how to leave the place for young people and enthusiasm. If you stay too long, you risk thinking of yourself as indispensable.

According to PEB, the company should adapt to the future, ready to be transmitted to the future generation. He thinks also about building the future. One of his sources of professional pride is the in-house training school that he launched, accredited to issue CPCs (Certificate of Professional Competence) for all the jobs practiced in the company.

He thinks that all individuals will eventually disappear, but the company must continue by adapting. This adaptation is the next step for the group, which is preparing to choose a successor. He confirmed that his son has expressed his intention to join the family business. This acceptance by the son to take over the management of the company was greeted with joy by the family. The joy felt by the CEO is related to the satisfaction of a desire—the success of an important project in his eyes—that of seeing his son take over the family business. During the interview, this state of satisfaction and well-being was expressed not only in his speech, but also through his smile, good humour, cheerfulness and sparkling eyes.

But PEB is not yet reassured; for the moment, his son has to complete training within the company and work as a simple employee. He will be assigned a managerial position later. "That does not mean I do not trust him", he stated. "But I'm afraid he cannot deal with all the issues". The fear felt by the CEO is an anticipation emotion. It is useful because it informs of a danger, a potential (or even real) threat, and it allows the individual experiencing the emotion to act.

> But running a business needs experience. Now it is more complex to manage than it was in the beginning. I want to be sure that the business will continue after I let go. I am sad because he is not ready yet. My sadness proves what the company means for me.

The sadness expressed by the CEO is linked to disappointment (even if it is temporary), a feeling of helplessness and an unfulfilled wish for the moment.

In principle, the choice of successor has been made, but the CEO is currently evaluating his performance and identifying his actual skills. The negative emotions felt by the CEO have been an obstacle to formalising the succession. The predecessor waits for the designated successor to prove himself before leaving him the reins of the company.

Case 2: Disgust, Anger and Fear

MH is the CEO of 'H', which is one of the leading wine producers in the north-east of France. Founded in 1639 and still active, this company produces high-end wines from its own vineyards and, as a wine merchant, markets products from other selected winemakers under long-term contracts. Strongly established in foreign markets, it exports nearly 80% of its wines.

When we first met MH, he had a simply inexhaustible enthusiasm for the discovery of extraordinary soil. Before you even take a walk in the vineyards or taste his wines, MH offers you a fundamental lesson in geography and geology. MH is not alone at the controls. Here, as you may guess, wine is a family affair. His father AH is never far from the cellars (where, pride of place, is the world's oldest active vat—constructed in 1715, it holds 1,800 litres. You have to see it.); his nephews MAH and JFH—the latter being the son of his late brother EH, who died in 2016—roam the world to carry 'the good word'; his cousin JPH also presides over the destiny of the company. However, it is MH who spoke to us with passion and insatiability about the soils he tirelessly explores, having worked 20 years ago on soil pits to understand the earth near its 250 scattered plots across 30 hectares. "This is how you learn the true nature of the soil: limestone, clay, granite, organic layer thickness, hydromorphy, structure, compactness . . .". When we discussed the subject of succession with MH, he got angry. His son wants him to let go of the family business and allow him to manage the firm instead. On this subject, MH's anger is a protective reaction. It results from frustration, a feeling of injustice, an attack on his power and his rights in the company. He raised his voice and frowned at the beginning of the conversation.

Indeed, his son—who has been working in the company for several years—asked him to resign and wanted him to convince the other family members to appoint him as CEO. The fact that his son took this approach hurt MH. Disgust, in this case, is the rejection of the action of a person (MH's son) who is considered a threat in this situation. When commenting on his son's behaviour, he asked us, "How did he come up with the idea?" MH's surprise was provoked by an unexpected event related to the revelation of his son's intentions, which went against his perception, his representations. MH's surprise was brief and gave way to another emotion.

"For the moment, it's out of the question!" He confirmed,

> It's not because I do not want him to take over the company! Thinking about and preparing for the succession of the company is a must. Followed rigorously at all stages of its development under the supervision of a member of the family, the wine, once in bottles, then stays on average two years in the cellars and is only labelled after a final quality control. He does not have the complete knowledge of our methods. How, under these conditions, can he take over the business? If he does not change his behaviour, I will not be able to defend his application before the family members.

It is fear that followed surprise for MH. In this case, it is an anticipation emotion. MH feels a potential threat to his situation. MH's reaction was to act by blocking the succession process. According to him, to take over the business, one must be capable and deserve it.

In this case, like Case 1, the emotions felt by MH were an obstacle to beginning the necessary steps towards the transfer of the company. Finally, to understand and manage emotions, company stakeholders need to listen to the messages coming from incumbent, like MH, and take one or more actions to change the situation.

Discussion

The purpose of this chapter was to propose that family business succession is an emotion-influenced process, which can affect the choice of a successor. For family firms, succession embodies the central issue to be addressed in order to survive. Prior studies already pointed to the fact that emotions affect decision-making processes in family firms (Shepherd, 2016; Holt and Pop, 2013). These emotions greatly influence the reasoning of the incumbents. In the aforementioned cases, emotions manifested themselves when choosing a potential successor. The emotions of the incumbents were a powerful engine, but they also had a dragging effect. Indeed, they blocked the incumbents, provoked undesirable outcomes and prevented them from acting to set up the succession process. In fact, the fear that the successor would fail to keep up with them prevented them from passing on their businesses, despite the urgency and the need to do so. Conversely, having managed to convince a descendant to take over the business provides great satisfaction, even enthusiasm. Positive emotions can stimulate, allowing the incumbent to be optimistic about the future of the company. Being attentive to one's emotions, to one's feelings, and putting the intensity of the emotion into words develops emotional awareness and helps people to better understand themselves and to better understand the other person. However, in both the cases discussed here, the incumbents seem to be too emotional to be able to mobilise those emotions as levers for a successful succession.

Entrepreneurs have invested considerable resources, time and energy into their businesses. It is not surprising that they do not pass on their businesses easily without first making sure they are in good hands. Entrepreneurs have also made a significant emotional investment in their business, which plays a central role in shaping their identities, and their personal and professional lives. For these reasons, they need to anticipate succession planning to be better prepared emotionally when the time comes. After the succession, entrepreneurs who were emotionally invested in their business reinvest their emotions in planning for their personal future. Emotions occur before and after the succession and have an impact on emotional recovery. Good preparation for succession planning probably helps to better control their emotions and thus should not slow down the action. If both incumbents and successors work to anticipate the future, they will understand the boundaries of their actions.

Succession requires careful anticipation, rigor and expertise. It can help the incumbent to be accompanied through the process by other professionals, such as consultants, lawyers, business lawyers, tax experts and accountants. An external consultant should not be limited to reviewing balance sheets, financial indicators or ratios; they should take into account the experience of the incumbent, including their personal and professional background. In the succession phase, it is imperative for the incumbent to be accompanied by a person who knows them. But what should they do if the advisor does not know the incumbent before this mission? We propose that the incumbent starts with a 'life story' to allow the advisor to know them and therefore be able to respond to both professional and personal issues.

We encourage incumbents to receive support throughout the succession process from an advisor. It seems to us that long-term support is necessary. This support must be global because it is difficult to accompany someone only on a professional level without knowing their global problems, including on a personal and family level. To succeed in their mission, a consultant must have a good knowledge of the professional and personal history of the incumbent. The advisor should be present at their side regularly, and remain available during the years of preparation and joint reign with the successor. Regarding the latter, an external consultant can undoubtedly help them to detach themselves from the family hierarchical relationship. This consultant must therefore be different from that of their predecessor because their objectives are different.

Conclusion and Implications

To conclude, emotions are a driving force and a real cohesive and motivational influence in a family business, but they can also endanger it and generate conflict. Indeed, in the case of succession in family businesses, the behaviour of the incumbent is influenced by their emotions, which push them to interact with their environment in order to ensure their survival, and that of the company and the family.

In terms of the implications for research, we believe that our work proposes a new angle that deserves further study. While family business research recognises the importance of emotions in making decisions and taking actions, no empirical study has yet examined the emotions of incumbents and their influence in succession. This chapter has aimed to shed new light on succession and its preparation by examining emotions. As for the managerial contributions, we point out the need for family incumbents and successors to have trusted advisors to accompany them during the succession process so that emotions do not constitute an obstacle to action. Finally, we must not forget that, in family businesses, emotions are triggered by interactions between the family and the company. They can have an impact not only on the succession, but also on the course of the history of the family business.

References

Barsade, S. (2002). "The ripple effect: emotional contagion and its influence on group behavior", *Administrative Science Quarterly*, 17, 644–675.

Berrone, P., Cruz, C. and Gomez-Mejia, L.R. (2012). "Socioemotional wealth in family firms: theoretical dimensions, assessment approaches, and agenda for future research", *Family Business Review*, 2(3), 258–279.

Brundin, E. and Härtel, C.E.J. (2014). "Emotions in family firms", in L. Melin, M. Nordqvist and P. Sharma (Eds.), *The Sage book of family business*, 529–548, London: Sage Publications.

Cahour, B. (2010). "Emotions, affects et confort comme nouveaux déterminants de l'activité et de l'usage", *Ergonomie, conception de produits et services médiatisés*, 273–305.

Cahour, B. and Lancry, A. (2011). "Émotions et activités professionnelles et quotidiennes", *Le Travail Humain*, 2(74), 97–106.

Cardon, M., Zietsma, C., Saparito, P., Matherne, B. and Davis, C. (2005). "A tale of passion: new insights into entrepreneurship from a parenthood metaphor", *Journal of Business Venturing*, 20(1), 23–45.

Carrau, C. (2019). "Familiales: emprises et entreprises", in E. Lamarque, T. Poulain-Rehm and P. Barnetto (Eds.), *Variations autour des PME et des entreprises de taille intermédiaire*, 235–244, Caen, France: Editions EMS.

Chrisman, J.J., Chua, J.H., Sharma, P. and Yoder, R.P. (2009). "Guiding family businesses through the succession process", *The CPA Journal*, 79(6), 48–51.

Cohen, A. and Sharma, P. (2016). *How successful family business develop their next leaders*, Oakland, CA: Berrett-Koehler.

Cosnier, J. (1994). *Psychologie des émotions et des sentiments*, Paris: Retz.

Cruz, C.C., Gomez-Mejia, L.R. and Becerra, M. (2010). "Perceptions of benevolence and the design of agency contracts: CEO-TMT relationships in family firms", *Academy of Management Journal*, 53, 69–89.

Damasio, A. (2003). *Spinoza avait raison; joie et tristesse, le cerveau des émotions*, Paris: Odile Jacob.

Daspit, J., Holt, D., Chrisman, J. and Long, R. (2016). "Examining family firm succession from a social exchange perspective", *Family Business Review*, 29(1), 44–64.

Dehlen, T., Zellweger, T., Kammerlander, N. and Halter, F. (2014). "The role of information asymmetry in the choice of entrepreneurial exit routes", *Journal of Business Venturing*, 29(2), 193–209.

Deschamps, B. (2014). *Des pratiques de transmissions au concept générique de transfert d'entreprise*, Note de synthèse des activités de recherche en vue du diplôme d'Habilitation à Diriger des Recherches, Université Grenoble.

DeTienne, D.R. (2010). "Entrepreneurial exit as a critical component of the entrepreneurial process: theoretical development", *Journal of Business Venturing*, 25(2), 203–215.

DeTienne, D.R. and Chirico, F. (2013). "Exit strategies in family firms: how socioemotional wealth drives the threshold of performance", *Entrepreneurship Theory and Practice*, 37(6), 1297–1318.

Duh, M., Tominc, P. and Rebernik, M. (2009). "Growth ambitions and succession solutions in family businesses", *Journal of Small Business and Enterprise Development*, 16, 256–269.

Ekman, P., Friesen, W.V. and Ellsworth, P. (1972). *Motion in the human face*, New York: Pergamon.

Gagné, M., Sharma, P. and De Massis, A. (2014). "The study of organizational behaviour in family business", *European Journal of Work and Organizational Psychology*, 23(5), 643–656.

Gersick, K.E., Davis, J.A., McCollom-Hampton, M. and Lansberg, I. (1997). *Generation to generation: life cycles of the family business*, Boston, MA: Harvard Business School Press.

Gómez-Mejía, L.R., Haynes, K.T., Núñez-Nickel, M., Jacobson, K.J. and Moyano-Fuentes, J. (2007). "Socioemotional wealth and business risks in family-controlled firms: evidence from Spanish olive oil mills", *Administrative Science Quarterly*, 52(1), 106–137.

Graebner, M.E. and Eisenhardt, K.M. (2004). "The seller's side of the story: acquisition as courtship and governance as syndicate in entrepreneurial firms", *Administrative Science Quarterly*, 49(3), 366–403.

Harrell, S. (1997). *Human families*, Boulder, CO: Westview.

Holt, R. and Popp, A. (2013). "Emotion, succession, and the family firm: Josiah Wedgwood & Sons", *Business History*, 55(6), 892–909.

Kellermanns, F.W., Eddleston, K.A. and Zellweger, T.M. (2012). "Extending the socioemotional wealth perspective: a look at the dark side", *Entrepreneurship Theory and Practice*, 36, 1175–1182.

Labaki, R. (2019). "La recherche sur les entreprises familiales: Une épopée de liaisons dangereuses", in E. Lamarque, T. Poulain-Rehm and P. Barnetto (Eds.), *Variations autour des PME et des entreprises de taille intermédiaire*, 195–208. Caen, France: Editions EMS, janvier.

Labaki, R., Michael-Tsabari, N. and Zachary, R.K. (2013). "Emotional dimensions within the family business: towards a conceptualization", in *Handbook of research on family business*, 2nd ed., Cheltenham Glos, UK: Edward Elgar Publishing.

Lazarus, R.S. (1991). "Cognition and motivation in emotion", *American Psychologist. psycnet.apa.org*.

Ledoux, J. (1998). *The emotional brain*, London: Weidenfeld and Nicolson.

Lépine, V. and Martin-Juchat, F. (2018). "Situations émotionnelles de cadres de santé: les émotions au cœur de l'action et de la communication", *Revue française des sciences de l'information et de la communication* [in ligne], 15. http://journals.openedition.org/rfsic/5114; https://doi.org/10.4000/rfsic.5114.

Nordqvist, M., Wennberg, K., Bau, M. and Hellerstedt, K. (2013). "Succession in private firms as an entrepreneurial process", *Small Business Economics*, 40, 1087–1122.

Radu-Lefebvre, M. and Randerson, K. (2020). "Successfully navigating the paradox of control and autonomy in succession: the role of managing ambivalent emotions", *International Small Business Journal*, 38(3), 184–210.

Schwarz, N. (2000). "Emotion, cognition, and decision making", *Cognition & Emotion*, 14, 433–440.

Shepherd, D.A. (2016). "An emotions perspective for advancing the fields of family business and entrepreneurship: stocks, flows, reactions, and responses", *Family Business Review*, 29(2), 151–158.

Stewart, A. (2003). "Help one another, use one another: toward an anthropology of family business", *Entrepreneurship Theory and Practice*, 27, 383–396.

Van der Merwe, S., Venter, E. and Ellis, S.M. (2009). "An exploratory study of some of the determinants of management succession planning in family businesses", *Management Dynamics, Journal of the Southern African Institute for Management Scientists*, 18(4), 2–17.

Van Hoorebeke, D. (2008). "L'émotion et la prise de décision", *Revue française de gestion*, 182(2), 33–44.

Wennberg, K. and DeTienne, D.R. (2014). "What do we really mean when we talk about 'exit'? A critical review of research on entrepreneurial exit", *International Small Business Journal*, 32(1), 4–16.

Whetten, D., Foreman, P. and Dyer, G. (2014). "Organizational identity and family business", in L. Melin, M. Nordqvist and P. Sharma (Eds.), *The SAGE handbook of family business*, 480–497. Thousand Oaks, CA: Sage Publications.

Zahra, S.A. (2003). "International expansion of U.S. manufacturing family business: the effect of ownership and involvement", *Journal of Business Venturing*, 18(4), 495–512.

Zellweger, T.M. and Dehlen, T. (2012). "Value is in the eye of the owner: affect infusion and socioemotional wealth among family firm owners", *Family Business Review*, 25(3), 280–329.

4 Family Business Transfer

A Stressful Event for Successors

Florence Guiliani and Luis Cisneros

Business transfer is one of the most studied subjects in family business research (Cisneros *et al.*, 2018). Succession is "an especially challenging event for all kinds of firms" (Miller, Steier and Le Breton-Miller, 2003, p. 515). Indeed, the economic, social and also human ramifications emphasise the critical nature of the subject. Paradoxically, while the legal, financial and tax dimensions are well researched, the emotional and psychological factors, which are the determining conditions for the success of family transfers, are often too briefly or superficially dealt with (Miller *et al.*, 2020; Bertschi-Michel *et al.*, 2020), despite there being so many questions about these different elements (Filser *et al.*, 2013).

In the context of family business succession, the family's influence means that emotions impact many of the main actors' coordinated activities and decisions, especially those involving both the incumbent and the successor (Bertschi-Michel *et al.*, 2020). Stressors can be the result of disagreements between the incumbent and their successor about values or the choice of successor, etc.; they can engender work-related stress or anxiety, and impact succession outcomes (Salvato and Corbetta, 2013). A better understanding of how stress is managed from the successor's perspective and how it affects outcomes of the succession process is therefore needed. Indeed, the management of stress during this time of change represents a significant research gap.

Moreover, the strong interrelation between the family and work spheres within family businesses (Aldrich and Cliff, 2003) can spread the stress felt by the successor. The succession can be a stressful event that affects both the family business and family. The impact of coping strategies on stress is key to reducing its effects. Miller *et al.* (2020, p. 55) argue that "the operation of a family business influences these resources and coping strategies available to a family and that those strategies, in turn, will influence the business". In this chapter, we explore how stress influences families (business families) and family businesses during succession. We thus ask the following research questions: in the different succession phases, what stressors emerge in the family business and the business family from the successor's perspective? Which coping strategies are used to deal with the event?

To answer these research questions, we build on the transactional theory of stress and coping (Lazarus and Folkman, 1984). The methodological approach consists of a qualitative study of four successors in SMEs who have successfully taken over family businesses. Our findings reveal familial and professional stressors that successors face during succession, how they induce stress, and how they affect both their psychological and physical health. Our findings further show the role of coping strategies in response to these stressors.

Theoretical Framework

The specificity of family business lies in the unique overlap between the family, ownership, management and individual relations within the company (Filser *et al.*, 2013). The succession represents the most critical issue a family business must manage to ensure its survival from one generation to another (Miller *et al.*, 2003; Giménez and Novo, 2020). Indeed, "only one third of family businesses survive into the second generation, and only about 10–15% make it into the third generation" (Le Breton-Miller *et al.*, 2004, p. 305). The transfer of a business is a complex professional life event in many respects for both the predecessor and the successor (Kets de Vries *et al.*, 2007). In the context of family businesses, it is a multidimensional process impacted by several variables, since this event can also affect personal lives (Kets de Vries *et al.*, 2007). There are many reasons for the emotional difficulty of the situation the successor faces.

The way the incumbent allocates the leadership step-by-step to the successor has been well represented in academic literature for years (Cisneros *et al.*, 2018). According to Handler (1994) and Cadieux (2007), the succession process can be divided into four main phases, namely Incubation, Implementation, Joint Management, New Leadership and Predecessor's Disengagement. (1) In Incubation, the predecessor is the dominant actor: he manages and controls the firm. During this first phase, the successor is initiated to the daily workings of the firm, acquiring family business culture, and he/she then either shows or does not show interest for the family business. (2) In Implementation, the successor joins the firm officially, and operational and administrative responsibilities are assigned to him/her. Generally, he/she evolves gradually within the company and shows his/her willingness to succeed the incumbent. The successor is chosen in a formal or informal way at this stage. (3) In Joint Management, the successor and predecessor lead the family business together. A programme is established for completing the transfer of leadership to the successor. Over time, more and more important projects and responsibilities are assigned to the successor. (4) In New Leadership and Disengagement, the predecessor retires and the leadership and ownership transfers are completed. The successor takes over the leadership of the organisation, signalling the end of the succession process.

Le Breton-Miller *et al.* (2004) show that in the context of successful successions, the most documented successor's attributes reducing both internal and external strains are: the quality of the relationship with the incumbent (respect, understanding, trust, cooperation and closeness), his/her motivation, interest and commitment to perpetuate family values, the freedom not to be a part of the family business, his/her managerial ability, competence, talent, experience, drive, credibility and legitimacy.

These attributes allow the successor to manage the family business, but do not always erase the psychological and physiological challenges created by transfers, especially family business transfers (Nikolaev *et al.*, 2020).

Succession Can Be a Stressful and Anxious Experience . . .

The issue of stressors in family business is important to address because it has been found to stimulate negative effects, such as worry, stress and anxiety (Conroy and Metzler, 2004). According to Bertschi-Michel *et al.* (2020, p. 83), "the succession process bears unique challenges that can affect the incumbent's and successor's emotions". The succession process exposes the successor to a palette of potential stressors which can increase stress levels and reduce well-being (Baron *et al.*, 2016).

From the successor's perspective, these challenges (stressors) are intensified by his/her direct connection to the incumbent, the business, work results, shareholders, and other family members who work there or depend on it. Detaching themselves emotionally, cognitively or even legally from their liability can prove very difficult (Wach *et al.*, 2018).

Lazarus's theory (1991) argues that stressors are dependent on the individual's perception of changes in their relationship to their environment, which will lead to their inability to fulfil their needs. Folkman *et al.* (1986, p. 572) define stress as "a relationship between the person and the environment that is appraised by the person as taxing or exceeding his or her resources and as endangering well-being". For these authors, stress is a two-way process that requires environmental stressors as well as an individual's subjective response to them. Indeed, the individual's evaluation of a stressful experience influences how he/she will react to it.

Stress and anxiety are highly interconnected in the entrepreneurial context (Baron *et al.*, 2016). In addition to family business stressors, a successor has to deal with familial stress. At the time of the transfer, the family business will have already existed for numerous years and will provide financial support to several family members. In this situation, intergenerational succession failures take on a whole new dimension and the stakes rise astronomically (Miller *et al.*, 2003). The high level of individual and family expectations increase the pressure, anxiety and stress for the successor.

The link between stress and health outcomes is well documented, both for its impact on physical health (the physiological and physical status of the body) and mental health. Long-term exposure to chronic stress can affect health and is an indirect risk factor for many diseases such as heart disease, intestinal diseases, different infections affecting the immune system and mental illness (anxiety and depression) (Cohen *et al.*, 2019). The links between exposure to stressful events and disease have also been studied in entrepreneurship literature (Shepherd and Patzelt, 2015; Baron *et al.*, 2016).

Nevertheless, empirical studies show that entrepreneurs can experience stress and still decide to pursue their entrepreneurial aspirations (Mitchell and Shepherd, 2011). Stress can generate both motivation and inhibition for entrepreneurial action (LePine *et al.*, 2004). Successors may experience both motivational and inhibiting stressors during the family transfer. Coping strategies are therefore perhaps the key to a smooth and stress-free succession.

. . . But Luckily, Coping Strategies Can Facilitate It

In their model of stress appraisal, Lazarus and Folkman (1984) include primary, secondary and reappraisal components. The primary appraisal occurs when an individual evaluates whether a stressor poses a threat. The secondary appraisal occurs when he/she assesses the resources or coping strategies available to counter any perceived threats. Finally, reappraisal refers to the process of continually reappraising the stressor and the resources available for responding to the stressor. In this chapter, we will only focus on the link between the stressor, the associated emotional effects and the coping strategies used by successors.

Lazarus and Folkman (1984, p. 141) define coping as "constantly changing cognitive and behavioural efforts to manage specific external and/or internal demands that are appraised as taxing or exceeding the resources of the person". In their definition, coping is a shifting process. For example, ineffective coping might result in more stress, whereas an effective one might result in relief (Segerstrom and Smith, 2019). The successor's coping strategy can be defined as cognitive and behavioural efforts to manage the taxing demands posed by the family business transfer.

Following Lazarus and Folkman (1984), the main coping strategy categories are problem-focused (managing or changing a stressful situation), emotion-focused (regulating emotional reactions to a stressor), meaning-focused (a stressor which, in the long-term, will bring enhanced meaning to the person's life) and social support-focused (using social support to minimise emotional response or resolve the issue).

In addition, Folkman and Moskowitz (2000) identify three classes of coping strategies in order to understand the positive outcomes of stress: positive reappraisal, problem-focused coping and the creation of positive events. Positive reappraisal refers to a cognitive process through which the individual focuses on the positive in every situation, such as discovering opportunities for personal growth. Problem-focused coping involves thoughts and instrumental behaviours to manage or resolve the stressor. The creation of positive events (meaning-focused) entails a positive psychological time-out by infusing ordinary events with positive meaning (Folkman and Moskowitz, 2000).

Avoidance-style coping also exists, and involves assertiveness or withdrawal. This coping style is related to more physical issues, while social-support coping is linked to fewer physical symptoms because it increases positive effects (Aldwin and Park, 2004). Fine *et al.* (2012) affirm that entrepreneur tends to be above average in their ability to cope with stress. In the succession context, the successor can cope with the challenge of succession by assuming different roles throughout the process and pass through a mutual role adjustment with the incumbent (Handler, 1990).

Method

Family business succession is a complex research topic (Cisneros *et al.*, 2018) and analysing it from the perspective of the health of the successors increases its complexity. This, in conjunction with the scarce literature linking succession and health, means our research is exploratory in nature (Yin, 2008), and it also legitimises using an inductive and qualitative approach (Eisenhardt, 1989). This approach allows us to capture various life experiences and offers a better understanding of the problem targeted (Sekaran and Bougie, 2003). It also permits us to gain deeper insights that might be used to create conceptual frameworks (Miles and Huberman, 1994).

In our study, we employed a semi-structured interview approach which is particularly useful for generating new knowledge in such exploratory situations (Yin, 2008). In addition, data was also gathered from various secondary sources such as webpages, financial records, newspapers and family participation in succession contests, conferences or workshops. After triangulating the data from primary and secondary sources, we compared (and contrasted) the information from each company to identify emerging insights.

In order to better understand how successors cope with stressors during the succession process, we followed De Massis and Kotlar (2014, p. 18) and used a polar-type sampling method to more easily observe *"contrasting patterns"*. We analysed extreme situations where the succession was successful so as to understand the emotional issues the successors experienced and how they solved them. Participants were identified through a regional contest on succession of family SMEs in the province of Quebec, Canada. The researchers' involvement in this context meant that they could select the winners of this contest—family businesses who had successfully transferred their business in the last five years. All participants had the majority share of the family firm capital. All the businesses grew and had a positive overall performance after the succession process concluded.

During the data gathering, the successors were actively involved in leading their companies. In each company, before passing the baton, the incumbent had been the managing director and primary owner. The four companies operate in different sectors and employ fewer than 250 employees (see Table 4.1). Our interview guide was based on the family business profile (company history, organisational context, family context and successor's profile), the family business succession process (four-stage model and incumbent-successor relationship), stress (thoughts, feeling and behaviours), and coping. We collected data through individual and semi-structured phone interviews (primary sources). Four interviews lasting one hour were conducted, recorded and transcribed.

Regarding data analysis, we separately cross-referenced the information from each company's interviews and secondary data. This strategy significantly reduced the retrospective rationalisation bias. Then, we coded the content of the interviews, formed categories and compared them with our literature review. It took several movements back and forth to model our results.

Table 4.1 Overview of the Sample

Company	Company A	Company B	Company C	Company D
Gender	Female	Female	Male	Male
Transition	2007–2009	2010–2016	2008–2014	2003–2014
Industry/Business sector	Manufacturer	Manufacturer	Energy	Manufacturer
Number of employees	110	225	150	150
Leading generation	2nd	2nd	3rd	2nd
Leadership position of successor	Co-President	President	President	President, CEO
Predecessor's position or disengagement	Retired, coach	Retired	Executive board	Business development consultant, ambassador

Findings

In this research, we try to understand how successors' health is affected during the succession process and what their coping strategies are. As can be seen in Table 4.2, we separated the responses into two main sources of stressors: organisational (family business) and familial (business family). We observed the emergence of emotional/psychological effects linked to these stressors. Finally, we identified coping strategies and their physical effects on the successors.

Discussion

Due to the complexity of the different stages, family firm succession can be perceived as challenging (Bertschi-Michel *et al.*, 2020). Each phase brings the successor its share of stressors, such as the succession planning (Incubation), potential miscommunication issues (Succession Project Implementation), uncertainty regarding the firm's future (Joint Management) or the incumbent's resistance to his/her new role (New Leadership). In this exploratory study, we identified stressors, individual subjective responses and how successors faced them, building on Lazarus and Folkman (1984).

We found four main categories of stressors linked to the family business (first source):

- The succession process: ambiguity due to the lack of formal planning and implementation, as well as the lack of clarity in either the choice of the next CEO or the expectations of the successor. These stressors provoked fear of failure, stress, anxiety and loss of meaning for the successors. The ambiguity was mainly present in the first two phases of the succession process.
- The successor's way of working: changes in the way the successor leads/manages the family business. Innovating, changing government structures, facing lack of growth, as well as changes in the way they communicate generate resistance and even opposition in both employees and family members working in the company. This, in turn, generates frustration, anger, fear of failure, stress, anxiety and cognitive overload. However, trying to improve or change the business model makes successors feel optimistic and boosts adrenaline.
- External issues to the company: crises or major external problems. A bad economic situation in the sector in which the company operates, as well as having problems with strategic external stakeholders provokes chronic stress, anxiety and a feeling of being powerless for the successors.
- The effort required by the successor to succeed: working hard and pushing themselves to succeed. Stressors engender ambivalent effects of fear of failure and eustress.

Table 4.2 Coping Mechanisms in Response to Familial or Business Stressors at the Four Stages of the Succession Process

Stages	Source	Stressors	Emotional and psychological effects	Coping strategy	Psychological/ physical effects	Example interview quotes
Incubation	Family Business:	Uncertainty related to method for choosing the successors. Misalignment between the FB goal and the successor's goals. Ambiguous succession planning process	Anxiety Fear of failure, loss of meaning Stress	Implementation of structured processes supported by external advisors. Acquisition of business social capital (relations with the stakeholders)	Reassurance Optimism Full of energy	I had to create my own work and find my own challenges in the FB (Company B) Without professional support, the transfer became a bit chaotic. The incumbent had a vision and I had another one. (Company D)
	Business Family:	Uncertainty caused by the incumbent's health issues. Disagreement between members of the previous generation. Conflicts split business family (loss of familial link). Lack of self-confidence (perception of lack of legitimacy by being the son/daughter of the incumbent)	Eustress (challenge), sadness Deception, anxiety, sadness Anxiety	Practicing introspection (self-reflection). Establishing family meetings to improve communication and getting family approval. Extended family avoidance. Evolve gradually within the FB as an employee (job crafting)	Boost of adrenaline Reassurance Optimism Courage	The disagreement created a lot of anxiety, because I was close to my cousin and since the transfer we are no longer in contact (Company C)

(Continued)

Table 4.2 (Continued)

Stages	Source	Stressors	Emotional and psychological effects	Coping strategy	Psychological/ physical effects	Example interview quotes
Succession project implementation	Family Business:	Ambiguous implementation of the transaction for acquiring company's shares (how much, when and how) Lack of communication between incumbents and family members working within the FB	Fear of failure Stress, anxiety Loss of meaning Frustration, anger	Closing transaction and establishing incumbent's disengagement (leaving the company or changing his/her role) Capitalise on past failing transfer experiences Establishing better communication channels with family and peers Implementing an advisory board Implementing a family council	Tiredness Hope Self-efficacy Courage Relaxed Optimism, eustress	Literally, for two years the incumbents postponed the transaction every month. Those two years were excruciating. (Company A) On the one hand, implementing a board was very helpful in formalising and somehow professionalising the company. Thanks to the board, we followed our actions more closely. . . . However, integrating outsiders into the company's board stressed family members. But on the other hand, the family council allowed us to reduce family tensions. (Company C)

	Challenges	Emotions	Coping strategies	Outcomes	Quotes
Business Family:	Resistance to change, the acceptance and respect of the new roles of each family member working within the FB Lack of self-confidence (perception of not being able to fulfil responsibilities)	Stress Doubts, anxiety, imposter syndrome	External coaching Communication with family (extended and nuclear) Practicing introspection (self-reflection) Having psychotherapy	Reassurance	I experienced a certain anxiety towards my brother and if he would be comfortable in his role in the FB, since I was chosen to be the President (Company C) I feel always a little fear of failure and that's ok, because I think it is crucial to have it—if you want to know your blind spots (Company D)
Joint management Family business:	Change resistance to improving (even reinventing) business model (restructuring, innovating, reorienting activities, etc.) Facing an external economic crisis Facing problems with financial stakeholders	Optimism, boost of adrenaline, anxiety Fear of failure Cognitive overload Frustration Chronic stress, powerless Stress, anxiety	Implementing a formal (and participative) strategic plan, shared vision and formal governance structure Having business family members' and subordinates' support Having a strong vision and strategy for the FB Presenting a new strategy and a business restructuring plan	Strong self-efficacy Eustress	There was a very formal event during which my father [incumbent] gave me a steel key, [as a] symbol of the transfer (Company D)

(Continued)

Table 4.2 (Continued)

Stages	Source	Stressors	Emotional and psychological effects	Coping strategy	Psychological/ physical effects	Example interview quotes
	Business Family:	Avoiding succession problems because of the incumbent health issues Escalation of negative emotional tensions related to the unwell incumbent reclaiming their voting shares Conflict with the incumbent, dealing with a lot of pressure and jealousy Conflict with another business family member (also a potential successor) Lack of self-confidence (perception of lack of competency)	Anxiety, worry, guilt Loss of meaning, depression, powerless Hostility, anger, anxiety, meanness, guilt Stress, frustration, hopeless Loneliness Anxiety, imposter syndrome	Implementing incumbent's new role within the FB Business partner, nuclear family and friends' support Spousal support (and alcohol use without abuse) Being member and participating in CEO associations and communities of leaders Nuclear family support Coaching Practicing an introspection (self-reflection) Discussing and exchanging with counterparts (other CEOs)	Exhaustion, insomnia Neck and shoulder pains Eczema Reassurance Optimism Reassurance	This period was like hell. He [incumbent] threatened me with lawyers, he panicked. He even physically threatened my partner. I put aside my father because he was toxic. (Company B) Belonging to an association of business leaders helped me a lot....I was able to exchange views with empathetic people who lived through the same business and family problems as me. (Company D)

| New leadership/predecessor's disengagement | Family business: | Concluding the transfer transaction Having a work overload Pushing him/herself to success (post-succession) and perceiving an uncertain future—family disappointment Facing a business degrowth Integrating external shareholders disturbed family shareholders Preparing the next generation | Anxiety Eustress Fear of failure Anxiety Frustration Stress | Past professional success Maintaining and enlarging (with more family members) family councils Looking for family support Having advice about incumbent's experiences Having peer support Improving communication channels with family shareholders and educating them on corporate financial issues | Pride, perseverance, high energy Boost of adrenaline Insomnia Reassurance | I have repayment pressure, and to do this I must grow the FB while continuing to generate family wealth. This kind of pressure makes me experience a lot of anxiety, but creates also a challenge. (Company D) A few months ago, the FB experienced a period of decline since I became president. For me, it was very difficult to deal with; I was disappointed with myself and I was afraid that my family would be disappointed with me too. (Company C) Calm after the storm and my body says now I have time to be tired (Company A) Once the succession process was over, I decided to not continue the family council meetings. . . . I soon realised my mistake; the relationship with my father started to degrade and a distancing with the other members of the family was created. (Company C) |

(Continued)

Table 4.2 (Continued)

Stages	Source	Stressors	Emotional and psychological effects	Coping strategy	Psychological/ physical effects	Example interview quotes
	Business Family:	Healing family relationships Lack of self-confidence (permanent doubts about his/her accomplishments as leaders and as parents)	Doubts, anxiety, imposter syndrome	Improving communication with extended family (through social activities) Applying a healthy lifestyle (nutrition, hockey) Trying to balance work and family Training in entrepreneurship and leadership skills	Arterial pressure, Less energy Physical wellness Eustress Strong self-efficacy	Energy level goes down whether we like it or not (Company B)

We identified three main stressors linked to the business family (second source):

- The successor's lack of self-confidence: they expressed a lack of confidence in themselves during the different phases of the succession process. They perceive themselves as having a lack of legitimacy, feel incompetent, believe that they will not be able to achieve what is expected of them, and even after successfully completing the succession process and growing the company, they question their own family and business achievements. This quasi-permanent impostor syndrome throughout the process causes anxiety and often makes successors doubt themselves.
- The relationship between predecessor and successor: damaged relationships and the incumbent's health problems generate avoidance and uncertainty. When those factors impact the succession process by delaying its development, successors feel anxiety, worry, guilt, depression, loss of meaning and powerlessness. If the negative emotional tensions are strong, they can provoke hostility, anger and mean feelings in the successor. When tensions between actors are linked to jealous conflicts, the successor tends to feel stress, frustration and powerless. Finally, the incumbent's health problems also cause sadness for the successors, although they also perceive it as a challenge which tells them to prepare themselves to succeed the incumbent.
- The relationship between the successor and the business family members: disagreement with members of the previous generation causes disappointment, anxiety and sadness for the successor. Also, conflicts and misunderstanding which split the business family stress and frustrate him/her. When conflict emerges with a member of his/her management team, who was also a potential CEO, the successor feels loneliness. On the other hand, when damaged family relations are healing, even if he/she feels anxiety, optimism is also present. Finally, preparing the next generation of successors makes him/her feel optimistic and eustress.

According to Handler (1990), mutual role adjustment must occur for both the incumbent and the successor to make it through the succession process. The successor will transform from first having no role or power, to an employee who carries out certain tasks, to a manager who fulfils most of the important tasks and finally to new leader (Handler, 1990). Our findings show that certain stressors experienced by successors can have positive (challenging) effects and/or a negative (hindrance) effect (LePine *et al.*, 2004). Stressors that involve the possibility of future gains and personal growth, like cognitive demands or time pressure, are described as challenge stressors. By contrast, stressors that entail constraints and strain, such as role conflict or role ambiguity, are characterised as hindrance stressors.

Folkman and Moskowitz (2000) address the question of the nature of stress; for them, the positive outcomes associated with stress and previous experiences that dispose individuals to appraise stressful situations as more of a challenge than a threat depend on their coping strategies. In our study, because of the ambiguity generated by the succession process, stressors in general are mostly perceived as a hindrance. The successors used problem-focused coping (Lazarus and Folkman, 1984) when they thought they had personal control over the outcome. In contrast, when the perceived control over the situation was low, they tended to choose avoidance-style coping (Aldwin and Park, 2004). This strategy was a way to regain control over their professional life. For example, the successor of company A decided to prospect other firms in order to fulfil her dream of business ownership. Due to the interconnection between family and business, when avoidance-style coping was used in the family business, it was also used in a business family context, especially in the relationship between the successor and the other business family members.

The stressors related to the successor's way of working and the company's external issues were perceived as challenging. The two main coping strategies used by the successors regarding challenge stressors was problem-focused coping and social support (Lazarus and Folkman, 1984). They used active coping strategies to take control and manage the underlying cause of distress. Some successors implemented a structured process supported by external advisors or established better communication channels with family and peers. Usually, problem-focused coping is used to cope with both internal (improving business model) and external organisational stressors (economic crisis), while social support is used to deal with interpersonal issues in both the family business and business family.

The stressors related to the effort required by the successor to succeed and their self-confidence are also challenge stressors, but the main coping strategy for them was positive reappraisal (Folkman and Moskowitz, 2000). For example, the successor in company D practices introspection to cope with imposter syndrome. This coping strategy brings reassurance and self-confidence by increasing his perception of personal growth.

To conclude, this exploratory research makes several contributions: it identified the main sources of stressors for successors and also their coping strategies during the succession process. It brings to light the fact that even though the successors were experienced, trained in their sectors, had evolved within the company and had been accompanied by advisors, they expressed a lack of confidence in themselves during all the stages of the succession process.

As for all exploratory research, ours is not without limitations. We only investigated four Canadian family businesses and their successful successions, therefore the results are not generalizable. It would be worthwhile to compare these results with failed successions. Another future research avenue based on our study could be to do a quantitative research.

References

Aldrich, H.E. and Cliff, J.E. (2003). "The pervasive effects of family on entrepreneurship: toward a family", *Journal of Business Venturing*, 18(5), 573–596.

Aldwin, C.M. and Park, C.L. (2004). "Coping and physical health outcomes: an overview", *Psychology and Health*, 19(3), 277–281.

Baron, R.A., Franklin, R.J. and Hmieleski, K.M. (2016). "Why entrepreneurs often experience low, not high, levels of stress: the joint effects of selection and psychological capital", *Journal of Management*, 42(3), 742–768.

Bertschi-Michel, A., Kammerlander, N. and Strike, V.M. (2020). "Unearthing and alleviating emotions in family business successions", *Entrepreneurship Theory and Practice*, 44(1), 81–108.

Cadieux, L. (2007). "Succession in small and medium-sized family businesses: toward a typology of predecessor roles during and after instatement of the successor", *Family Business Review*, 20(2), 95–109.

Cisneros, L.F., Ibanescu, M., Keen, C., Lobato-Calleros, O. and Niebla-Zatarain, J.C. (2018). "Bibliometric study of family business succession between 1939 and 2017: mapping and analyzing authors' networks", *Scientometrics*, 117(2), 919–951.

Cohen, S., Murphy, M.L. and Prather, A.A. (2019). "Ten surprising facts about stressful life events and disease risk", *Annual Review of Psychology*, 70, 577–597.

Conroy, D.E. and Metzler, J.N. (2004). "Patterns of self-talk associated with different forms of competitive anxiety", *Journal of Sport and Exercise Psychology*, 26(1), 69–89.

De Massis, A. and Kotlar, J. (2014). "The case study method in family business research: guidelines for qualitative scholarship", *Journal of Family Business Strategy*, 5(1), 15–29.

Eisenhardt, K.M. (1989). "Building theories from case study research", *The Academy of Management Review*, 14(4), 532–550.

Filser, M., Kraus, S. and Märk, S. (2013). "Psychological aspects of succession in family business management", *Management Research Review*, 36(3), 256–277.

Fine, S., Meng, H., Feldman, G. and Nevo, B. (2012). "Psychological predictors of successful entrepreneurship in China: an empirical study", *International Journal of Management*, 29(1), 279–292.

Folkman, S., Lazarus, R.S., Gruen, R.J. and DeLongis, A. (1986). "Appraisal, coping, health status, and psychological symptoms", *Journal of Personality and Social Psychology*, 50(3), 571.

Folkman, S. and Moskowitz, J.T. (2000). "Positive affect and the other side of coping", *American Psychologist*, 55(6), 647.

Giménez, E.L. and Novo, J.A. (2020). "A theory of succession in family firms", *Journal of Family and Economic Issues*, 41(1), 96–120.

Handler, W.C. (1990). "Succession in family firms: a mutual role adjustment between entrepreneur and next-generation family members", *Entrepreneurship Theory and Practice*, 15(1), 37–52.

Handler, W.C. (1994). "Succession in family business: a review of the research", *Family Business Review*, 7(2), 133–157.

Kets de Vries, M.F.R., Carlock, R.S. and Florent-Treacy, E. (2007). *Family business on the couch: a psychological perspective*, West Sussex: John Wiley & Sons.

Lazarus, R.S. (1991). *Emotion and adaptation*, Oxford: Oxford University Press.

Lazarus, R.S. and Folkman, S. (1984). "Coping and adaptations", in W.D. Gentry (Ed.), *Handbook of behavioral medicine*, 282–325, New York: The Guildford Press.

Le Breton-Miller, I.L., Miller, D. and Steier, L.P. (2004). "Toward an integrative model of effective FOB succession", *Entrepreneurship Theory and Practice*, 28(4), 305–328.

LePine, J.A., LePine, M.A. and Jackson, C.L. (2004). "Challenge and hindrance stress: relationships with exhaustion, motivation to learn, and learning performance", *Journal of Applied Psychology*, 89(5), 883.

Miles, M.B. and Huberman, A.M. (1994). *Qualitative data analysis: an expanded sourcebook*, Thousand Oaks, CA: Sage Publications.

Miller, D., Steier, L. and Le Breton-Miller, I. (2003). "Lost in time: intergenerational succession, change, and failure in family business", *Journal of Business Venturing*, 18(4), 513–531.

Miller, D., Wiklund, J. and Yu, W. (2020). "Mental health in the family business: a conceptual model and a research agenda", *Entrepreneurship Theory and Practice*, 44(1), 55–80.

Mitchell, J. and Shepherd, D. (2011). "Afraid of opportunity: the effects of fear of failure on entrepreneurial decisions", *Frontiers of Entrepreneurship Research*, 31.

Nikolaev, B., Shir, N. and Wiklund, J. (2020). "Dispositional positive and negative affect and self-employment transitions: the mediating role of job satisfaction", *Entrepreneurship Theory and Practice*, 44(3), 451–474.

Salvato, C. and Corbetta, G. (2013). "Transitional leadership of advisors as a facilitator of successor's leadership construction", *Family Business Review*, 26(3), 235–255.

Segerstrom, S.C. and Smith, G.T. (2019). "Personality and coping: individual differences in responses to emotion", *Annual Review of Psychology*, 70, 651–671.

Sekaran, U. and Bougie, R. (2003). *Research methods for business, a skill building approach*, New York: John Willey & Sons.

Shepherd, D.A. and Patzelt, H. (2015). "Harsh evaluations of entrepreneurs who fail: the role of sexual orientation, use of environmentally friendly technologies, and observers' perspective taking", *Journal of Management Studies*, 52(2), 253–284.

Wach, D., Stephan, U., Gorgievski, M.J. and Wegge, J. (2018). "Entrepreneurs' achieved success: developing a multi-faceted measure", *International Entrepreneurship and Management Journal*, 1–29.

Yin, R.K. (2008). *Case study research: design and methods*, 4th ed., Thousand Oaks, CA: Sage Publications.

5 The Making of Family Entrepreneurs

How Heirs Become Entrepreneurs and Take Over a Family Business

Paulette Robic, Dominique Barbelivien and Nicolas Antheaume

The aim of this chapter is to understand how heirs turn into entrepreneurs and take over the reins of a family business. We study the case of a French fifth-generation family business (FB) belonging to a complex family, i.e., involving several predecessors and successors from several different branches of the same family. We consider that becoming a family entrepreneur requires a long process of socialisation and testing that is anything but natural. It is particularly complex when the family itself is complex. In sustainable FBs, the family makes the entrepreneurs it needs. This chapter explains the nature of this making-of process.

We use a model developed by Gersick *et al.* (1999) on the passing down of a business from one generation to another. Our firm corresponds to a rarely investigated case. This is due to the complexity of the family, and to data availability issues on how family entrepreneurs are made out of a population of heirs who all have a potential claim to the succession.

In the next section, the framework proposed by Gersick *et al.* (1999) is enriched with the theoretical concepts of socialisation and commitment. The last section presents the case of a fifth-generation FB named Gravels (not the real name for confidentiality reasons). The case was developed based on data we collected on three successions: from the second to the third, the third to the fourth and the fourth to the fifth generations. Starting with the third generation, we observed an increasingly formal and complex process of incubation, testing, then selection and choosing, intended to make family entrepreneurs emerge while avoiding the pitfalls of a business succession.

A Framework for Understanding the Making of an Entrepreneur

Apart from Gersick *et al.* (1999), the literature says little about handovers of FBs owned by extended, complex families. It says even less about the way family entrepreneurs emerge from a pool of heirs. The framework we chose belongs to the research approach developed by Nordqvist and Zellweger (2010). They argue that to understand the trajectory of FBs, it is vital to analyse the family itself. In our case we study how heirs—i.e. individuals from the family- are turned into entrepreneurs. We first present the framework of Gersick *et al.* (1999). We then enrich it with the concepts of socialisation and commitment.

Stages and Transitions in the Business Handover Process, According to Gersick et al. (1999)

Gersick *et al.* (1999) remodel the framework of Lansberg (1983) and Davis and Tagiuri (1982) into a dynamic analysis framework. The typical life cycle of a firm which remains managed by the family is divided into three stages. The first stage is the period when the business is led by a single owner-manager. The second is the period when the firm is managed by a group of siblings and, finally, the third sees the arrival of a consortium of cousins as managers. The transition phases between these stages correspond to intergenerational handovers.

The first transition, when the firm is still developing and its founder is approaching retirement age, concerns the handover from a sole owner to his children. The second transition is a handover to a consortium of cousins. The complexity in this situation is significantly higher, as there are many options for the choice of a successor. Gersick *et al.* (1999) model this handover as a process in which stability alternates with disruptions that move the firm from one step to another during its life cycle as part of a transition towards greater complexity in governance of the family firm. The making-of process for family entrepreneurs is a part of this transition.

According to Gersick *et al.* (1999) the handover process is divided into six major stages (Figure 5.1).

First comes the continuous accumulation of pressures. The dynamics of change are rising, but invisibly, because organisational routines are strong enough to resist them. As time passes, the feeling by managers that succession issues should be addressed increases. Pressures gradually introduce disturbances that highlight the inadequacies of certain organisational routines. The second and third stages are the trigger, then the announcement of disengagement. Any trigger can set off the actual transition period. The owner(s)-manager(s) thus show(s) a desire to disengage and pass on the baton. The fourth stage is the exploration of alternatives. Once disengagement has been announced, the managers examine all of the possible options. The exploration stage is critical for achieving convergence between the participants' dreams, skills and feasible compromises.

Figure 5.1 The Six Stages in the Choice of a Successor

Source: Author created

The fifth and sixth stages correspond respectively to choosing a solution, then to an act of commitment by the successors. The exploration phase ends with a choice. In the family entrepreneur making-of process, the choice of people results from a socialisation process. The designated successor, or successors, must then clearly display their personal commitment (accept their selection) and also commit to other fiscal, legal and organisational choices.

While this model clearly describes the different phases of the handover, it cannot explain how, at each step, heirs can become family entrepreneurs. To meet this objective, we refer to the concepts of socialisation and commitment.

Socialisation and Commitment: Vital Ingredients for the Making of Family Entrepreneurs

Anticipatory socialisation (Merton, 1968; Durkheim, 1922) and social capital (Bourdieu, 1980, 1994) on one side, and commitment (Labaki, 2007) on the other side, are two concepts that can be mobilised to understand family firms.

The Socialisation Process and its Specificity in FBs

First comes primary socialisation, which takes place in childhood, with the family as the principal socialising body. Then comes secondary socialisation, which intervenes at a later stage in the construction of the individual outside of the family circle. Socialisation can be seen as a conditioning process. Family and society educate the individual. According to Durkheim (1922), this socialisation proceeds from unconscious, unintentional processes in the family, theorised by Bourdieu (1980) through the concept of *habitus*. These processes strongly determine individual social and career trajectories. Other authors, such as Berger and Luckman (1967), reject this determinism and demonstrate that the individual is also constructed by active appropriation and positioning in relation to the influence of his/her environment, leaving some room for free will. Mouline (2000) and Lubinski (2011) observe that in family firms, the dimensions of socialisation are difficult to separate from one another. Even at a very young age, heirs can witness how central the family firm is to the family's concerns. Similarly, at a later age, the family continues to play a decisive role. This cannot be ignored when occupational socialisation takes places in the family firm.

Lubinski (2011) shows the consequences of this interdependency on the choice of vocation and the place where it is exercised. In general, these two choices are made in sequence (first the vocation, then the place where the occupation will be exercised). In the case of FBs, being an heir to the family firm conditions the place of work. At a very young age, the heirs ask themselves whether or not they want to work in the family firm. The answer to this question influences their occupational vocation in such a way that the usual process is reversed: the choice of where to work is made before the choice of a career. This underlines a strong ambition by the current owners to influence the future genera-tion's choices.

Socialisation in family firms thus corresponds to an incubation period for the heirs. They are endowed with the social capital and values that enable them to take part in the adventure of the FB. The process also tests them at a young age by producing a commitment that can be assessed by the current managers involved in the process of selecting successors.

Towards a Conceptualisation of Commitment as a Product of Socialisation

Commitment can be viewed as the product of the heir's socialisation (Gersick *et al.*, 1997; Labaki, 2007). In the making of a family entre-preneur, there are two targets for commitment. The first target is family members who run the FB. They need to commit to the incubation, testing and selection of the future generation of family entrepreneurs. The sec-ond target is the upcoming generation. They must commit to the process imposed upon them.

Commitment first corresponds to being part of a social group which the individual identifies with in terms of values and attitudes (attitudinal commitment). It also corresponds to behaviour patterns and deeds that are considered important, this time because of the efforts put into them (behavioural or continuity commitment). Sharma and Irving (2005) break this type down into calculative commitment (to avoid losing investments already made in the family firm and the family; to avoid feeling guilty for working elsewhere), and imperative commitment based on the perceived need to belong to the FB. These commitments are dynamic, intertwined and systemic in nature. The members of a family commit to family ties and to the action of the FB through the commitment of the family mem-bers concerned. The managers of the FB commit to a long-term view of the firm and to the family's ongoing involvement in it.

Using the Theoretical Framework

This theoretical framework combining the research on FB handovers with the research on socialisation and commitment will now be used to analyse the case of a family firm (Gravels).

Gravels is interesting for its age, currently five generations old; its size, which is the consequence of a succession of dynamic general managers;

and the complexity of the family itself, which has led Gravels to formally organise its handovers in the last two generations.

The case study was constructed on the basis of a historical and genealogical analysis. It highlights the links between family events and the strategy of the family firm. Individual interviews using a non-directive method with nine family members related to three generations provided further details of this 'making of' process, enabling comparisons with the theoretical framework. Collective meetings and a questionnaire sent to the 17 members of the fifth generation completed these interviews, along with a press review.

Overview of the Gravels Case

Gravels was founded by Charles-Maxime Gravels at the end of the 19th century, in Boncamp, north-west of France. In 2017 Gravels celebrated its 120th anniversary and was still a FB, operating in the quarry and public works sectors. It now has around 1,400 employees, and sales of above €254 million.

Although since January 2012 the founder's family was no longer the sole manager of operations, it was totally in control of strategy and still owned all the capital. 71% of the shares were held in equal proportions by the seven members of the fourth generation—Andrew, John-Malcolm, Gareth-Alfred, Mickael, Yannis, Mark and Victoria-Rose—who were all approaching retirement age. The rest of the shares were held by the members of the fifth generation.

Only family owners are members of the supervisory board. As for the executive board, Patrick Orion was appointed chairman in 2012. He is not a family member, but has been a manager in the FB for a long time. Three members of the fourth generation currently work in the firm: Andrew, Mickael and Gareth-Alfred. The latter, currently chief environmental officer, is the former chairman of the executive board. In the last five years, they have been joined by four members of the fifth generation.

The links between the firm's legal structure, family events and corporate strategy are described in Figure 5.2. The firm's legal form has changed as necessary through its successive handovers to facilitate transfers of shares to the various heirs. Periods of significant strategic development are marked by stability at the helm of the firm, while growth is slower in transition periods, particularly when they are consecutive to a crisis (such as a sudden death in the family). This reflects the strong interweaving of events in the family and business spheres. One point to note from the intricate Gravels family tree is that for the first two generations, the problem of succession was solved by the non-involvement of some children in the business. The owner-manager chose one successor among

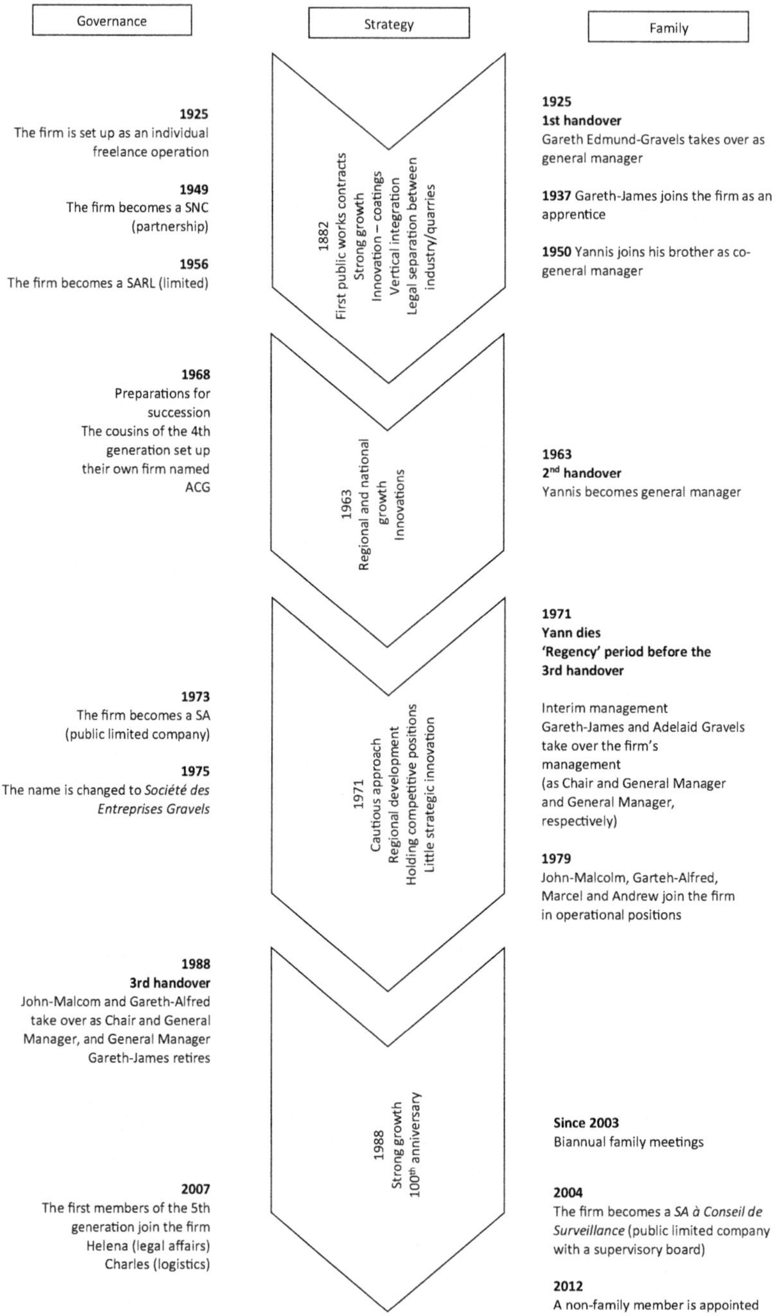

Governance

1925
The firm is set up as an individual freelance operation

1949
The firm becomes a SNC (partnership)

1956
The firm becomes a SARL (limited)

1968
Preparations for succession
The cousins of the 4th generation set up their own firm named ACG

1973
The firm becomes a SA (public limited company)

1975
The name is changed to *Société des Entreprises Gravels*

1988
3rd handover
John-Malcom and Gareth-Alfred take over as Chair and General Manager, and General Manager
Gareth-James retires

2007
The first members of the 5th generation join the firm
Helena (legal affairs)
Charles (logistics)

Strategy

1882
First public works contracts
Strong growth
Innovation – coatings
Vertical integration
Legal separation between industry/quarries

1963
Regional and national growth
Innovations

1971
Cautious approach
Regional development
Holding competitive positions
Little strategic innovation

1988
Strong growth
100th anniversary

Family

1925
1st handover
Gareth Edmund-Gravels takes over as general manager

1937 Gareth-James joins the firm as an apprentice

1950 Yannis joins his brother as co-general manager

1963
2nd handover
Yannis becomes general manager

1971
Yann dies
'Regency' period before the 3rd handover

Interim management
Gareth-James and Adelaid Gravels take over the firm's management
(as Chair and General Manager and General Manager, respectively)

1979
John-Malcolm, Garteh-Alfred, Marcel and Andrew join the firm in operational positions

Since 2003
Biannual family meetings

2004
The firm becomes a *SA à Conseil de Surveillance* (public limited company with a supervisory board)

2012
A non-family member is appointed

Figure 5.2 Governance Strategy and Family Involvement in the FB

Source: Author created

his children, leaving the others aside. As a result, there are branches of the family tree that have lost all connection with the family firm.

Since the third generation, two branches of the family have been involved, giving rise to a large number of cousins. The succession currently in preparation, from the fourth to the fifth generation, will involve seven brothers and sisters (the predecessors) and 17 cousins, their children (the successors).

An analysis of the family tree shows an increasing number of family members. As time passes, selection for the top position at the firm takes place from a growing number of potential successors. From generations 1 to 2, there were six potential successors; from G2 to G3, there were four; from G3 to G4, there were seven, and now, from G4 to G5, there are 17 potential successors.

Analysis of the Case Based on the Theoretical Concepts Chosen

In the literature on family firm handovers, there are very few investigations of families that have a large number of children and a complex structure including several branches. As a result, it is particularly instructive to study the third-to-fourth and fourth-to-fifth generation successions.

Using the Gersick et al. Model (1999): a Good Fit With the Case

In the two handovers studied, we observe the six stages described in the Gersick *et al.* model (1999): accumulation of developmental pressures, trigger event, disengagement, exploring alternatives, choosing and personal commitment.

The handover to the fourth generation resulted from the premature death of the firm's 47-year-old family co-owner and manager, Yannis Gravels (trigger event and disengagement). He had set developmental pressures in motion before dying, using various ways to prepare and then select his successor(s) from among the seven cousins. Yannis Gravels' death was followed by an interim period during which his widow, Adelaid Gravels-January, and his brother Gareth-James Gravels, co-managed the firm until their children could take over. This period lasted eight years. During that time, 12 cousins from the fourth generation were prepared for succession in differentiated ways (adapted to the skills of each individual) to the needs of the firm (exploration). This exploration was triggered by Yannis Gravels' death and lasted until the heirs were deemed ready. At that point, a choice was made between the cousins, deciding who would take over the reins of the business. The commitment was materialised when management responsibilities changed and were handed over to the chosen heirs.

The handover from the fourth to the fifth generation is going through similar stages, but is not yet complete. The exploration of alternatives is still ongoing, and the choices are not yet final. Although the present managers have announced that they will retire soon, they are still in power.

A closer look at the process of making family entrepreneurs shows that education, experience and working outside the family firm are important factors.

When the fourth generation arrived, a charter was drafted, setting out how family members can join the firm. It stipulates that family members must have previous work experience outside the FB. The fourth and fifth generations respected this rule. This charter forces heirs to prove their skills elsewhere. This is a test for candidates for the top job in the FB.

The preparatory phase of the fourth generation included an unusual decision by Yannis Gravels and his brother. They obliged the 12 cousins in the fourth generation to jointly set up their own micro-business. It became a subcontractor for Gravels. This experiment gave all the cousins real-life experience of an entrepreneur's work. It had the advantage of exposing them to the reality of business life while they were very young, and also revealed the aptitudes of some of them for taking over the FB.

The difficulty of exploring all possible alternatives, given the large number of cousins in the fourth generation, led to this unusual but effective selection process. We see it as a commitment by the third generation to keep the family involved in the FB. The testing of heirs is multidimensional: higher education, experience outside the family firm, initiation inside the firm and a real-life entrepreneurship experiment. All these steps had to be successfully completed to qualify for a management position in the FB.

Yannis's decision to make this process mandatory brought out the entrepreneur profiles the family was looking for. After an interim period, two cousins from the fourth generation, judged as best-suited, took over the helm. Gravels regained the pace of growth it had reached before its manager's premature death. Exploring alternatives and choosing, which Gersick *et al.* (1999) describe as difficult, were prepared and implemented successfully despite the presence of several potential successors.

These choices combined a search for the 'best man' with a certain respect for past conventions. The oldest of the male children 'naturally' took over, as together with the second-oldest male child with whom he worked, he proved to be an excellent choice. He considers this state of affairs perfectly natural, and he refers to his skills, which he began to acquire at a very young age. Their mother clearly had no wish to hang on any longer than necessary (disengagement). For the fourth generation, getting to the top management position in the FB depended partly on skills and partly on gender. However, all the cousins were given equal shares regardless of gender and management skills.

The same stages of Gersick *et al.*'s model (1999) are now being experienced by the family for the handover to the fifth generation. The 17 members of this generation are aged between 25 and 30. They come from seven different branches of the family. Many of them could claim the position of top manager. In this case, the trigger is that their parents are reaching retirement age and have begun disengaging from the firm. The executive board is now chaired by a non-family member until a family member shows his/her ability to take over.

The preparation of the fifth generation was adapted to the current social context and made more formal. Rather than imposing things, the aim was to elicit a desire to take part in the selection. Daughters are no longer excluded. The common features shared by this handover and the previous one concern the requirement of higher education, work experience outside the FB and an initiation period in the family firm. Gaining entrepreneurial experience by setting up a business has been replaced by other systems which are described in the following.

Apart from family meetings, where informal but often crucial discussions take place, and the firm's annual general meetings, which are instead very formal, the Gravels family has set up what it calls its 'family university' to teach and incubate future successors. One share was also given to each member of the fifth generation, entitling them to attend general meetings, as even the youngest are shareholders. This is a sign of commitment by the predecessors to convergent objectives, both for the family's continued involvement in the firm and for the perpetuation of the family's values and traditions.

The Gravels University has now become the institution through which the family values are passed on. It combines technical training in management with seminars on the meaning of belonging to a FB designed to elicit a greater commitment from participants. In this way, the predecessors want to foster commitment to the family's continuing involvement in the firm. They do so by providing training and creating emulation designed to make family entrepreneurs emerge from a pool of heirs.

A Model Enhanced by the Concepts of Socialisation and Commitment

The types of commitment listed by Labaki (2007) can also be used to understand how the socialisation of heirs takes place in practice.

First, the interview with Yannis Gravels's widow showed how the firm played an important role in the family's everyday life. The family home was the firm's registered office until the 1970s, and it is still next door to the head office. The children were exposed to the FB's activities from a very early age. For example, since the family home was the head office, they often met the firm's management executives, and thus came into contact with the general manager's everyday life. This was particularly crucial after Yannis Gravels's death: two management executives hired shortly before he died played the role of mentors for the young cousins. Adelaid considered it very important to encourage contacts with male role models, to educate and guide her sons in particular. Also, the family has hunting lands to which it invites customers for hunts, and to which the children were also invited. This shows the predecessors' commitment to the convergence of objectives between the family firm and the family.

Second, in parallel to this primary socialisation, the parents urged their children to seek higher education and choose subjects possibly related to the firm's business activities (predecessors' commitment to convergence of objectives), and required them to display their skills through an initial experience working outside the family firm.

Through this learning in their teenage years on the field, the heirs of the fourth generation were consciously and unconsciously conditioned to choose a career in an area that, while being of interest to them, could also correspond to a need for the FB. Once again, this reflects the predecessors' commitment to convergence of objectives. This also illustrates the theory put forward by Lubinski (2011). Joining the family firm was the first subject put on the table. It was experienced by some as a natural, moral obligation and by others simply as an option to be taken up if an individual was interested and deserved it. Thus, the choice of where to work came before the choice of a profession.

As for the fifth generation, the family University first contributed to commitment from inside the family. It gave everyone an opportunity to show their commitment, and alongside this the charter defined the ways through which commitment could be proven and tested. In a second phase, the system enabled the expression of many forms of commitment, reflecting how each person identified with the family-FB system. The nature of the commitment is an outcome of the tests through which the fifth generation went through by taking part in the family University (regular attendance, preparatory work, etc.). It contributed to the process of selecting the heirs. Based on Lansberg's three-circle model (1983), it is possible to position family members and determine their level of commitment.

A first category comprises family members with no role in governance (no shares in the firm) or operational decision-making bodies. Their career takes place outside the FB. They only belong to the family sphere and their commitment to the business as defined by Labaki (2007) is low or non-existent.

A second category is family members who are shareholders only and play no active role, even in that capacity. They have financial expectations (return on capital). Their level of commitment is higher than for the previous category, but dedication to the cause of the FB remains low.

These family members are unwilling or unable to become managers in the FB. Several members of the fifth generation are in this situation. This appears to result from their choosing a career and family life that does not closely correspond to the firm's needs, even after they took part in the family University. This attitude, which marks a difference from the previous generation, is notably due to the role played by daughters-in-law. They want their careers to matter as well, and that may lead to periods spent outside of France, obliging their husband to leave the family firm, at least for a short while.

A third category is family members involved in the governance bodies; they are active family shareholders, making an important contribution to corporate strategy, particularly through their skills. Sharma and Irving (2005) call this 'behavioural commitment'. These family members' past and present acts are consistent with the objectives of the FB. The fourth generation is in this situation, even after their operational involvement has ended. It also applies to some members of the fifth generation who are currently engaged in the socialisation/selection process that is designed to bring out the fourth and final category.

The fourth category corresponds to family members who are shareholders and operational managers, devoted to the FB. For these people, the making-of process can be declared successful. They have been 'produced' by the socialisation processes. They have demonstrated their skills and have been identified by their predecessors. Among the potential fifth generation successors, several cousins are now showing a desire to be part of this category.

Conclusion: How to Bring out the Right Manager From a Large Number of Potential Successors

We identified a three-stage making-of process which is the ultimate expression of the socialisation process.

First, there is an incubation stage. It was mostly implicit to start with and evolved into formal strategies aimed at preparing heirs. This included a family charter which defined the steps to follow to join the firm, and the systematic attribution of one share to every member of the family. This incubation stage is an internal component of the first phase of a handover, i.e., the period of growing pressure for change.

Second, there is a testing stage. It runs partly concurrently with the incubation stage. Through socialisation arrangements, the present managers can test the heirs and assess their commitment through their involvement (family meetings, the microbusiness for the fourth generation, the family University for the fifth generation). This stage takes over from incubation when the heirs are in higher education and begin their career with a job outside the FB before potentially joining it. This testing stage is part of the exploration of alternatives. The heirs' academic and occupational trajectories are compared with the needs of the FB in order to identify the best possible configurations. During this stage, the heirs acquire the skills and legitimacy they need to take over the FB. They have an opportunity to display their entrepreneurial capabilities.

Third, there is a selection and choosing stage. The generation in charge considers the match between the heirs' backgrounds and the needs of the FB, but also how successful they have been so far, in order to select the best candidates. This stage is not always free of the prejudices specific to each generation.

Labaki's work (2007) contributes to understanding the outputs of the socialisation process and to the dynamics which make families move from one stage to the next in Gersick *et al.*'s model (1999). Some heirs turn into family entrepreneurs and take over the FB after a formally defined and managed process that is designed to produce evidence of commitment. The family's size and complexity become an advantage. The larger the pool of potential successors, the higher the chances that a competent heir will emerge and take over the management of the FB.

Overt competition is avoided in two ways. First, the commitment generated by socialisation acts as a deterrent. Attitudinal, imperative and calculative commitment play a strong role (desire to belong to the family, potential guilt of being excluded, desire not to lose the result of past efforts). Second, clear rules are established. They reduce uncertainty by obliging each member to follow them.

Avenues for future research include developing case studies from diverse countries in order to identify what is universal and what is specific to different national cultures.

References

Berger, P. and Luckman, T. (1967). *The social construction of reality: a treatise in the sociology of knowledge*, London: Penguin Press.

Bourdieu, P. (1980). *Questions de sociologie*, Paris: Les Editions de Minuit.

Bourdieu, P. (1994). *Raisons pratiques*, Paris: Seuil.

Davis, J.A. and Tagiuri, R. (1982). "Bivalent attributes of the family firm: familly business sourcebook", in *The advantages and disadvantages of the family business*, Santa Barbara, CA: Owner Managed Business Institute.

Durkheim, É. (1922). *Éducation et sociologie*, Paris: Presses Universitaires de France.

Gersick, K.E., Davis, J.A., Hampton, M.M. and Lansberg, I. (1997). *Generation to generation: life cycles of the family business*, Cambridge, MA: Harvard Business Press.

Gersick, K.E., Lansberg, I., Desjardins, M. and Dunn, B. (1999). "Stages and transitions: managing change in the family business", *Family Business Review*, *12*(4), 287–297.

Labaki, R. (2007). "Toward a conceptual model of commitment in family business", in *Dimensions of family business research*, 120–140, Jyväskylä, Finland: University of Jyväskylä Publishing Series.

Lansberg, I.S. (1983). "Managing human resources in family firms: the problem of institutional overlap", *Organizational Dynamics*, *12*(1), 39–46.

Lubinski, C. (2011). "Succession in multi-generational family firms. An exploratory study into the period of anticipatory socialization", *Electronic Journal of Family Business Studies (EJFBS)*, *5*(1-2), 4–25.

Merton, R.K. (1968). *Social theory and social structure*, Enl. ed., New York: Free Press.

Mouline, J.P. (2000). "Dynamique de la succession managériale dans la PME familiale non cotée", *Finance Contrôle Stratégie*, *3*(1), 197–222.

Nordqvist, M. and Zellweger, T.M. (2010). "A qualitative research approach to the study of transgenerational entrepreneurship", in M. Nordqvist and T. Zellweger (Eds.), *Transgenerational entrepreneurship: exploring growth and performance in family firms across generations*, 39–57, Cheltenham and Brookfield: Edward Elgar Publishing.

Sharma, P. and Irving, P.G. (2005). "Four bases of family business successor commitment: antecedents and consequences", *Entrepreneurship Theory and Practice*, *29*(1), 13–33.

6 Succession and Family Business in Between Emotional and Financial Issues

The Role of a Governance With a Two-Tier System[1]

Céline Barrédy

Despite the large amount of research on governance, few address the interest of the choice of the two-tier governance system composed of a management board strictly separated from the supervisory board. This is particularly true concerning family business whereas, in the context of succession, this structure seems to be relevant for many. Only the changes made by the classical board of directors monopolise the discussions. Recently, partnerships limited by share have taken the attention concerning its potentiality in terms of succession (Charlier, 2014), but very few have considered the two-tier system in a context of family business succession.

The two-tier board is nevertheless original. It was born in Germany and extended in Continental Europe. In France, this system became a legal option of incorporation in 1966 through the reform of the corporate law. It was designed to meet the limits of the classical board of directors. Indeed, this structure was no longer relevant for the form of organisation that separates the functions of management and control. This reform was intended to establish management's independence from shareholders. Since its creation, this structure has only been moderately successful, however, a new momentum has been initiated since 1990 (Godard, 1998), boosting its representation (Barrédy, 2005). The link with family businesses arose from the fact that the majority of listed firms with a two-tier system have a family character. In 2000, 16.75 % of family businesses were organised through a two-tier system, whereas only 8.28% of non-family businesses were organised in the system (Barrédy, 2005; Belot *et al.*, 2014). Today, in 2020, it is more than 22% of family businesses that are organised with a two-tier system, with only 10% of non-family business using the system. Family businesses change their governance structure for a two-tier system at the time of the succession (Barrédy, 2005). The two-tier board is more likely used by family businesses managed by a descendant (inheritor) (Belot *et al.*, 2014). What is the link between the two-tier structure and succession in a family business?

The main issue of this research is to understand the interest, in France, of adopting a two-tier system for a family business at the time of the succession, particularly regarding the issue of continuity.

The chapter is structured as followed: at first, we present the literature review, then we develop the methodology, and conclude with the results and contributions.

Literature Review

The Specificities of the Two-Tier Structure

This structure is characterised by three characteristics:

- It legally requires a split between management and control functions into two[2] separate bodies. The D board, appointed by the S board, is responsible for the management of the company.[3] In contrast to a one-tier system, the D board is legally responsible and its chairman represents the company among partners. As a result, they are not required to be shareholders of the firm. In addition, the D board is independent of the S board, as one of its members may not simultaneously be part of the S board and vice versa. Collusion between the two bodies of the system is therefore reduced. The S board, elected by the general assembly of shareholders, has no management prerogative and focuses on the permanent control of the management, carried out by the D board. It establishes the link between the management and the general meeting. It depends on the D board to obtain the expected information for its mission, even if the S board has a right of investigation.[4]
- The collegiality of the D and S boards is an important aspect, especially for the D board, whose members are collectively responsible in front of the S board and the shareholders.
- The relationship between the D and S boards should lead to the development of a teamwork table. The clarification of the respective prerogatives strengthens the complementarity of the missions of each. Respect for these roles determines the balance of the structure, especially with regard to the S board, which has the broadest power.

The Contributions of Shareholder Theories of Governance

While Economic Analysis of Law has made a significant contribution to the field of governance (La Porta *et al.*, 1998), the interests of the two-tier system for family companies is not significantly developed. We will successively discuss the contributions and limitations of the three theoretical aspects of governance to understand this phenomenon in the context of succession.

Based on the agency theory, the organisation costs associated with the ownership structure separating management from ownership can be reduced by specialising management and control functions (Fama and Jensen, 1983). To what extent can this approach fit with the family firm, particularly in the context of succession? When the family business is listed, at first, it pits family shareholders against other shareholders. As stipulated in the agency theory, the family transfers part of the risk to shareholders and values its discretionary consumption on the firm. Entrenchment theory confirms the opportunism of owner-managers, especially when they own more than 25% of the shares (Morck *et al.*, 1988). This leads to agency relations of type two, where the family majority shareholders could enter in conflict with minority family shareholders (Charlier and Lambert, 2013).

At the time of succession, conflicts can arise from a divergence of interests between family members as shareholders, managers and employees (Lank and Neubauer, 1998). The asymmetry of information between managers and shareholders leads to inequality in the access to resources and the risk associated with family investment, which is by nature undiversified, and leads to divergent financial interests as well as emotional conflicts that lead to sub-optimal financial decisions (Schulze *et al.*, 2002). A two-tier system would make it possible to pre-empt or resolve these conflicts by formalising the family-business relationship and clarifying roles and responsibilities (James, 1999). However, these theories concern companies with diluted ownership. Applied to a family company, they anticipate an inevitable dispersion of ownership (Fama and Jensen, 1983). For James (1999), the clarification of roles in family firms results in a gradual separation of family and business. At this point, these theories lead to predict the disappearance of the family character of those firms, which is not consistent with the empirical observation. The governance system must protect specific investments in the family firm (Rajan and Zingales, 1998) to encourage the partners to join the 'team', in particular the succession team. A way to increase the specific investment protection is to delegate this mission to an independent arbitrator (Blair and Stout, 1999). As mentioned by Bughin *et al.* (2010), the choice between an internal or external successor is quite a dilemma. Both bring very different cognitive resources to the company and the family. Therefore, by the collegiality of the S and D board, the two-tier system could bring a solution by helping creating teams of both internal and external successors.

It is not only the succession team that needs to be protected, but also the whole family. The question is no longer to oppose the family and the company, but to integrate them. The S board could be the link between the management board and all the family shareholders.

The time of the succession also raises a question of resources and potential cognitive conflict. The governance structure can be seen as a means of facilitating access and coordination of resources to capture and exploit strategic opportunities (Foss, 1993) the team of family successors can't bring to the company. The sustainability and continuity of family firms are conditioned by the access and coordination of resources coming from outside the family and by the resolution of subsequent cognitive conflicts (Wirtz, 2000). The two-tier structure can be considered as 'a relay' for succession (Vancil, 1987). It would allow the incumbent to evaluate his successor and transfer the know-how and legitimacy necessary for his functions. Burkart *et al.* (2003) show that the choice of a successor outside the family raises the point of the legal protection provided to family shareholders. These contributions do not make it possible to understand why the chairman of the D board is often part of the family, nor why only few companies change their structure at this stage. The contributions of theories of governance are fragmented in understanding the interest in this structure by the family firms that are listed. There is still a lack of understanding of the relevance of the two-tier system for those firms. It is presented as a means of mitigating the effects of family presence, which may eventually lead to its distance from the company. The research must therefore be oriented towards a methodology that, based on practice, will make it possible to identify the reasons that led to the adoption of this structure and its relevance for family businesses.

An Exploratory Methodology Focused on Managerial Experience

The empirical observations and the theoretical problem raised have led to a qualitative exploratory methodological approach. An exploratory study helps in understanding the reasons for the structural change through the experience of managers to identify recurrent processes and evolves towards a theory. It allows apprehension and analysis of the complex processes in depth (Hlady, 2002), the different situations related to them and the motivations of the actors involved. The research covers the 44 French family firms listed on the stock exchange that are organised with a two-tier system.

The originality of the approach is to mobilise two complementary methods of access of data and analysis. The first is a thematic study of the justifications for the adoption of a two-tier system in the annual reports. Since these communications do not aim to be transparent, a second approach mobilises multiple case studies to understand the processes underlying the decision and its implementation by focusing on interactions with stakeholders in order to focus on the family influence on governance decisions. These two steps distinguish between explicit and implicit reasons of adopting the two-tier system.

Explicit Reasons and Their Logics of Association

They are analysed on the basis of the annual reports, which contain the arguments developed by the directors to convince the shareholders to support the proposal of adopting a two tier system and enhance its interests for the company (Jacquot and Point, 2000). The management controls the level and type of in-course training. The assumption that the content of these reports is deliberately limited and coded is therefore acceptable. The presence, absence and weight of the themes are not fortuitous. The second postulate defines reasons as a homogeneous assemblage of several themes, materialised by groups of words, bearing common meanings, isolable (Bardin, 2001), appearing under various contents. Extracts are coded according to the frequency of occurrence of empirical themes. The choice of annual reports was selected while respecting the diversity of the companies in the initial population in terms of the intensity of family ownership (the family is more than 50% shareholder for 55% of the individuals in the sample).

Two complementary techniques, conducted using SPAD software, were mobilised to extract the reasons explained from the themes. A multiple correspondence factor analysis was carried out on the themes, and made it possible to extract four significant axes with an explained variance of 74.17%. These axes are made up of interrelated themes. The analysis provides new factors by positioning each theme in the reference frame made up of these axes. The hierarchical classification to obtain the typology of explicit reasons then focused on the themes based on their factors (Table 6.1).

The division into seven classes was retained so that seven explicit reasons could be identified. The logics of association of these reasons were identified from an analysis of multiple correspondences.

Table 6.1 Summary of Optimal Partitions

Number of optimal partitions	Inertia Interclass	Skip from aggregation level	Commentary
Scores proposed by the SPAD software			
Split into 3 classes	0.8786	4.77	This partition is not retained: class n° 3 is too heterogeneous.
Split into 5 classes	1.4686	2.38	This score is complementary; it helps in the interpretation.
Split into 7 classes	1.8693	3.16	This score is much more interesting.

The Study of Implicit Reasons Was Conducted by Seven Case Studies

This method best corresponds to the study of the governance of the family firm, driven simultaneously by emotional relationships and a concern for performance, leading interactions between the leader, the family community and other partners. Studying it requires access to and analysis of data that may shed light on the origin of the organisational crisis and understanding the value of this structure. The case method, 'spatial and temporal analysis of a complex phenomenon by conditions, events, actors and implications' responds to the 'why and how' through access to actors' perceptions of their value system, concerns, logic, experience and interpretation of facts. The context of the event, an essential aspect of its understanding, can be considered. Our objective being the emergence of unexpected concepts and the evolution towards a theory by the discovery of regularities, a multi-case study was privileged. It requires a careful sampling based on essential criteria (Eisenhardt, 1989).

Theoretical representativeness requires that each case has sufficient common features with the others. All cases are homogenous—they are French family firms, organised with a two-tier system. The variety of cases is also ensured because they have been selected according to the richness of the data to better understand all the phenomenon, in particular from the influence of the family on governance (weight of the family in the ownership, separation of ownership and management, and number of generations). The potential for discovery is also an essential criterion. The actors were selected for the richness of the data they could formulate and their openness to in-depth investigation. The chairman of the D board and the chairman of the S board could, by their function, their responsibility in changing and their influence on the family-corporate relationship, bring diversified and complementary perceptions and representations of the phenomenon. Very sensitive data on family relationships have been collected. Finally, the number of cases was determined on the basis of research validity criteria: saturation of theoretical concepts and empirical data (Eisenhardt, 1989). Case 6 revealed empirical and conceptual redundancies. Case 7 did not provide anything additional. The cases are presented in Table 6.2. The collection of data was mainly carried out through semi-directive interviews repeated three times by actors over the entire period.

The interviews were gradually oriented towards decision-making and the interest of the company structure. Secondary accounting data and family history data enriched the exchanges. This iterative technique made it possible to validate the analyses internally with the actors and to deepen the results by exploiting the incomplete studies of the previous collections. The interviews were then empirically coded to facilitate their comparison and carry out the intra-case analysis by using the role

Table 6.2 Case Characteristics*

Cases	Creation	Size (turnover)	Capital owned by the family	Chairman of the D Board**	Chairman of the S Board
Radiall 1*	1952	177 M €	> 50%	F (son of the last CEO)	F (last CEO-founder)
2	1913	320 M €	< 33%	F (son-in-law of the last CEO)	F (wife of the last chairman-descendant)
3	1966	344 M €	> 50%	F (son of the last P-DG)	F (last CEO-founder)
4	1849	41 M €	> 50	NF	F (last CEO-descending)
5	1893	4,5MM€	> 50 %	F (family member by marriage)	F (widows of family branch leaders—former CEO)
6	1941	5 MM€	> 50%	NF	F (last son CEO)
7	1855	622 M€	< 33%	F (niece of the last CEO)	NF

* Companies will remain anonymous with the exception of the Radiall case.

** Family: F; Non-Family: NF.

matrix (Huberman and Miles, 2003) to compare the actors' perceptions of their role in the company and in the family. The empirical codes have been structured into five categories that clarify the process to arrive at the results: 'Perception of the concept of governance', 'Perception of the family business', 'Context of the choice of structure', 'Origin of choice' and 'Perceived interest of the structure'. In a second step, the concepts structuring the final theorisation were created from the confrontation of cases.

The Results: The Two-Tier System at the Service of Succession Sustainability and Family Continuity

Results reveal that theoretical aspects of governance are not competing but complementary to understand the interest of the two-tier system in a family business succession. The results show two aspects of the phenomenon: explicit reasons are descriptive and overlook the family dimension while implicit reasons bring the understanding and analytical dimension by putting the family back at the heart of change.

Explicit Reasons: Focus on Performance
and Organisational Change

The explicit reasons are grouped into three logics. The logic of 'resources' is only composed of an explicit reason: 'Separation of functions and access to skills'. There is a clear link between two-tier systems and access to resources in terms of skills. This issue, raised by the theory of resource, particularly forces the family subjected to having access to external resources to develop the company.

The logic of 'strategy and performance', which combines three explicit reasons: 'Organisational catch-up and optimisation of human resources', 'Performance and change' and 'New strategic step'. Two perspectives emerge. The first is adaptive and aims to use this structure to increase organisational performance. The second is prospective. This structure would facilitate strategic change and improved performance. This logic reveals the link between organisational form, strategy and performance at the time of succession.

The logic of 'executive transmission' combines three explicit reasons: 'Departure of the CEO and collegiality of the executive', 'Continuity and power of influence of the former CEO' and 'Transmission and sustainability'. It mobilises the concepts of entrenchment and focuses on the continuity and sustainability of the company. For the actors, this structure simultaneously facilitates the achievement of a team success and the influence of the last CEO on the values and strategy of the company for which he is the guarantor. He is associated with continuity. The transmission process is focused on it and clearly dissociates continuity and sustainability. This structure would make it easier to choose successors from outside the family.

The explicit reasons do not create an understanding of how this structure responds to these arguments. In addition, the role played by the family in making the decision to change is overlooked. The implicit reasons provide an analysis of the underlying mechanisms.

The Implicit Reasons: Focus on the Relationship Between Performance and Family Continuity

The implicit reasons emanate from the family context and the destabilising events that drive the decision.

The Family, Economic and Financial Context

The family context is understood by the representation that social leaders have of the family's role in the relationship and its influence on their decision-making process. This study shows that the legality and role of the family presence depend on the image conveyed by the company to its environment, especially the stock market. Thus, when the company is successful, the market would be neutral in terms of family involvement. On the other hand, the family would be responsible for difficulties because of the negative perceived influence of family relationships on performance. The shareholder approach therefore dominates this context.

The chairman of the D board in case 2 stated: "The family is the scapegoat for the market in the event of underperformance, the market considers that it is responsible for the difficulties. However, in normal times, when everything is going well, it is neutral".

The chairman of the S board in case 3 added: "The market may be tempted to think that the passion they crystallise (family ties) only has a negative influence on the company's performance".

The family is not seen as a source of organisational efficiency. It is performance that determines the legitimacy of the family influence. This relationship to the environment explains the absence of the family for explicit reasons. At the same time, the actors are very attached to family continuity, which encourages them to balance performance and family continuity. In addition, the decision to transfer management is influenced by a negative economic and financial context, caused by a management considered to be 'archaic'. The objective is to introduce 'new ideas' to stimulate a new dynamic (cases 2, 4 and 6).

This context is complemented by event factors that drive the change decision.

Destabilising and Triggering Factors

These factors are spontaneously mentioned by the actors to justify their choice. However, they do not allow it to be fully understood because they are events and not a decision-making process, and not all companies facing them adopt this structure. The implicit reasons come from the process that leads to considering the interests of this form. The main one is the transmission of the executive and the second one, which is related to the transmission, is taxation on personal wealth. This argument is never mentioned publicly. Upon leaving office, the CEO loses his exemption on the shares he owns. Paying this tax often means selling your shares, and considering giving up family continuity. The chairman of the S board keeps this exemption and allows his successors to be exempted by investing in the D board.

Governance Issues and Interest of the Two-Tier Structure

The two-tier structure meets the challenge to strengthen family involvement. Companies that adopt the two-tier structure face a significant risk of family disengagement due to the context and destabilising factors. Its consequences would be of two kinds: the family members involved in the business would see the probability of a reduced return on their investment and family continuity would be threatened. However, family involvement is not an exogenous factor, but a process that is under development. In these companies, two forms of commitment are involved. First, intra-generational involvement concerns the maintenance of the implication of family members belonging to the same generation as the leader. It requires specific governance mechanisms since conflicts arise from the relationship between majority shareholders and minority family members. This conflictual relationship is enhanced by the context of transmission. The originality of the situation lies in the reversibility of the conflictual relationship. The human and financial investment of family leaders depends on the commitment of minority family members. On the other hand, minority family shareholders limit their potential for financial diversification by keeping their assets in the family business. They expect financial performance, but also other incentives to agree. Engaging family members is therefore crucial to maintaining family influence over the company. Involving minority shareholders is an incentive factor favoured by the two-tier structure. Indeed, family continuity is established by balancing the family's perception of being a specific asset and the specific contribution that the company provides to it. The collegiality of the two boards makes it possible to establish a family democracy. Representatives of minority family branches may participate in the tasks of these two boards without unbalancing decision-making power because of the collegiality. Correlatively, unlike a traditional board of directors, this structure provides a formal organisation and a rigorous delimitation of individual roles. It strengthens control between boards and promotes the family's sense of belonging.

Intergenerational commitment causes concerns about the involvement of new generations in the family continuity. It is also exacerbated by transmission, but it exists before it, because family members are placed in a family continuity scheme that encourages them to develop arrangements to maintain power in family hands. Thus, the manager—the majority family shareholder—is responsible to the other members of the family for the choices inherent in his succession and the successor is responsible for the family continuity and sustainability of the company with regards to his predecessor. This is manifested by a doubt about the successor's ability (his son, nephews, son-in-law in any case) to assume this responsibility, leaving the manager with the feeling of risk-taking in the choice of his successor. The latter also takes a significant risk. This situation exists only because both generations have entered an escalation of commitment (Staw, 1981) to family continuity.

Balance can only be achieved if the governance mechanisms provide them with reciprocal protection. This is very related to the super-principal agent (Villalonga *et al.*, 2015) who considers the overall family interest in playing a significant role in the family business. The two-tier system allows the placement of different family shareholders on the S board and the D board.

Two configurations have appeared. In the first case (cases 2, 4, 5, 7), the generation initiating the change guarantees the maintenance of an already old family continuum and its value towards past generations, for future generations.

The chairman of D board in case 5 stated: "To engage the family, it is necessary to ensure the diversity of opportunities for representation of the family branches".

The chairman of the D board in case 4 stated:

> Family continuity is a moral obligation for the heir. Each heir is only the link in a huge chain that surpasses him. He had no responsibility for the creation of the company, nor for its development. It is a legal right that confers formal enjoyment of these assets. He is only the steward of the capital that has been transmitted to him and this morally deprives him of his right of use because this capital was entrusted to him by his fathers, to be honored, maintained, valued and transmitted to the following generations. His responsibility is increased and made more complex by accepting the management, he is the guarantor of family continuity.

It is the 'agent' of past, present and future generations who delegates the valuation of their investments. In the second configuration (cases 1, 3, 6), the initiators of the change are the founders of the company. The 'escalation of commitment' to continuity is also marked; the successor allows the creator to perpetuate his work. Risk taking is present for both generations.

In both cases, the family leaders responsible for this continuity develop organisational arrangements limiting their responsibility for the possible loss of family character, in particular by diversifying the profiles of successors. One or more family successors are appointed and 'freely submit', regardless of their interest in the succession. They are always accompanied by non-family managers on the board of directors, some of whom take the chair (cases 4, 6).

In case 2, the company was founded at the beginning of the 20th century by the family of the wife of the last CEO. As the latter had a son, he planned to transfer the management to him. The father and son entered into conflict to the point that the father pushed his son aside and called his son-in-law to succeed him. The latter accepted after several requests from his father-in-law. It was a 'challenge' for him.

> Some people told me I was crazy to accept. Then my father-in-law asked me to find a way to reintegrate his son into the company. It was necessary to find a management position for him. He is the son, not really trained, very submissive, even crushed by his father. The son accepted and joined the board.

The collegiality of the management board provides an answer by transmitting this responsibility to a team that operates under the control of S board chair, generally until his death, by the last CEO. The risk of error in the selection of a successor is reduced by the diversity of team members. In addition, the collegiality of S board allows the last CEO to surround himself with other family members, representing minority branches, who also participate in the appointment of the team of successors. The risk of questioning the choice of management is also reduced and protects continuity. The two-tier structure is in line with the strategy of protecting the power of leaders. Family members only agree to lead if the organisation adequately protects their power and investment from risk. The conclusion of Burkart *et al.* (2003) is extended to the choice of the family successor. The family manager, upon leaving the management, may no longer be able to benefit from his past investment in the company. With regard to its human capital, by transferring management in a traditional structure it can no longer exercise any real influence. The two-tier system allows him to maintain a strong influence on the company's operations and to perfect his entrenchment by investing the S board, as he appoints, controls and can dismiss the management team. Its utility function is changing in favour of the valuation of its capital and to the detriment of its satisfaction to be managed. Its individual approach is part of the collective commitment. The two-tier structure responds to a managerial logic: access and coordination of resources external to the family.

The form of this structure allows the family to facilitate its access to external skills. External managers are placed on the D board to provide their managerial skills and transfer them, through learning, to the family successor. The latter can therefore exercise his power of family representation while being supported in his activity (cases 2, 3 and 4). External directors are also co-opted on the S board to extend new skills complementary to those of family members. Collegiality makes it possible to diversify the controls, which are no longer exclusively family-based. Frequently being themselves officers or directors of other companies, the external directors make it possible to open up the family circle and facilitate the development of a relational network. In all cases, 'experts' play the role of arbitrators, in the partnership sense, in decision-making and in the justification of results.

Conclusion

The two-tier system, through the strict separation of management and control functions and the collegiality of the D and S boards, is a governance tool for family business at the time of succession that works by leveraging:

- The family dynamics of strengthening the commitment of family members,
- The individual entrenchment dynamics of influential family actors, and
- The managerial dynamics of access of resources necessary for sustainability and family continuity.

The theories of governance are complementary at each of these levels to interpret the choice of the two-tier system in the context of succession. Addressing shareholders, the explicit reasons for choosing the two-tier system show that managers mainly communicate on access to non-family resources and the performance of the executive at the time of transmission, distinguishing between the imperatives of continuity and sustainability. The voluntary absence of a family reference reinforces the interest of case studies that place family involvement at the centre of the decision-making process. The family becomes the pivot around which the arguments related to non-family resources and individual logic are articulated from a performance perspective.

As a limitation, the research could be extended to a wide sample, by modelling the family business governance cycles beyond the two-tier board.

The governance of the family business cannot be approached from the usual corporate governance angles. The family is the essential actor, and the objective of continuity it pursues, combined with that of sustainability and company performance, makes it specific.

Notes

1. This chapter is inspired from the following paper: Barrédy, C. (2008). Gouvernance de la société familiale cotée. *Revue française de gestion*, (5), 1–19. This publication in the handbook has been explicitly authorised by the Revue Française de Gestion and the Editor Lavoisier.
2. French Corporate Law Code (art L225–68).
3. French Corporate Law Code (art. L225–58, art. L225–64).
4. French Corporate Law Code (art. L. 225–68).

References

Bardin, L. (2001). *L'analyse de contenu*, Paris: PUF.

Barrédy, C. (2005). *Le choix de la SA en directoire et conseil de surveillance dans la société familiale cotée comme mode de gouvernance*, PhD Thesis, University Montesquieu Bordeaux IV, Bordeaux.

Belot, F., Ginglinger, E., Slovin, M.B. and Sushka, M.E. (2014). "Freedom of choice between unitary and two-tier boards: an empirical analysis", *Journal of Financial Economics*, 112(3), 364–385.

Blair, M.M. and Stout, L.A. (1999). "A team production theory of corporate law", *Virginia Law Review*, 85(2), 247–328.

Bughin, C., Colot, O. and Finet, A. (2010). "Entreprises familiales et gouvernance cognitive: quelle transmission?" *Management Avenir*, 7(37), 14–33.

Burkart, M., Panunzi, F. and Shleifer, A. (2003). "Family firms", *Journal of Finance*, 58(5), 2167–2202.

Charlier, P. (2014). "La société en commandite par actions: un outil de transmission pour l'entreprise familiale cotée", *Finance Contrôle Stratégie*, 17(3), 5–30.

Charlier, P. and Lambert, G. (2013). "Modes de gouvernance et performances des entreprises familiales françaises en fonction des conflits d'agence", *Finance Contrôle Stratégie*, 16(2), 1–26.

Eisenhardt, K.M. (1989). "Building theories from case study research", *Academy of Management Review*, 14(4), 532–550.

Fama, E.F. and Jensen, M.C. (1983). "Separation of ownership and control", *The Journal of Law and Economics*, 26(2), 301–325.

Foss, N.J. (1993). "Theories of the firm: contractual and competence perspectives", *Journal of Evolutionary Economics*, 3(2), 127–144.

Godard, L. (1998). "Les déterminants du choix entre un conseil d'administration et un conseil de surveillance", *Finance Contrôle Stratégie*, 1(4), 39–61.

Hlady, M. (2002). *Case study, Application to management research*, Brussels: DeBoeck University.

Huberman, A.M. and Miles, M.B. (2003). *Analyse qualitative des données*, 2nd ed., Paris: DeBoeck University.

Jacquot, T. and Point, S. (2000). "Le management symbolique des ressources humaines: une analyse du langage des dirigeants en Europe", *Revue de gestion des ressources humaines*, 38, 116–132.

James, H.S. (1999). "What can the family contribute to business? Examining contractual relationships", *Family Business Review*, 12(1), 61–71.

La Porta, R., Lopez-de-Silanes, F., Shleifer, A. and Vishny, R.W. (1998). "Law and finance", *Journal of Political Economy*, 106(6), 1113–1155.

Lank, A.G. and Neubauer, F. (1998). *The family business*, London: Palgrave Macmillan.

Morck, R., Shleifer, A. and Vishny, R.W. (1988). "Management ownership and market valuation, an empirical analysis", *Journal of Financial Economics*, 20, 293–315.

Rajan, R.G. and Zingales, L. (1998). "Power in a theory of the firm", *The Quarterly Journal of Economics*, 113(2), 387–432.

Schulze, W.S., Lubatkin, M.H. and Dino, R.N. (2002). "Altruism, agency and the competitiveness of family firms management", *Decision Economic*, 23(4–5), 247–259.

Staw, B.M. (1981). "The escalation of commitment to a course of action", *Academy of Management Review*, 6(4), 577–587.

Vancil, R.F. (1987). *Passing the baton: managing the process of CEO succession*, Boston, MA: Harvard Business School Press.

Villalonga, B., Amit, R., Trujillo, M.A. and Guzmán, A. (2015). "Governance of family firms", *Annual Review of Financial Economics*, 7, 635–654.

Wirtz, P. (2000). *Politique de Financement et Gouvernement d'Entreprise*, Paris: Economica.

7 Succession and Strategic Renewal in Family Firms

Insights From a French Family Firm[1]

Didier Chabaud, Mariem Hannachi and Hedi Yezza

Strategic renewal (SR) has generated considerable interest in recent years. We will use Sharma and Chrisman's (1999, p. 19) definition of the term as "corporate entrepreneurial efforts that result in significant changes to an organisation's business or corporate level strategy or structure". Alongside the research done over the past 30 years in the area of strategic renewal, there has also been an increasing focus on family firms.

Researchers are examining the role of SR in family firms more and more (Salvato *et al.*, 2010) in order to better understand their commitment to entrepreneurial behaviour over the long term (Zahra, 2018) and their ability to cope with change. This entrepreneurial behaviour depends on the particular features of the company, the family members involved in the business management and the family system. The change in CEO through a business transfer can have an impact on the entrepreneurial behaviour of family firms.

This chapter aims to understand how family SMEs deal with strategic renewal to ensure longevity, particularly through the succession process. This approach offers an opportunity to get a better grasp of the organisational processes underlying this process.

We start by delving into the concept of strategic renewal and the characteristics of the succession process in the context of family SMEs. After presenting our case study, we discuss the mechanisms of SR to shed light on the peculiarities of the choices available to a family SME. Finally, we consider the scope and limitations of our approach.

Literature Review

As Teece (2019) points out, for most companies, long-term survival is not guaranteed, and most of them disappear before they can be handed off to the next generation. In order to be successful, companies have to develop a regenerative capability. The need for this capability is greater among family firms (Zahra, 2018). Therefore, strategic renewal appears to be an appropriate theoretical lens through which to study them.

Despite the growing attention that SR is receiving as a research domain (Schmitt *et al.*, 2018), there is still a lack of consensus when it comes to defining and conceptualising it. We will try to fill this gap before investigating how the context of family firm succession may potentially affect its content and effects.

Conceptual Overview of Strategic Renewal

In the medical field, 'renewal' refers to the phenomenon through which an organism replaces a part that has been lost or damaged (on its own, after an accident or because of an experiment). In management science, the term refers to a deliberate action that drives a firm to alter its path of dependence (Volberda *et al.*, 2001). Thus, the firm learns and explores new ways of using its core competencies and competitive approaches (Floyd and Lane, 2000).

Over the past 30 years, authors have unanimously considered SR to be an answer to changing and turbulent business conditions (Agarwal and Helfat, 2009), in line with the assertion of Huff *et al.* (1992) that the term 'strategic regeneration' is a substitute for 'strategic change'. From this perspective, SR appears to be a kind of entrepreneurial activity (Zahra, 2018) implemented by established or mature companies to either combat the dangers resulting from maturity, decline (Baden-Fuller and Stopford, 1992), or internal and external changes (Capron and Mitchell, 2009); or face the threats posed by dynamic and complex business conditions. Thus, various studies acknowledge that SR is a multidimensional and multi-level concept (Volberda, 2017) and may be viewed as an answer to the challenges arising from external or internal factors (Teece, 2019). One of its goals is to keep the company afloat.

Going further, it will be necessary to identify the process and content of strategic renewal (Agarwal and Helfat, 2009) and to look at how companies manage to renew themselves by initiating SR and clearly identifying its purpose (Schmitt *et al.*, 2018). To this end, we have to be aware that SR is not an easy task; it is only one possible option given the changes, and several paths can be taken to renew the firm, leading to consider its temporal and sequencing aspects.

More generally, the company has to face its routine and the resulting inertia. Thus, the managers' and company members' willingness to safeguard the company's longevity and success is a necessary, if inadequate, condition to enable the firm's strategic renewal. Firms must continuously seek new opportunities to guarantee renewal and anticipate crises or a change in their environment. At the same time, they also need to have a reactive capacity to deal with the environmental changes they face. This leads Baden-Fuller and Volberda (1997) to assert that the company can react in three ways to changing business conditions:

1. It can avoid change by adopting a strategy of inertia.
2. It can accept change by processing it externally through an 'outsourcing' strategy, for example, by signing contracts, alliances and partnerships allowing it to capture new technologies or new ideas.
3. It can implement an internal adaptation and renew itself. This is where strategic renewal comes in, and we have noticed that it implies an entrepreneurial behaviour, as the manager will have to redefine some aspects of the firm's structure, grasp new market opportunities and/or innovate.

One can consider these ways as the first level of options for the managers—SR being only one of the possible responses to change.

The strategic renewal process can be implemented by top management (Glaser *et al.*, 2015) or middle management (Canales, 2013)—and even non-managerial actors (Pettit and Crossan, 2019). In a top-down approach of SR, the manager may envisage four mechanisms by superimposing two methods of managing change (spatial separation and temporal separation) on two types of change consequences ('revitalisation' and 'reordering'). This leads to the content aspect of SR. Four mechanisms derived from two parameters allow an organisation to call for SR (Baden-Fuller and Volberda, 1997). The first parameter depends on the way change is managed: changes can be made either locally on functions (spatial separation) or globally on the organisation as a whole (temporal separation). Spatial separation aims to limit the risks associated with change and only affects certain functions at a time; it comes with a downside, however, as it requires more time to develop the business. Making major changes to all functions at the same time allows for faster adaptation, but is also likely to lead to greater disruption. Therefore, it would be wiser for the company to alternate periods of change with periods of stability in order to avoid running out of steam or falling victim to chaos (temporal separation). The second parameter that distinguishes SR mechanisms concerns the nature of the changes made (i.e., revitalisation or redevelopment). Revitalisation is when the change aims to alter the organisation's core competencies, redefine them or even acquire new ones. If, by contrast, the aim is to alter the relative importance of core skills and routines, the change falls under the redevelopment category (Bégin *et al.*, 2011).

Another dimension regarding SR within firms involves an understanding of how firms renew themselves and what their SR sources are. On the one hand, some scholars argue that SR is a set of dynamic capabilities that make it possible to configure internal and external resources (Capron and

Mitchell, 2009). On the other hand, and according to scholars and organisational learning theory, firms' capacity to acquire multiple and diverse identities allows them to increase their contextual knowledge and their ability to pursue incremental and discontinuous renewal strategies (Brusoni and Rosenkranz, 2014). Thus, success is linked to a recognition of the responsibilities and benefits resulting from a resolution of the tensions associated with exploration and exploitation (Lengnick-Hall and Inocencio-Gray, 2013).

Although various questions and issues have been studied and raised in strategic renewal literature, some specific contexts, such as succession in family firms, have received little attention.

Succession and Strategic Renewal in Family SMEs

Succession is defined by the transfer of direction and ownership from one generation to another (Le Breton-Miller *et al.*, 2004), which involves the successor becoming more involved and the incumbent gradually disengaging (Handler, 1990). The integration of the successor in a family firm structure can be accompanied by a new orientation and new strategic choices. Owing to the commitment of family members to a multigenerational transfer, we contend that they prefer SR to inertia or outsourcing. Family firms will necessarily come up against changing business conditions. Thus, their desire to keep the business in the family and transfer it from one generation to the next ensures continuity of the family's name and reputation. Family CEOs have to focus on SR to adapt the company to the market and/or technological changes rather than accepting the inevitability of business failure (by choosing inertia) or transferring ownership to external stakeholders. These non-economic goals could be regarded as drivers to maintain the family firm's survival and SR (Zahra, 2018). The integration of a potential successor plays a driving role in the design, initiation and implementation of both strategic renewal (Mitchell *et al.*, 2009) and firm continuity. In the same vein, Jaskiewicz *et al.* (2015) introduce the concept of entrepreneurial legacy, which engages both the previous and the current generations in new strategic activities by adding new products and services, as well as new technologies or innovations, and entering new markets. These authors highlight the importance of succession by choosing family members as potential CEOs to preserve family cohesion. This strategic transition maintains the family firm's tradition and reinforces its history.

Methods

Longitudinal Case Study

Multigenerational family SMEs seemed like very appropriate venues in which to track changes and observe any recurrent patterns of strategic renewal. We sought to understand how a company that was founded in

1826 and is still managed by the sixth generation of the same family has dealt with events over time that might otherwise have led to failure. Using longitudinal analysis and employing archival data using multiple sources allow for an in-depth analysis of the case study (Zahra, 2018). Using a 'revealing' case (Yin, 2018; Gioia *et al.*, 2013) has a strong potential to clarify a phenomenon and fill a theoretical gap (Langley and Abdallah, 2011). This choice was also justified by the opportunity to have access to the family CEO, other family members and employees open to sharing (private) information about sensitive issues and answering "unusual research questions" (De Massis and Kotlar, 2014, p. 17).

We used two sources of data collection. The primary data consisted of 20 semi-structured interviews with family members involved in the company's management, including the current CEO, the previous CEO (who joined the company in 1946) and some of the longest-working employees at the company. We interviewed several people to ensure construct validity (Yin, 2018). The use of multiple data collection tools and information sources strengthened data credibility (De Massis and Kotlar, 2014). Data were collected in face-to-face setups (with an average interview duration of 50 minutes). All the interviews were recorded and transcribed. Additional data came from the company archives from 1932 to the present day, the stock transfer register, confidential notes and internal reports. The study was supplemented by conference notes from a former director and books (Malon, 2006; Bonin, 2008).

By using data collected over three years, it was possible to reconstruct the events chronologically. This approach has the advantage of allowing an in-depth analysis of the company being studied and makes it possible to consider the context in which the company has developed (Yin, 2018).

Brief History of the Company

We will now lay out the story of the family SME in an episodic format and identify the points marking renewal in the company. The company was founded by Frédéric Guillaume Foerster (FGF) in 1826, in Le Havre (France). For more than 194 years, the company has managed to continue its main line of activity—namely, trade—despite the many changes it has undergone. In this respect, the desire for successive directors to preserve the family's legacy has allowed the company to survive when many other companies operating in the same business folded. Figure 7.1 illustrates the succession of family and non-family directors in the company from the year it was founded until the present day.

Trading in Tropical Products and Shipping

FGF based his business on the tropical products trade, which was supplemented by sail shipping. The founder and his son focused their business

Figure 7.1 Successive Directors of ERDC Since 1826

Source: Author created

activities on trading with the United States, the West Indies and the French colonies, importing products that were little-known in France at the time and exporting national specialities. By 1868, the company had no fewer than nine sailing boats, which allowed the company to not only transport its own goods\, but to also earn additional profits by offering freight services to other trading companies. At the time, it traded in many tropical commodities (coffee, cocoa, tropical woods, etc.).

When he succeeded his uncle in 1890, Edmond RD kept up the existing activities of the business while also trying to diversify the range of traded products. In 1907, he managed to buy a stake in SIAPP, one of Guadeloupe's largest sugar/rum companies, which was in a state of bankruptcy at the time. Thus, the company gained a monopoly on its activities in France—a lucrative business, even if it was a minor one.

The arrival of steamboats at the start of the 20th century sounded the death knell for sail shipping. Following this major technological innovation that greatly reduced transport times and because the company's main line of business was trade/import, the directors decided not to renew the merchant fleet. They gradually abandoned the shipping business to focus on trade and to develop the company in this area by creating a subsidiary (SHIC-Société Havraise Indochinoise) in Indochina. This company was created in 1926 in Saigon and consolidated the policy of expansion and diversification.

Indochina and the Transition Towards Coffee/Cocoa

In 1930, Edgar RD took over from his father and sought to further grow and expand the company. After the growth of its business in Indochina, the parent company, which changed its name to ERDC in 1933, opened an office in Marseille and subsidiaries in Saigon (Vietnam) and Phnom Penh (Cambodia). However, the political and economic instability in Indochina and the outbreak of World War II slowed down trade and affected profits. The group's responsiveness in terms of anticipating change after facing setbacks because of the changing business conditions allowed it to set up new offices in Phnom Penh, Paris and Bordeaux. In this way, it was able to carry on trading and look for new opportunities, for example, by starting to trade with Côte d'Ivoire, one of the leading coffee and cocoa producers, at the start of the 1940s.

Succeeding his brother Edgar at the head of the company, Jean RD became the firm's CEO in 1948. Although the dangers of the war in Indochina ultimately caused the group to close its subsidiary there, it did not cease trade with this part of the world altogether. With the fall of Dien Bien Phu in 1954 forcing the subsidiary to move to France, as well as the closure of the Saigon agency in 1960, the closure of the Marseille office in 1962 after the independence of Madagascar, the ending of trade with this territory and the subsequent reduction in trade with Indochina, the parent company was also forced to close its Phnom Penh office in 1965.

While this series of closures was taking place, culminating in the loss of its SHIC subsidiary, the company was simultaneously developing its business in the coffee and cocoa trade with Côte d'Ivoire, which provided the group's business with a new burst of momentum.

Specialising in Coffee

In 1964, Jean's nephew Hubert RD became the new CEO after many years of experience in the company's various subsidiaries. Although the group had been trading coffee since its early years, it was not until the middle of the 1940s that it decided to pay more attention to this commodity, partly because of the political problems dogging Indochina at the time. An African subsidiary (SHAC-Société Havraise Africaine de Commerce) was opened in Abidjan in 1952. The main reason was to sell Robusta coffee and cocoa, and to provide Africa with a platform from which to send international exports. SHAC recorded a loss during its first year in business. Despite this loss, however, the CEO recognised it as an opportunity for the group to make its reputation in the local market and to prepare for the future. In the 1960s, the subsidiary began to make a profit and expanded its structure. The positive development of the coffee/cocoa business continued until the start of the 1970s when the group decided to open other SHAC subsidiaries in Côte d'Ivoire to sustain the thriving coffee/cocoa industry. It also opened a second factory, in San-Pédro, in 1970.

However, because of the upheaval that accompanied decolonisation in Africa, this success could not last indefinitely. The company's assets in the country were gradually confiscated, and SHAC finally closed shop there in 1987. And yet, continuing to believe in the future of coffee, the group successively bought Interocéanique, a coffee-trading business, in 1980, followed in 1988 by Maison Jobin, which specialised in trading and distributing coffee to wholesalers. At the same time, it set up SCRD (Société Commerciale Raoul-Duval) to look after all of the group's coffee businesses.

Searching for Diversity

Managed in tandem by Gilbert and Hubert RD (fifth-generation first cousins), the group began to make a series of takeovers from 1965 onwards to diversify the group's activities and to reduce its dependence on a single source of provisions. After assessing several businesses, this diversification drive generated several takeovers:

- 1970: SNRMIA, in the agrifood industry;
- 1975: a company manufacturing snail-shelling equipment;
- 1982: Havraidex, a company specialising in fibres, honey and brooms; and
- 1983: CFE, a company specialising in vegetable extracts for use in the tanning, cosmetics and animal food industries.

Although these takeovers contributed to the group's growth, most of them have since been resold or closed.

Restructuring the Group Around Extracts and Wood

Globalisation and increasing transparency in the coffee trade, along with growing risks in the mid-1990s, forced margins down considerably. The group decided to focus on greatly developing CFE, which has been managed since 1999 by François (sixth generation), and the wood business, with Havraidex. Although the continued decline in prospects for the coffee business ultimately convinced the directors to dispose of it in 2006, the past decade has been characterised by a desire to develop other activities to safeguard the group's long-term future.

The work of CFE, which is based on the ability to develop and formulate products using vegetable extracts, requires the company to expand into new territories. Therefore, a site was purchased in Nicaragua in 2004 to open up the possibility of cultivating the plants that are required to supply the group and to set up an on-site processing plant.

When the decision was made to suspend activity in the coffee trade, the director had to consider how CFE and wood activities, which had previously played a marginal role in the business, could be developed. While the operations of many actors whose businesses make use of timber are still based on the large-scale exploitation of resources, the directors of the family group are keen for an environmentally friendly—or sustainable—exploitation of such resources. When the leaders of Gabon decided to protect the country's forests through legislation, measures were implemented at ERDC to invest there. The company embarked on this project in 2006, buying a concession and setting up a sawmill that made it possible to make better use of the resources on-site and to ensure the exploitation was at an acceptable scale. Today, this local operation has some 30 employees and is in its first year of production.

The past 194 years have seen the family group transform from an international trading concern involved in transport and shipping to a group specialising in vegetable extracts and wood. This transition has been made possible by several episodes in the group's history that characterised its growth first in Indochina, then in Africa. Even though the group appeared to have coffee and cocoa as its central activities, it was always looking to maintain a certain degree of diversity in its business. At the same time, it is clear how the directors have tried to revitalise the business every time the group faced a new set of challenges.

Results

Despite the changing business conditions, which were not always conducive to the growth and prosperity of ERDC, the company has always tried to safeguard the long-term survival of its family heritage for future generations. This desire to protect the company over the long term has been backed up by the firm's entrepreneurial ability to seize the opportunities that came its way.

The five episodes presented in this chapter illustrate the group's strategic choices and the actions implemented to address changes in the business conditions. The strategic orientations made during these episodes were triggered by the arrival of a new CEO. Faced with pressures because of business conditions, political events, competition and new technologies, the group found itself in a position where it ended up either disposing of or selling parts of its business, a strategy Baden-Fuller and Volberda (1997) refer to as 'outsourcing'. ERDC has always tried to establish itself in new business areas and set up new sources of supplies before disposing of or selling a business. Therefore, the desire to safeguard the long-term survival of the group, backed up by the entrepreneurial spirit of successive directors at the company, which enabled them to seize opportunities, has also played a decisive role in choosing which strategy to adopt in order to best respond to the changing business environment. Therefore, the choice of SR mechanisms has not been a systematic one, but instead depends on the situation the company has found itself in.

In the case of sail shipping, which was by no means an insignificant aspect of the group's business, the arrival of steamboats, seen as a major technological innovation, triggered the SR process, as the director decided not to renew the fleet.[2] This decision meant redefining both the mission of the firm and its activities. Diversification began with the opportunity to acquire participation in the SIAPP distillery, while simultaneously establishing a subsidiary in Indochina to boost its business in the tropical products trade. It only abandoned the shipping industry when it had set up its business in Indochina and had consolidated its trading activities. In this area, the company looked into other possibilities, buying the SIAPP (regeneration) and making the most of its maritime trade and business skills by forming the SHIC subsidiary in Indochina (venturing).

Next, as business slowed in Indochina, the group began to look into new destinations to continue trading in tropical products. This led to the start of its business in Côte d'Ivoire, and gradually the group set up its subsidiary SHAC there (venturing). In the beginning, as the business in Côte d'Ivoire was not profitable, ERDC continued its operations in Indochina but also gradually reduced them before finally suspending its presence in the 1970s, when SHAC's business was flourishing. Within the SHAC subsidiary, the group also specialised within the coffee industry by implementing a vertical integration of activities, creating new subsidiaries and becoming involved in activities outside of trade (regeneration). Finally, anticipating its loss of the Côte d'Ivoire subsidiary, the group seized all the opportunities that became available, diversifying its sources of coffee provisions by taking over Maison Jobin and Interocéanique (rejuvenation) and entering new areas of business with SNRMIA and Havraidex company (reordering).

Figure 7.2 highlights the overlapping nature of the various strategic renewal initiatives and shows how the group has always tried to establish itself in a new area of business when an existing area is under threat. The case study of this family SME illustrates the SR approach taken when faced with pressures resulting from the various business conditions.

Discussion

The company's entrepreneurial spirit and ability to seize opportunities have allowed it to overcome the paradox of change and stability and to adapt to a changing business environment. This paradox should not be considered a counteracting force in family firm renewal (Sievinen *et al.*, 2019).

Previous research has investigated strategic renewal by addressing one or more aspects of this concept (Schmitt *et al.*, 2018). Firstly, we contribute to the literature by examining the set of dimensions of the

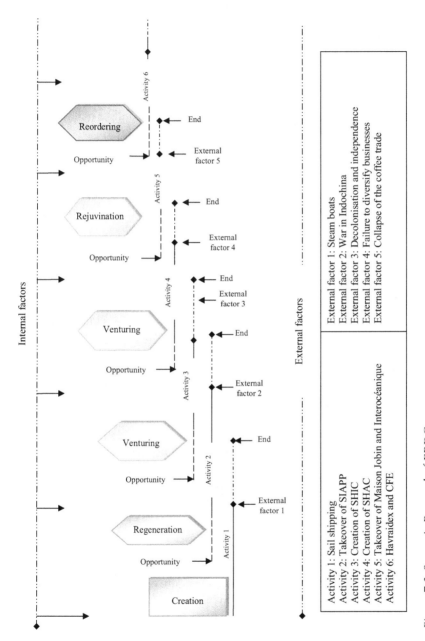

Figure 7.2 Strategic Renewal of ERDC

Source: Author created

SR: (1) the context and when firms renew themselves; (2) their antecedents and how firms renew themselves; (3) its process and who initiates and implements the SR; (4) their outcomes and why firms renew themselves; and, finally, (5) content and the mechanisms through which SR is carried out.

To contribute to the understanding of what characterises strategic renewal in a specific context, we analysed a family SME. Secondly, strategic succession is seen as a central element to nurture transgenerational entrepreneurship (Jaskiewicz *et al.*, 2015). We reinforce this idea by emphasising that succession can be also considered a catalyst of strategic renewal in a family SME.

As we focused on a single case, we cannot hope to provide a general observation applicable to all family firms. However, we were able to demonstrate how the family dimension—and the desire to pass the company on to the next generation—helps to explain the spirit of SR.

This study sheds some light on an interesting process of overlap between, on the one hand, mature or declining activities and, on the other hand, the start and growth of new ventures. From this, we can derive the following practical lesson: To guarantee its strategic renewal over the long run, a firm must continually be on the look-out for opportunities; therefore, it should nurture its entrepreneurial orientations. Moreover, the manager must be committed to keeping the firm in business. In the case of a family firm, however, this dedication to the future may be facilitated by the presence of new generations who want to pursue the family tradition and business continuity (Miller and Le Breton-Miller, 2005; Randolph *et al.*, 2018). Finally, it also means that the family firm must not be afraid of failing. Sometimes the efforts might not bring the desired success, but to be sure to have a heritage to pass on to the next generation, the family firm's managers must go on innovating and investing in the future, no matter whether it takes the form of new products, new lines, new ventures or new partnerships. As Abdelgawad and Zahra (2019) point out, failing to respond quickly to environmental shifts and implementing SR activities can endanger these firms' survival.

Conclusion

The succession process, through the involvement of new family members in family business management, offers an opportunity to renew and regenerate a company's vision, orientation and strategy to ensure its longevity and survival. The entrepreneurial behaviour of potential successors is informed by education, family business history through past entrepreneurial achievements and family cohesion and culture. However, it is necessary to pay attention to the counterproductive effect due to the absence of a shared vision between family members, which can generate interminable conflicts ending in the failure and even the disappearance of the business.

Notes

1. The authors wish to express their gratitude to Lucie Bégin for her contribution to this paper.
2. One of the reasons why they abandoned the shipping business is the size of the investment that would have been required to renew the fleet, which vastly exceeded the resources of the small-sized family business.

References

Abdelgawad, S.G. and Zahra, S.A. (2019). "Family firms' religious identity and strategic renewal", *Journal of Business Ethics*, 1–13.

Agarwal, R. and Helfat, C.E. (2009). "Strategic renewal of organizations", *Organization Science*, 20(2), 281–293.

Baden-Fuller, C. and Stopford, J.M. (1992). *Rejuvenating the mature business: the competitive challenge*, London: Routledge.

Baden-Fuller, C. and Volberda, H.W. (1997). "Strategic renewal: how large complex organizations prepare for the future", *International Studies of Management and Organization*, 27(2), 95–120.

Bégin, L., Chabaud, D. and Hannachi, M. (2011). "La transmission/reprise des PME: une occasion de régénération stratégique", in L. Cadieux and B. Deschamps (Eds.), *Le duo cédant/repreneur*, 12–30, Québec: Presses de l'Université du Québec.

Bonin, H. (2008). *CFAO 1887–2007*, Paris: Publication de la SFHOM.

Brusoni, S. and Rosenkranz, N.A. (2014). "Reading between the lines: learning as a process between organizational context and individuals' proclivities", *European Management Journal*, 32(1), 147–154.

Canales, J.I. (2013). "Constructing interlocking rationales in top-driven strategic renewal", *British Journal of Management*, 24, 498–514.

Capron, L. and Mitchell, W. (2009). "Selection capability: how capability gaps and internal social frictions affect internal and external strategic renewal", *Organization Science*, 20(2), 294–312.

De Massis, A. and Kotlar, J. (2014). "The case study method in family business research: guidelines for qualitative scholarship", *Journal of Family Business Strategy*, 5(1), 15–29.

Floyd, S.W. and Lane, P.J. (2000). "Strategizing throughout the organization: managing role conflict in strategic renewal", *Academy of Management Review*, 25(1), 154–177.

Gioia, D.A., Corley, K.G. and Hamilton, A.L. (2013). "Seeking qualitative rigor in inductive research: notes on the Gioia methodology", *Organizational Research Methods*, 16(1), 15–31.

Glaser, L., Fourne, S.P. and Elfring, T. (2015). "Achieving strategic renewal: the multi-level influences of top and middle managers' boundary-spanning", *Small Business Economics*, 45(2), 305–327.

Handler, W.C. (1990). "Succession in family firms: a mutual role adjustment between entrepreneur and next-generation family members", *Entrepreneurship Theory and Practice*, 15(1), 37–52.

Huff, J.O., Huff, A.S. and Thomas, H. (1992). "Strategic renewal and the interaction of cumulative stress and inertia", *Strategic Management Journal*, 13, 55–75.

Jaskiewicz, P., Combs, J.G. and Rau, S.B. (2015). "Entrepreneurial legacy: toward a theory of how some family firms nurture transgenerational entrepreneurship", *Journal of Business Venturing*, 30(1), 29–49.

Langley, A. and Abdallah, C. (2011). "Templates and turns in qualitative studies of strategy and management", in D.D. Bergh and D.J. Ketchen (Eds.), *Research methodology in strategy and management*, Vol. 6, 201–235, Emerald Group Publishing.

Le Breton-Miller, I., Miller, D. and Steier, L.P. (2004). "Toward an integrative model of effective FOB succession", *Entrepreneurship Theory and Practice*, 28(4), 305–328.

Lengnick-Hall, C.A. and Inocencio-Gray, J.L. (2013). "Institutionalized organizational learning and strategic renewal: the benefits and liabilities of prevailing wisdom", *Journal of Leadership & Organizational Studies*, 20(4), 420–435.

Malon, C. (2006). *Le Havre Colonial de 1880 à 1960*, France: Presse Universitaire de Caen.

Miller, D. and Le Breton-Miller, I. (2005). *Managing for the long run*, Boston, MA: Harvard Business School Press.

Mitchell, J.R., Hart, T.A., Valcea, S. and Townsend, D.M. (2009). "Becoming the boss: discretion and postsuccession success in family firms", *Entrepreneurship Theory and Practice*, 33(6), 1201–1218.

Pettit, K.L. and Crossan, M.M. (2019). "Strategic renewal: beyond the functional resource role of occupational members", *Strategic Management Journal*, 41(6), 1112–1138.

Randolph, R.V., Li, Z. and Daspit, J.J. (2018). "Toward a typology of family firm corporate entrepreneurship", *Journal of Small Business Management*, 55(4), 530–546.

Salvato, C., Chirico, F. and Sharma, P. (2010). "A farewell to the business: championing exit and continuity in entrepreneurial family firms", *Entrepreneurship & Regional Development*, 22(3), 321–348.

Schmitt, A., Raisch, S. and Volberda, H.W. (2018). "Strategic renewal: past research, theoretical tensions and future challenges", *International Journal of Management Reviews*, 20(1), 81–98.

Sharma, P. and Chrisman, J.J. (1999). "Toward a reconciliation of the definitional issues in the field of corporate entrepreneurship", *Entrepreneurship: Theory and Practice*, 23(3), 11–27.

Sievinen, H.M., Ikäheimonen, T. and Pihkala, T. (2019). "Strategic renewal in a mature family-owned company—a resource role of the owners", *Long Range Planning*, 101864.

Teece, D.J. (2019). "Strategic renewal and dynamic capabilities: managing uncertainty, irreversibilities, and congruence", in A. Tuncdogan, A. Lindgreen, H.W. Volberda and F. van den Bosch (Eds.), *Strategic renewal: core concepts, antecedents, and micro foundations*, 21–51, London: Routledge.

Volberda, H.W. (2017). "Comments on 'mastering strategic renewal: mobilising renewal journeys in multi-unit firms'", *Long Range Planning*, *50*(1), 44–47.

Volberda, H.W., Baden-Fuller, C. and Van den Bosch, F.A. (2001). "Mastering strategic renewal: mobilising renewal journeys in multi-unit firms", *Long Range Planning*, *34*(2), 159–178.

Yin, R.K. (2018). *Case study research and applications: design and methods*, New York: Sage Publications.

Zahra, S.A. (2018). "Entrepreneurial risk taking in family firms: the wellspring of the regenerative capability", *Family Business Review*, *31*(2), 216–226.

Part III

Internal Business Transfers to Employees

Transfer to employees is currently the least studied type of transfer in management research. This is relatively surprising inasmuch as this type of transfer is often favoured by predecessors. For business owners, employees are the second-best choice of successor, with their children in first place. To their eyes, long-term employees deserve to be successors because they may well have spent years with the company and proven themselves in their work. Transferring the business to these employees can be a form of recognition and reward for their involvement. It is also a way of ensuring the continuity of the transferred company, as employees are both eager to keep their jobs and best able to preserve the company's know-how. In this respect, transfer to employees constitutes one third of business transfers in many countries of Europe.

As few researchers have been interested in transfers to employees, this part of the handbook consists of only two chapters.

In Chapter 8, **Towards a Better Understanding of SME Employee Buyouts,** which draws up an inventory of the available knowledge on business transfers to employees, **Catherine Thévenard-Puthod** and **Cédric Favre** detail the different forms that this type of transfer can take. The authors identify not only the advantages in each stage of the transfer process that employees may enjoy, but also the specific difficulties that they may encounter. Drawing up a few avenues for future research, they invite researchers to take an interest in this type of transfer, which is still little studied.

Chapter 9, **Is a Workers' Cooperative an Effective Means for Transferring SMEs?,** is devoted to the specific features of a very particular form of employee buyout: the transfer to a workers cooperative. **Marie-Christine Barbot-Grizzo** provides an overview of this form of transfer, highlighting its weight on a global scale and its specific characteristics. She lists the obstacles to be overcome by predecessors and successors, as well as the key factors for the success of this type of transfer.

8 Towards a Better Understanding of SME Employee Buyouts

Catherine Thévenard-Puthod and Cédric Favre

A SME can be transferred to different types of individual buyers, depending on the degree of proximity of the buyer to the owner-manager who wishes to sell his/her firm. There are four types of cases: family successions, transfers to one or more employees of the company, transfers to a third party, and transfers called mixed or hybrid, because they bring together different types of buyers (for example, family successors and employees, or employees and external buyers; Thévenard-Puthod, 2020). Historically, researchers have focused on family succession (e.g., Le Breton-Miller *et al.*, 2004; Marshall *et al.*, 2006; Scholes *et al.*, 2007; De Massis *et al.*, 2008), even though this type of transfer has been declining for several years.[1] More recently, particularly in France, several researchers have been interested in external transfers (Picard and Thévenard-Puthod, 2004; Bornard and Thévenard-Puthod, 2009; Kamei and Dana, 2012; Nordqvist *et al.*, 2013; Wiklund Nordqvist and Hellerstedt, 2013). Employee buyout[2] is currently the least studied type of transfer, even though in some countries, such as France,[3] it constitutes one-third of business transfers (according to the '*Cédants et Repreneurs d'Affaires* [Business Assignors and Buyers]' association). It is also likely to grow, due to a favourable legislative framework and a context of growth in social entrepreneurship (Garcia and Beltrami, 2014; Audebrand, 2017). Finally, despite statistical data showing greater success for this type of transfer,[4] buyouts by one or more employees are complex (Bargues *et al.*, 2017), and failures can occur.

This chapter therefore proposes to inventory the few available studies on employee buyouts, in order to have a better vision of this particular process. It is structured as follows: in the first part, we present the different forms of employee buyouts and the few studies found on this subject. In the second part, we identify the advantages that employees have in the early stages of the transfer process, as well as the obstacles they face. Finally, we present the levers they hold and the difficulties they can encounter once the transfer of company ownership is completed.

A Wide Variety of Forms of Employee Buyout

The first difficulty that researchers face when they study employee buyouts is the variety of forms that the phenomenon covers (Gunderson Sack et al., 1995). As shown in Table 8.1, an employee can take over a company alone or as a team. Among the teams, we can distinguish between a buyout with peers—in other words, by a team of employees—and mixed or hybrid takeovers, including other types of buyers (children of the seller or external buyers, as in the case of MBO/MEBO or MBI[5]). Finally, among buyouts by a team of employees, a distinction can also be made between buyouts in SCOPs (Cooperative and Participating Companies or Worker Cooperatives; Chapter 3.2, Barbot-Grizzo, this volume), where each employee can become an owner of the company, and buyouts in which the former employees are owners of traditional private limited companies and may have an unequal distribution of company shares.

This diversity of forms can undoubtedly explain the limited and dispersed nature of the research on employee buyouts. A review of the literature (Table 8.1) reveals a very small number of studies focusing on this kind of firm transfer.

Table 8.1 The Different Forms of Employee Buyouts

	INDIVIDUAL BUYOUT	*TEAM ACQUISITION*			
		Team of peers (with other employees)		*Hybrid teams*	
		In worker cooperatives	*In traditional private limited companies*	*With one or more children of the predecessor*	*With one or more external buyer(s) or financial investors*
Main studies identified in the literature	Deschamps, 2003; Barbot-Grizzo, 2012; Cadieux et al., 2014; Thévenard-Puthod et al., 2014	Huntzinger and Jolivet, 2010; Barbot-Grizzo et al., 2013 Barbot-Grizzo, 2013; Garcia and Beltrami, 2014; Bargues et al., 2017	Bah, 2014 Deschamps and Thévenard-Puthod, 2019	Thévenard-Puthod, 2020	Gunderson et al., 1995 Howorth et al., 2004; Scholes et al., 2007

At first glance, this review shows that researchers have embraced all types of employee buyouts, since at least one study is found in each box of Table 8.1. However, employee buyouts often occupy a marginal place in those studies. Most of the time, the empirical part of these articles, based mainly on qualitative methodologies, contains one or more case studies involving employee buyouts, but without this kind of transfer explicitly being the central subject of the research. Only a handful of articles focus specifically on employee buyouts (Gunderson *et al.*, 1995; Huntzinger and Jolivet, 2010; Barbot-Grizzo, 2013; Barbot-Grizzo *et al.*, 2013; Bah, 2014; Garcia and Beltrami, 2014; Bargues *et al.*, 2017), and often only in the specific case of worker cooperatives.

Consequently, in order to better understand the specific features of employee buyouts, whatever their form, we divided the process into two main stages:

1. The upstream part of the process, which includes the preparation of the predecessor and the employee(s) for the transfer of the company, the negotiations between the predecessor and the buyer(s), and all the legal and financial steps that must be taken for the transfer to take place.
2. The downstream part of the process, which includes a possible transition phase with the seller and then the post-transfer management phase, when the seller definitively leaves the company with the former employee(s) alone at the helm.

The following paragraphs therefore identify the potential assets and pitfalls that employees may face during those two steps of the takeover process, indicating how situations may vary depending on the type of takeover (alone or in teams, in a traditional company or in a worker cooperative).

Strengths and Pitfalls of Employees in the Upstream Part of the Transfer Process

Motivations of Predecessors and Employees at the Heart of the Process

Employees who embark on the process of buying out the company that employs them may benefit from the favour of predecessors. Predecessors can be more inclined to transfer their companies to known people than to outsiders (Jacques-Jouvenot and Schepens, 2007). The literature on business transfer shows that whatever the reason for the transfer (retirement, illness, loss of profitability or wish to change the company's direction), SME managers committed to their businesses are often concerned about their sustainability (Cabrera-Suàrez *et al.*, 2001; Howorth *et al.*, 2004;

Le-Breton-Miller *et al.*, 2004; DeTienne, 2010; Scholes *et al.*, 2007; Favre-Bonté and Thévenard-Puthod, 2013). Owners want their companies to continue developing, maintain employee jobs and firm know-how, continue relations with privileged partners (customers, suppliers) and, in the case of family firms, extend the history of what is often several generations of work (Dalziel, 2008). The selection of a buyer is therefore very painstaking (Graebner and Eisenhardt, 2004; Dalziel, 2008), with sellers sometimes going so far as to relegate the financial aspects to the background (Graebner and Eisenhardt, 2004; Favre-Bonté and Thévenard-Puthod, 2013), or even postpone the operation because they have not found the ideal candidate. Passing the firm on to employees can therefore constitute a guarantee for the founder that the company will not close or be relocated (Bah, 2014), at least in the short term. In addition, although several studies show that company managers prefer to pass on their business to their children (Calabro *et al.*, 2018; Discua Cruz *et al.*, 2013; Royer *et al.*, 2008), long-term employees can also be considered reliable successors. They have spent a long time within the company and have proven themselves in their work. In line with the 'socio-emotional wealth' perspective, which shows the influence of the emotional in the decisions of family business owners (Minichilli *et al.*, 2014; Calabro *et al.*, 2018), the transfer of the company to employees could be considered as a form of recognition and reward from a manager to employees (Thévenard-Puthod, 2020).

Legal incentives can also be added to the list of factors motivating the predecessor, since in France, in companies with less than 250 employees, the manager must inform employees about the possibilities of buying out the company at least once every three years. For firms with less than 50 employees, employees must even be notified by the predecessor at least two months before the sale of the company. As a result, sellers and employees are now more aware of the potential of employee buyouts.

However, it can also happen that predecessors may find it difficult to engage in the transfer process for fear of disclosing sensitive information to employees, such as the company's detailed accounts or managers' remuneration (Barbot-Grizzo *et al.*, 2013; Barbot-Grizzo, 2013; Bah, 2014).

Apart from this aspect, the main difficulty upstream of the process lies more on the employees' side. The literature regularly highlights the lack of entrepreneurial motivation in employees, given the workload of an entrepreneur (Bah, 2014). They may also have doubts about the predecessor's real motivations for the sale, as the transfer may be seen as an indication of the company's poor health (Gunderson *et al.*, 1995; Bah, 2014). They must therefore pluck up courage to embark upon the entrepreneurial adventure. As such, the formation of a team can strengthen the motivation of employees to take over, as it allows a better distribution of entrepreneurial risks (Almeida and Wolfenzon, 2006). By reducing their anxiety, the formation of a team reduces the employees' reluctance to embark on a buyout and encourages them to act (Thévenard-Puthod, 2020).

However, in the particular case of worker cooperatives, founding a succession team is not always sufficient. Employees may be reluctant to invest part of their savings and take a financial risk in a company that ultimately offers little profitability (Gunderson *et al.*, 1995; Barbot-Grizzo *et al.*, 2013). The legal constraints of the worker cooperatives only offer a limited distribution of interest on shares, and their repayment in the event of departure cannot lead to a capital gain, since these shares will be sold at the nominal price, possibly increased by the cost of inflation. The granting of a large part of the profits in the form of profit sharing (minimum of 25%) and the incorporation of a part of the profits into non-distributable reserves (minimum of 16%) greatly reduces the return on investment of the co-operators.

From Negotiating the Sale Price to Seeking Financing

The general literature on business transfers presents the negotiation phase as being very delicate, and the same is generally true for employee buyouts, even though employees are in less of an asymmetric information situation than an external buyer would be (Howorth *et al.*, 2004). While some studies show that finding a buyer who meets their expectations takes precedence over the financial amount of the transaction in the predecessor's motivations (BPCE, 2017), owners nevertheless naturally tend to overvalue their companies (CNCFA barometer-Epsilon, 2014). It is difficult to objectively evaluate a cherished possession that represents the accumulation of several years of effort, success, failure and invested capital (Astrachan and Jaskiewicz, 2008). This can result in differences in price estimates between the employee(s) and the seller.

The financing of a buyout usually requires a significant initial financial investment. However, employees, especially if they are not in remunerative management positions, often do not have sufficient financial resources to finance their project (Gunderson *et al.*, 1995; OSEO BDPME, 2005) and may also lack knowledge about the sources of financing they could utilise (Thévenard-Puthod *et al.*, 2014). This can be a major obstacle to buyouts, although some measures can facilitate the operation. In cases where the transfer is planned in advance and the predecessor is not in a hurry to sell, employees can buy the business by gradually increasing their equity interest until they obtain full ownership. Sellers can also contribute financially to the buyout by granting employees a vendor loan (Barbot-Grizzo, 2013). This risk assumption by sellers (potential loss of capital gain in the event of the company's failure) demonstrates their attachment to the company and reassures the banking institutions that will provide the main financing for the operation. Another solution is to create a holding company, which will take on the loan necessary to buy back the shares and then repay it, thanks to the dividends generated. However, employees must make a personal contribution of between 20% and 30% of the transaction amount. In this context, buyouts by a team of employees facilitate obtainment of additional resources by calling upon the social networks of the various partners (Thévenard-Puthod, 2020). Banks, private equity firms and business angels may be more inclined to participate in the financing of the buyout when a team is involved in the project. In addition, SMEs with comfortable levels of profitability can be subject to a management buyout (MBO). Investment funds are indeed fond of this arrangement, in which they provide, on average, 15% to 20% of the total financing, because they are reassured of management continuity. Finally, in France, the *Confédération générale des SCOP* [The General Confederation of Worker Cooperatives] has set up a range of financial tools to facilitate the financing phase of worker cooperative buyouts and has assembled a group of preferred banking partners.

Strengths and Disadvantages of Employees in theDownstream Part of the Transfer Process

A Facilitated Transition From Predecessor to Employee(s)

A transition period between predecessor and employee ownership is often considered essential in the business transfer literature, although it does not always take place (Picard and Thévenard-Puthod, 2004). In small firms, information systems are often limited (Thévenard-Puthod *et al.*, 2014), and it is generally the former managers who centralise all the information about the company (informal agreements with certain customers or suppliers, pricing, deadlines to be met, stock situation, age of machines and equipment, etc.). However, while employees have the advantage of their familiarity with the company in which they work and its industry, they often only know part of it. Managers of very small firms generally have difficulty delegating and involving their employees in strategic decisions (Bah, 2014). Employees will therefore have to benefit from a transfer of knowledge from the seller. The transfer of management generally starts before the deal is signed (Barbot-Grizzo *et al.*, 2013), since employees are already present in the company, but it does not really take place until the transfer of ownership has been formally completed.

As in any period of cohabitation at the head of the company between a predecessor and one or more successors, there may be conflicts related to differences in perspectives of the required management mode (for example, the place of technical know-how in the daily work of the manager, the choice of HRM practices or the use of IT; cf. Cabrera-Suàrez *et al.*, 2001). Some managers may have difficulty letting go and accepting a different way of running the business than their own. In addition, there may sometimes be a generational and cultural gap between a self-made founder of retirement age and a younger buyer, who may have earned a diploma (at university or in a business school) before being hired in the company. Nevertheless, this essential transfer of tacit knowledge related to management and strategic aspects seems more likely to take place between a seller and former employees than in the case of an external takeover, where the protagonists only get to know each other during this transition phase (Bornard and Thévenard-Puthod, 2009). In the case of employees, joint working habits have developed before the takeover can attenuate differences in perspective (Barbot-Grizzo *et al.*, 2013).

A Successful Post-Transfer Management Phase Influenced by the Ability to Take on a New Role and Develop New Skills

Once at the head of the acquired firm, it would seem likely that employees, who come with some knowledge of the company from their previous period of employment and a possible longer transition phase, will take over the company smoothly, making fewer mistakes than an external buyer would. As employee-owners, they may be more willing to adjust pay in order to preserve jobs and to avoid strikes (Gunderson *et al.*, 1995). Internal dynamics may also change through improved worker motivation, effort and commitment to the firm (Gunderson *et al.*, 1995). However, the few available studies show that employees do not really encounter fewer difficulties in the post-buyout management phase than other types of buyers (Eurochambres, 2006). This can be explained by various factors.

First, an employee who buys out a company alone does not necessarily master all the skills needed to be a SME manager. For example, in the craft industry, Picard and Thévenard-Puthod (2004) show that when buyers are only technically trained, the daily management of the company can be problematic (accounting, sales, human resources, purchasing, etc.). Buyers from the craft industry are often penalised because they may lack sales skills, creating a risk to the sustainability of the acquired company's customer portfolio (Picard and Thévenard-Puthod, 2004). Moreover, their position as an employee has not necessarily enabled them to acquire management skills, which can affect their strategic acumen and ability to lead a team (e.g., recognise and reward the contribution of each employee, ensure their well-being, be able to identify missing skills; Barach *et al.*, 1988).

However, a team-based buyout allows employees to benefit from a greater diversity of knowledge and know-how (Thévenard-Puthod, 2020), and to introduce a specialisation of tasks that can be very appropriate in relation to the volume of work needed. In a team, some employees may have worked in the company for several years, in different positions. They therefore benefit from a good knowledge of the various aspects of the company and how they function. They are fully familiar with the processes and have developed shared working habits (Barbot-Grizzo *et al.*, 2013). This continuity makes the takeover process more seamless. This last point is an important factor for the company's other stakeholders, primarily customers and suppliers. Observing that a team of employee buyers is taking over the company's reins helps to reassure them about the company's continuity and the consolidation of collaboration habits.

The main difficulty lies undoubtedly in whether other employees accept the change of ownership. The buyout by an employee raises two problems. On the one hand, it can be difficult for former employees to assume their change of role from colleague to manager (Cadieux and Deschamps, 2011). On the other hand, their former colleagues must recognise the legitimacy of their new boss. The literature shows that without the confidence of the remaining employees, dysfunctions can quickly appear (loss of motivation, reduced productivity or quality of work, or even resignations), damaging the health of the transferred company. In the very specific case of worker cooperatives, the intervention of the General Confederation of SCOP, which acts as a representative of employees' interests, favours the emergence of trust between the various internal actors of the company (Barbot-Grizzo *et al.*, 2013).

The final difficulty found in the literature concerns a possible reluctance on the part of former employees to question how the acquired company is operated and thus to promote changes that would make it possible to revitalise and grow the purchased firm (Bah, 2014). The company could find itself in a *status quo* position and not take full advantage of the momentum that a new manager could have given it.

Difficulties of Team Leadership: From Disagreements Between Members to the Possible Break-up of the Buyout Team

While building a team of employees seems to remove many of the obstacles related to the buyout, it can also lead to leadership problems and rivalries between partners.

The business transfer literature underlines the need to bring out a leader in all types of entrepreneurial teams (Gunderson *et al.*, 1995; Farrington *et al.*, 2012). However, taking on leadership is not self-evident and can generate conflicts, especially if the partners hold equal shares in the capital of the acquired company. For example, in the particular case of worker cooperatives, even if the number of shares held is not necessarily identical for each employee, one of the founding principles is 'one person = one vote'. The appointment of a new leader is therefore made by the decision of all the members. In hybrid teams made up of employees and the founder's family members, Thévenard-Puthod (2020) showed that the heirs have a privileged position over non-family employees in obtaining leadership.

The presence of conflicting objectives and differing work attitudes, as well as differences in values and personalities, may prove incompatible in the long term (Francis and Sandberg, 2000; Lung *et al.*, 2013), and are also potential sources of conflict that can undermine the effective functioning of a buyout team. However, few empirical studies on collective employee buyouts can attest to the significance of these conflicts. One research conducted on hybrid teams (Thévenard-Puthod, 2020) points out that conflicts can be significant and be related to 1) the selection of team members by the predecessor, 2) too much heterogeneity in the composition of the team and 3) a lack of strong ties among team members. Those conflicts can result in one type of member (children or employees) exiting the team.

Finally, Table 8.2 summarises all the advantages and difficulties that employees can potentially encounter upstream and downstream of the buyout process, depending on whether they buy the company alone or with other team members.

Conclusion

The objective of this chapter was to synthesize the knowledge on employee buyouts, a form of transfer often forgotten in research on business transfers, even though it represents a significant percentage of these operations. We first showed the extreme variety of the phenomenon, which may explain the difficulty for entrepreneurship researchers to grasp it. Then, based on the rare studies specifically focused on employee buyouts and the broader literature on business takeovers, we highlighted the specific features of this buyout process, and therefore the particular strengths and difficulties that this type of buyer can face upstream and downstream of the process. It appears that these vary strongly depending on whether the buyout is done by an individual or a collective. This literature review, even if it does not claim to be exhaustive, is therefore a first attempt at a global vision of the employee buyout phenomenon.

We invite researchers to pursue further research in this little-explored field. Indeed, many questions are still outstanding, opening up avenues for future research. First, apart from a few studies dealing with the particular case of worker cooperatives, no research has carried out a real empirical review of the particular difficulties or, on the contrary, of the key success factors for employee buyouts, whether individual or collective, throughout the process. The elements identified in this article,

Table 8.2 Summary of the Strengths and Levers Used by Employees at Each Stage of the Process in the Different Types of Buyouts

	UPSTREAM OF THE PROCESS		DOWNSTREAM OF THE PROCESS	
	Advantages	*Difficulties*	*Advantages*	*Difficulties*
Employee buyouts in general	Easy target search Favour of the predecessor	Reluctance of the predecessor to disclose sensitive information to employees A lack of entrepreneurial motivation in employees	Knowledge transfer facilitated by previous presence in the company Less risk of slip-ups	Possible lack of competence in employees Change of role to be assumed and accepted by other employees Reluctance to make changes that may be necessary
Individual buyout		Sense of greater entrepreneurial risk Finance the buyout	One captain on board for decision-making	More pronounced lack of skills
Team buyout	Stronger motivation of buyers (reduction of perceived entrepreneurial risk) Financing facilitated		Greater diversity of knowledge and know-how	Problems of leadership and rivalry between partners Cognitive and effective conflicts
Peer teams — Worker cooperative	Strong support from dedicated organisations (e.g. CGSCOP in France)	Legal and financial constraints on motivation		
Classic company				
Mixed Teams — With child(ren) of the predecessor		Formation of the team often influenced by the predecessor		Too much heterogeneity
With external actor(s)				Employees in asymmetric position with children

often based on parallels drawn from the literature on family succession or external takeovers, deserve to be compared with empirical results, which could greatly enrich these reflections. Case studies on individual buyers on the one hand, and on collective teams of employees on the other hand, could be instructive in better assessing the real experience of employees at all stages of the transfer process. This could reveal specific needs of employees in terms of entrepreneurial support. It would also be relevant to study the functioning of employee teams more closely. Most of the available studies focus on the financial performance of MBO and MBI operations (Bruining and Wright, 2002; Bacon *et al.*, 2004; Bruining *et al.*, 2004; Howorth *et al.*, 2004) and are quantitative in nature. They do not allow to truly understand what is happening within these teams. Moreover, there is no specific research on teams of employees in the classic company format. The only studies available focus on worker cooperatives and do not address all aspects of the buyout (e.g., how they function after the buyout). Nor is there any research on mixed teams of employees and external buyers. Consequently, studies on different types of teams (teams of employees only, either traditional or in cooperative form, teams combining former employees and family successors, teams of employees and external buyers) could provide knowledge on how these teams are formed (their emergence mode and criteria for choosing members) and how they operate (the emergence of the leader, the distribution of tasks, the mode of governance, the management of possible conflicts). Finally, these qualitative studies should be supplemented with quantitative studies to measure the performance of these different types of employee buyouts, with regard to family successions and external transfers.

Notes

1. Several studies show that the children of entrepreneurs, having perceived very early on the constraints inherent in entrepreneurial life and the personal sacrifices of their parents, sometimes prefer to opt for careers as employees in other firms rather than take over the family business (Zellweger *et al.*, 2011).
2. In this research, we differentiate between employee buyout and employee share ownership (ESO). In the first case, employees take control of all or a majority of the company's equity in order to run it; in the second case, it is more a measure designed to provide opportunities for employees to share in the rewards of work and motivation to work harder (Trewhitt, 2000).
3. According to Eurochambres (2006), employee buyout is also very significant in other European countries such as Bulgaria (20% of operations), Slovakia (31.6%), Slovenia (35.3%), Belgium (37.5%), and the Netherlands (38.9%). Despite the lack of reliable statistics, some authors illustrate the importance of the phenomenon in North America, too (Gunderson *et al.*, 1995).
4. The average failure rate for business transfers is 21% six years after the transfer (OSEO BDPME, 2005). If we take the average default rate as 100, it rises to 126 when the takeover is carried out by an external buyer and falls to 80 in the case of employee buyout; 27 in family successions.

5. A MBO (*Management Buy Out*) is the takeover of a company by a group of employees (generally four to six senior managers) who will use their personal funds and external sources of financing (bank loans or private equity). A MBI (*Management Buy In*) is the takeover of the company by external entrepreneurs who may nevertheless include one or more employee managers of the company in the shareholder team (Bacon *et al.*, 2004; Howorth *et al.*, 2004).

References

Almeida, H.V. and Wolfenzon, D. (2006). "A theory of pyramidal ownership and family business groups", *The Journal of Finance*, 61(6), 2637–2680.

Astrachan, J.H. and Jaskiewicz, P. (2008). "Emotional returns and emotional costs in privately held family businesses: advancing traditional business valuation", *Family Business Review*, 21(2), 139–149.

Audebrand, L.K. (2017). "Expanding the scope of paradox scholarship on social enterprise: the case for (re) introducing worker cooperatives", *M@n@gement*, 20(4), 368–393.

Bacon, N., Wright, M. and Demina, N. (2004). "Management buyouts and human resource management", *British Journal of Industrial Relations*, 42(2), 325–347.

Bah, T. (2014). "Vers une compréhension des freins à la transmission des PME aux salaries", in Gilles Lecointre (Ed.), *Le Grand Livre de l'Economie PME 2015*, 547–567, Paris: Gualino Lextenso éditions.

Barach, J.A., Gantisky, J. and Ourson, J.A. (1988). "Entry of the next generation: strategies and challenge for family business", *Journal of Small Business Management*, 3, 12.

Barbot-Grizzo, M.C. (2012). "Gestion et anticipation de la transmission des TPE artisanales: vers une démarche pro-active du dirigeant propriétaire", *Management & Avenir*, 2, 5–56.

Barbot-Grizzo, M.C. (2013). "Opportunités et difficultés des transmissions de PME en SCOP: Quelles solutions?" *Entreprendre et Innover*, 17(1), 72–82.

Barbot-Grizzo, M.C., Huntzinger, F. and Jolivet, T. (2013). "Transmission de PME saines en Scop: Quelles spécificités?" *Revue Internationale de l'Economie Sociale*, 330, 57–71.

Bargues, É., Hollandts, X. and Valiorgue, B. (2017). "Mettre en œuvre une gouvernance démocratique suite à une reprise en SCOP. Une lecture en termes de travail institutionnel", *Revue Française de Gestion*, 43(263), 31–50.

Bornard, F. and Thévenard-Puthod, C. (2009). "To better understand the difficulties of an external takeover through the approach of social representations", *Revue Internationale PME*, 22(3–4), 83–108.

BPCE. (2017). *BPCE observatory notebook*. www.bpce.fr.

Breton-Miller, I., Miller, D. and Steier, L.P. (2004). "Toward an integrative model of effective FOB succession", *Entrepreneurship Theory and Practice*, 28(4), 305–328.

Bruining, H., Bonnet, M. and Wright, M. (2004). "Management control systems and strategy change in buyouts", *Management Accounting Research*, 15(2), 155–177.

Bruining, H. and Wright, M. (2002). "Entrepreneurial orientation in management buy-outs and the contribution of venture capital", *Venture Capital: An International Journal of Entrepreneurial Finance*, 4(2), 147–168.

Cabrera-Suàrez, K., De Saà-Pérez, P. and Garcia-Almeida, D. (2001). "The succession process from a resource- and knowledge-based view of the family firm", *Family Business Review, 14*(1), 37–48.

Cadieux, L. and Deschamps, B. (2011). "La dynamique cédant/repreneur: lecture à partir des transitions de rôle dans une transmission/reprise externe", in L. Cadieux and B. Deschamps (Eds.), *Le duo cédant/repreneur, pour une compréhension intégrée du processus de transmission/reprise des PME*, 67–84, Québec: Collection Entrepreneuriat et PME.

Cadieux, L., Gratton, P. and St-Jean, É. (2014). "La carrière repreneuriale: contexte et défis", *Revue de l'entrepreneuriat, 13*(1), 35–50.

Calabro, A., Minichilli, A., Amore, M.D. and Brogi, M. (2018). "The courage to choose! Primogeniture and leadership succession in family firms", *Strategic Management Journal, 39*(7), 2014–2035.

Dalziel, M. (2008). "The seller's perspective on acquisition success: empirical evidence from the communications equipment industry", *Journal of Engineering and Technology Management, 25*(3), 168–183.

De Massis, A., Chua, J.H. and Chrisman, J.J. (2008). "Factors preventing intrafamily succession", *Family Business Review, 21*(2), 183–199.

Deschamps, B. (2003). "Reprise d'entreprise par les personnes physiques (RPP): premiers éléments de réponse à la question de son intégration dans le champ de l'entrepreneuriat", *Revue de l'Entrepreneuriat, 2*(1), 59–71.

Deschamps, B. and Thévenard-Puthod, C. (2019, June 24–26). "Support for women entrepreneur through their personal and professional networks: the case of women successors", *EURAM Conference*, Lisbon.

DeTienne, D.R. (2010). "Entrepreneurial exit as a critical component of the entrepreneurial process: theoretical development", *Journal of Business Venturing, 25*(2), 203–215.

Discua Cruz, A., Howorth, C. and Hamilton, E. (2013). "Intrafamily entrepreneurship: the formation and membership of family entrepreneurial teams", *Entrepreneurship Theory and Practice, 37*(1), 17–46.

Eurochambres. (2006). *A helping hand for SMEs mentoring business transfer*, Analysis Report, Brussels, August 2009.

Farrington, S.M., Venter, E. and Boshoff, C. (2012). "The role of selected team design elements in successful sibling teams", *Family Business Review, 25*(2), 191–205.

Favre-Bonté, V. and Thévenard-Puthod, C. (2013). "Resource and skill transfers in subcontractor SME acquisitions: influence on the long-term performance of acquired firms", *European Management Review, 10*(3), 117–135.

Francis, D.H. and Sandberg, W.R. (2000). "Friendship within entrepreneurial teams and its association with team and venture performance", *Entrepreneurship Theory and Practice, 25*(2), 5–26.

Garcia, L. and Beltrami, V. (2014). "SCOP and takeover of companies in difficulty: prospects for greater efficiency", *Le Revue des Sciences de Gestion, 269*, 121–128.

Graebner, M.E. and Eisenhardt, K.M. (2004). "The seller's side of the story: acquisition as courtship and governance as syndicate in entrepreneurial firms", *Administrative Science Quarterly, 49*(3), 366–403.

Gunderson, M., Sack, J., McCartney, J., Wakely, D. and Eaton, J. (1995). "Employee buyouts in Canada", *British Journal of Industrial Relations, 33*(3), 417–442.

Howorth, C., Westhead, P. and Wright, M. (2004). "Buyouts, information asymmetry and the family management dyad", *Journal of Business Venturing*, *19*(4), 509–534.

Huntzinger, F. and Jolivet, T. (2010). "Transmission d'entreprises PME saines en Scop au regard de la relève de la direction: une étude exploratoire de faisabilité en France", *Revue internationale de l'économie sociale*, *316*, 58–71.

Jacques-Jouvenot, D. and Schepens, F. (2007). "Transmettre et reprendre une entreprise: de l'Homo œconomicus à l'Homo memor", *Revue du MAUSS* (1), 377–391.

Kamei, K. and Dana, L.P. (2012). "Examining the impact of new policy facilitating SME succession in Japan: from a viewpoint of risk management in family business", *International Journal of Entrepreneurship and Small Business*, *16*(1), 60–70.

Lung, A., Foo, M.D. and Chaturvedi, S. (2013). "Imprinting effects of founding core teams on HR values in new ventures", *Entrepreneurship Theory and Practice*, *37*(1), 87–105.

Marshall, J.P., Sorenson, R., Brigham, K., Wieling, E., Reifman, A. and Wampler, R.S. (2006). "The paradox for the family firm CEO: owner age relationship to succession-related processes and plans", *Journal of Business Venturing*, *21*(3), 348–368.

Minichilli, A., Nordqvist, M. and Corbetta, G. (2014). "CEO succession mechanisms, organizational context, and performance: a socio-emotional wealth perspective on family-controlled firms", *Journal of Management Studies*, *51*(7), 1153–1179.

Nordqvist, M., Wennberg, K. and Hellerstedt, K. (2013). "An entrepreneurial process perspective on succession in family firms", *Small Business Economics*, *40*(4), 1087–1122.

Observatoire CNCFA EPSILON de la Transmission de PME. (2014, November). *Baromètre de la transmission de PME en France*, 5th ed. https://app.epsilon-research.com/Auth/Login?returnUrl=/File/Download/66.

OSEO BDPME. (2005, June). *La transmission des petites et moyennes entreprises; l'expérience d'OSEO BDPME*, étude n°6203.02. www.oseo.fr/IMG/pdf/Oseo_transmission.pdf.

Picard, C. and Thévenard-Puthod, C. (2004). "La reprise de l'entreprise artisanale: spécificités du processus et conditions de sa réussite", *Revue Internationale PME*, *17*(2), 93–121.

Royer, S., Simons, R. and Boyd, B. (2008). "Promoting family: a contingency model of family business succession", *Family Business Review*, *21*(1), 15–30.

Scholes, M.L., Wright, M. and Westhead, P., Burrows, A. and Bruining, H. (2007). "Information sharing, price negotiation and management buy-outs of private family-owned firms", *Small Business Economics*, *29*(3), 329–349.

Thévenard-Puthod, C. (2020). "Hybrid succession teams: understanding their formation and conditions for success", *Journal of Small Business Management*. www.tandfonline.com/doi/full/10.1080/00472778.2019.1700690.

Thévenard-Puthod, C., Picard, C. and Chollet, B. (2014). "Relevance of tutoring as a support mechanism for the individual buyer after the takeover. An empirical study on a European scale", *Management International*, *18*(4), 80–96.

Trewhitt, L. (2000). "Employee buyouts and employee involvement: a case study investigation of employee attitudes", *Industrial Relations Journal*, *31*(5), 437–453.

Wiklund, J., Nordqvist, M. and Hellerstedt, K. (2013). "Internal versus external ownership transition in family firms: an embeddedness perspective", *Entrepreneurship Theory and Practice*, *37*(6), 1319–1340.

Zellweger, T., Sieger, P. and Halter, F. (2011). "Should I stay or should I go? Career choice intentions of students with family business background", *Journal of Business Venturing*, *26*(5), 521–536.

9 Is a Workers' Cooperative an Effective Means for Transferring SMEs?

Marie-Christine Barbot-Grizzo

Small to medium-size enterprises (SMEs) represent the vast majority of companies in all developed countries (80% to 99%, depending on the definition and number of employees). Correlatively, a majority of business transfers occur within this category dominated by family businesses with sole proprietary or closely held family ownership. There is no consistent set of statistical data regarding these transfers, but all estimates point towards their economic importance. The European Commission estimated that in 2013, on average, 450,000 SMEs[1] change ownership each year in the EU, representing 2 million jobs. The French banking group BPCE estimates that in 2019, the number of European SMEs and intermediate-size business transfers reached 100,000, involving 10 million jobs. According to the same organisation, in France alone, 51,000 transfer operations representing 750,000 jobs were carried out during the period from 2013–2016.

These business transfers are triggered by various human and economic factors, frequently including the retirement of the owner. They are made to family members, third parties, and also to one or more employees (Chapter 1, Deschamps, this volume). The process of transfer to employees varies greatly depending on management structure adopted and the repartition of capital and ownership rights. The transfer can be implemented as a straight purchase by the employees with the creation of a holding company (Estève, 1997; Bah, 2011), as buyout by the company managers (Howorth *et al.*, 2004), or via the creation of a workers cooperative, which makes the employees co-entrepreneurs in a joint venture (Barbot-Grizzo *et al.*, 2013; Chapter 3.1, Thévenard-Puthod and Favre, this volume).

The transfer of business ownership and management to employees by the creation of a cooperative, called Scop ('*Société Coopérative et Participative*') in France, is a potentially advantageous alternative for the seller-owner and employees, providing a cost-effective and efficient transfer that minimises business disruption. From a macro-economic standpoint, it potentially constitutes a very attractive solution for many

SMEs in many countries with proven unique economic and societal benefits. This is recognised by several country governments, the European Commission, and national and international cooperative network associations, which are actively promoting this model of business transfer. They are cooperating on the development of legal and economic incentives to facilitate these transfers and maximise their chances of sustainable success. However, this model is currently not often used, despite the fact that a well-defined legal framework exists in many countries including Germany, France, Spain, Italy and Canada (Quebec) (Roelants *et al.*, 2012). The reason is that implementation of such transfers is frequently difficult because human prejudices and emotions easily hinder the rational thinking and planning necessary for an orderly process and successful transaction (Barbot-Grizzo, 2013). Indeed, the success of such transfers requires that a reasonable consensus is established among all stakeholders at the inception, particularly regarding expectations and objectives, and that transparency is maintained throughout the process.

This chapter, after presenting the context and current development of worker cooperatives, their structure, and legal framework, analyses the economic and human context and specificities of business transfers to worker cooperatives. It focuses on the implementation challenges, and analyses and synthetizes the factors likely to increase the chances of success. Focusing on the French example, the analysis summarises many years of research[2] on this specific mode of business transfer for which there are few publications.

Context and Specificities of Worker Cooperatives

Importance of the Cooperative Sector

The cooperative sector represents an important economic force in all industries in many countries. According to the International Co-operative Alliance (ICA),[3] there are currently 3 million businesses worldwide organised as cooperatives, and 1.2 billion cooperative members, which includes employees, customers/users and entrepreneurs holding shares. The corresponding total employment of 280 million people represents approximately 10% of world's employed population, and the top 300 cooperatives have revenue of 2.1 trillion US dollars.[4] In Europe alone, 5.4 million of employees work in 160,000 cooperatives that have 123 million members (Confédération générale des Scop, 2019).

These aggregated figures cover a wide variety of situations in each country. The International Labor Office issued guidelines in 2018 to promote the development of consistent worldwide statistics regarding cooperatives to make pertinent economic analyses possible globally and for each region and country. Most importantly, the guidelines define the following four main categories of cooperatives based on the nature of the relationship of its members with it: producers, workers, consumer/ users (including financial service cooperatives) and multi-stakeholder cooperatives.[5]

Worker cooperatives, the main focus of this chapter about businesses transfers, are the only cooperatives in which the majority of capital is held by employees/workers. They exist in numerous countries, but their numbers vary greatly from one country to the other, and that number is not related to their economic size. Notably, there are only 465 worker cooperatives in the United States employing 7,000 people and generating $550 million annual revenues.[6] In Europe, the European confederation of industrial and service cooperatives[7] (CECOP, 2020) has 35,000 worker cooperatives registered. In France, the number of worker cooperatives reached 2,391 at the end of 2019, according to CG Scop[8] (Scop network in France), employing 53,700 people and generating 5.6 billion Euros in revenue.[9]

There are several factors driving the creation of worker coopera-tives. In France, according to CG Scop, worker cooperatives created to launch new businesses represented 65% of the total and 56% of employment, and those related to transfers 22% of the total and 29% of employment at the end of 2019. Contrary to prevalent beliefs, the French worker cooperative approach is not only used for the trans-fer of bankruptcy businesses,[10] with only 9% of new enterprises. The Confédération générale des Scop (2019) also reports that the five-year survival rate of these transfer cooperatives range from 69% for trou-bled businesses to 74% for healthy businesses, which compares quite favourably with those related to new (cooperatives) businesses, at 64%. Similar positive survival results are reported in studies regard-ing Italy and Spain for the transfer to cooperatives (CECOP-CICOPA Europe, 2013).

Characteristics of Workers' Cooperative Transfers

In France, the transfer of a company to a worker cooperative requires the setting up of a 'Scop', a profit-making, incorporated, legal entity whose employee-associates own a majority of the capital (51%) and voting rights (65%). It operates according to principles of democratic manage-ment, which all cooperatives in the world follow. Each employee-associate is a partner with one voting right, regardless of the amount of capital held. The partners elect the general manager for four or six years, and are involved in all major decisions affecting the operations and strategy of the company, including investments and allocation of profits. These fun-damental principles of ownership and management are included in the legal framework of worker cooperatives in Europe,[11] the United States,[12] and Canada.[13]

The allocation of profits focuses on maintaining employment and the long-term viability of the cooperative and its employees. The French Scop statute contains legally binding rules regarding the allocation of profits. These rules include the requirement for the company to retain a minimum of 16% of net income, and allocate a minimum of 25% to the employees. The percentage paid out to associates/shareholders (dividend) cannot exceed the sum of these two figures. Data published by CG Scop show that, on average, for the year 2018, 46% of net income was retained by cooperative companies, 42% was distributed to all employees and 12% was paid as dividends to shareholders—both employees and outside associates. These profit-sharing rules constitute a source of motivation for the employees entering into a cooperative structure to take over their company and give a sense to their commitment.

More generally, the cooperative structure for the transfer of an established business can be a potentially beneficial solution for all parties involved: owners-managers, employees and third parties (customers, suppliers, bankers, government agencies, etc.), and *in fine* for the whole civil society. If not solely motivated by short-term financial return, the owner/seller could derive significant tangible and intangible benefits by avoiding the problems and costs often associated with selling to third parties, and ensure a smooth transfer (Huntzinger and Jolivet, 2010) and a better chance for the survival of the business. Transfers to employees could save jobs and support local economic activity, usually at a lower cost (Roelants *et al.*, 2012) than transfer to third parties, and prevent the unnecessary disappearance of thousands of enterprises every year. Furthermore, although never mentioned by the various stakeholders interviewed in field surveys, this status provides significant tax advantages for the seller, the cooperative company and its employees.

Another external factor plays a significant role in the development of cooperatives in general and of worker cooperatives in particular. It is the determinant support provided by the networks of cooperative organisations which promote the cooperative model as an attractive tool for developing entrepreneurship. An example is the European organisation CECOP that groups national organisations in 15 countries, including 40,000 cooperatives in manufacturing industries and services, employing 1.3 million people across Europe.[14] The organisation contributes to the development of employee cooperative as an attractive business transfer model through exchanges of good practices at the national and international levels, and the promotion of favourable contextual factors pertaining to representation, network and legal framework. In France, the Scop network actively promotes business transfers using the cooperative approach. It carries out advertising campaigns in multiple media, and uses social networks to broadcast positive testimonials by managers and employees to the general public, and advocates this type of transfer to businesses and financial consultants. It lobbies the government to foster this type of transfer for healthy companies, not just companies in difficulty facing bankruptcy. These efforts contributed to the development of a new incentive legislative framework for employees in 2014.[15]

This new legal framework includes measures favouring salaried employees with the objective of making this type of transfer easier and more attractive to them. But, theirs effects are currently minimal on transfers. This French legislative approach contrasts with the one adopted in Italy, for example, where the creation of employee cooperatives is encouraged by a specific ad hoc legislation aimed at companies facing severe financial difficulties with the objective of saving them from bankruptcy and liquidation (Di Stephano, 2018). Different countries have adopted different legislations regarding transfer to worker cooperatives, and provide more or less incentives to workers and owners; some have none, like Japan,[16] for example.

According to CECOP-CICOPA Europe (2013),[17] the fact that, in Europe, the transfer of businesses to employees using the worker cooperative model is currently most developed in France, Italy and Spain can be explained by these three factors: a legal and regulatory framework favourable to salaried employees, financing and tax incentives, and a structured network of collaborators.

The Two Components of the Transfer Process

The transfer of a company includes two closely correlated fundamental transactional processes: the transfer of company ownership and the transition to new top management (Donckels and Lambrecht, 1999). For transfers to third parties, these two issues are usually dealt with simultaneously (Deschamps, 2000; Picard and Thévenard-Puthod, 2004), but for transactions involving family members (Hugron, 1991) or employees (Cadieux and Brouard, 2009), they need to be, and are, addressed separately most of the time. Clearly, this is the case when the successor to the top manager is not the main shareholder, as in the transfer to a Scop, and the distinction between these two components becomes crucial.

The transfer of general management to a cooperative of employees is viewed as a critical priority (Barbot-Grizzo, 2019). It needs to be timely to avoid disruptions in the management of day-to-day operations and customer service, and for this reason must be initiated and implemented before that of ownership transmission. The legal transfer of ownership which involves the purchase of capital stock by the cooperative of employees is handled by actors (banks, lawyers, consultants) not directly involved with running the business, and can thus be easily handled independently. Financing itself is often facilitated by specialised lending organisations with the help of the cooperative network in many countries. Additionally, when there are serious financing issues, some owners may agree to a seller credit as proof of confidence in their employees and the viability of the business. For these reasons, financial issues are generally[18] considered less challenging than management transfer, which needs to be explored as far in advance as possible and alternatives evaluated.

The following three contrasting examples illustrate these points among the studied cases. A CEO thus trained his successor for three years. A second initiated the transfer of management immediately after the creation of his company to all employees recruited gradually over a period of 12 years. In these two cases, the steps and transactions necessary to transfer ownership to employees were completed in few months. On the other hand, in the third case, a worker cooperative was created to transfer the business in less than 12 months without distinguishing ownership and management transfers. The change of status led to the election of new co-managers. But the outgoing CEO, who has become an employee, continues to manage the new Scop without having a precise retirement date. A number of conditions have to be satisfied in order to realise all the steps necessary for the transfer of ownership and actual management transfer.

Worker Cooperative Transfers: Success Factors and Obstacles

Many factors influence the viability of a business transferred to employees through a cooperative, including on-going sound strategic and operating management. However, decisions made before and during the transfer process, including choices regarding the general management and ownership structure, are critical and depend on the context, motivations, expectations and objectives of the parties involved in the transaction.

Context and Management

Anticipation and preparation of the company and its stakeholders have proven to be key ingredients for any successful business transfer. Business planning is a well-documented success factor in many studies related to family transfers (Ward, 1987; Davis and Harveston, 1998; Sharma *et al.*, 2003). The circumstances of the transfer can be deliberate or forced upon the actors, as in the case of the company facing severe financial conditions, for example. This will obviously impact the planning process and the alternatives available to structure the new company. Anticipation of a future transfer involves managing the value of the company, including investments aimed at preserving its competitive position (Barbot-Grizzo, 2012).

The psychological preparation of the potential seller is also to be considered for any transfer project (Cadieux, 2005; Bah, 2009; Barbot-Grizzo, 2012).

On the other hand, in the case of a transfer to the company employees through a cooperative, a forward-looking, progressive preparation of all the salaried employees is a definite positive factor. This can be achieved through practicing a participative management style at all levels, associating employees to decisions affecting their jobs, allocation of key resources and the future of the company. That kind of management brings a definite advantage when a transfer is considered, as employees are then familiar with business management issues (Estève, 1997; Bah, 2009; Barbot-Grizzo *et al.*, 2013). Clearly, the promotion from employee to employee-associate—and for some, to leading management—cannot be improvised, and requires foresight and planning. Ideally, this process involves preparation very early for both the owner-seller and the employees to help them build skills with training projects. Several cases analysed show the benefit of distinctive human resources management focusing on information exchanges and transparency carried out several years in advance. The specific actions identified towards employees' involvement include: regular information, exchanges regarding important decisions, promotion of team work and autonomy, delegating down responsibilities for decisions, and increasing competencies and skills through on-going training.

The transfer to employees is predominantly initiated by the owner-manager rather than by the employees themselves, who play a critical role in the management of the negotiation and transfer process (Barbot-Grizzo, 2013). The smaller the size of the company to be transferred the more critical is the role of the SME's owner-manager prior to, during and after the transfer, as he alone can create a supporting and positive dynamic. He/she must questions himself/herself about their intention to hand down their company, the appropriate timing and the potential value of the business without their active participation (Barbot-Grizzo, 2012). He/she should also be prepared to commit the appropriate amount of time required to make the operation a success. This complexity makes careful and flexible planning a prerequisite for achieving the objectives of the transfer to everybody's satisfaction, a capability unfortunately often lacking in small enterprises. Decisions regarding timing may depend or be influenced by the situation of the company, the objectives and constraints of the owner-seller, or the readiness of employees to embrace the new challenge they are facing.

Motivation and Involvement of the Stakeholders

Regardless of the type of transfer, the human factor remains paramount throughout the process. The attitude of the actors involved, and the type of relationships they have established, directly affect decisions and out-comes (Handler, 1990; Kets de Vries, 1996; Howorth *et al.*, 2004). The personality and behaviour of the owner-manager greatly influences the transfer's outcome (Handler, 1994; Kets de Vries, 1996; Cadieux, 2005; Bah, 2009). The owner-manager's career path and personal experience (Barbot-Grizzo, 2019), real motivations, and often other family members impact the choice of alternatives and process steps for the transfer.

The motivations of the owner-manager interact with those of salaried employees, whose expectations, desires and commitment are paramount for the success of the transfer. As in many human undertakings, shared desire to succeed by all key participants remains one of the top success factors in what becomes a true joint venture. To reach that objective, mutual trust among the main actors involved (Thévenard-Puthod and Picard, 2006; Barbot-Grizzo *et al.*, 2013) is very important for success-ful implementation, particularly for transfer to outside family members because it facilitates transfer of know-how (Howorth *et al.*, 2004). One of the specificities of the process studied is the development of trust between the actors involved within the company, but also with external agents of the Scop network that is paramount to the success of this type of collective project (Barbot-Grizzo *et al.*, 2013).

Indeed, the supporting role of agents of the Scop network is also an important success factor. All owner-managers and employees surveyed underline their key contribution as advisors with expertise covering all aspects of the transfer project—technical, financial, legal and social. These consultants focus on representing employees' interests and assist them to facilitate the process. They are present at all stages according to expressed needs. Paid training courses are also offered to future suc-cessors and associates. In many other countries, specialised consulting resources exist to support the establishment of a cooperative entity and implementation of business transfer. In fact, these business transfer pro-jects have reached a higher level of success and efficiency in Italy, France and the UK (Wales), where the support of a cooperative network is avail-able compared to other countries that do not have access to this assis-tance (Roelants *et al.*, 2012).

This comprehensive and focused support is a determinant for reach-ing an informed choice and the free consent of all stakeholders for all the operations necessary for the transfer of ownership and management transition. This consensus is required for a successful transfer because it creates an environment in which shared objectives and increased moti-vation contribute to sustaining the enterprise and concomitant stable employment for all. In this environment, the choice of a leader-successor to the owner-manager is crucial. Frequently, it is accomplished by the owner-seller selecting a successor, a decision then ratified by the employ-ees. It also happens that this choice is left directly to the employees. The selection of a successor can be made among the existing employees of the company. He/she can be also recruited externally if the manager believes that the skill set needed is lacking internally. In one of the cases analysed, an entrepreneur recruited and trained his successor for five years while gaining the confidence of other employees before transmitting his company to a cooperative. Another leader recruited and trained his team gradually; two potential successors then volunteered for a co-direction and finally proposed a single potential successor. In practice, there are many alternatives to a basic scheme.

When the successor is elected by the associates and officially becomes the new general manager, a transition period is desirable, including coaching by the owner-seller as in other types of transfers (Cadieux, 2005). Depending on the main actors' professional experience, a period of few months to 18 months is generally necessary to achieve the transfer of business management, providing that the respective roles of the owner-seller and successor are clearly specified early on. After the effective transfer of management, it is up to the new team made up of employees to make this intangible capital grow by managing the business profitably. This is facilitated by their commitment to the company which is now a common project in which they have financial and emotional ownership.

Main Obstacles

The feasibility conditions to be met to achieve successful and sustainable transfers to worker cooperatives intrinsically contain the factors that often make these transfers difficult to implement.

Every year, thousands of viable businesses disappear because no transfer solution can be found. There are also numerous obstacles which could make identifying a viable solution difficult or even prevent a successful or timely completion of a well-defined one. Usually, the main difficulties are not financial but psychological. Financial issues, whether related to the structuring of the ownership transfer deal or its financing are a challenge that can be overcome most of the time with, if need be, the help of consultants or government agencies.

Human factors associated with the different individuals implicated in the transfer deal are often a source of difficulties that are harder to resolve. For example, the potential owner-seller may not consider the employees as potential reliable co-entrepreneurs and buyers (Cadieux and Brouard, 2009; Bah, 2011; Murphy *et al.*, 2017). Indeed, among the different solutions for transfers to employees, the owner-seller's choice is more likely to be a transfer to a close employee rather than to the majority of employees through a Scop. Frequently, that doubt is shared by customers and suppliers. Another human-related obstacle is the reluctance of owners to fully disclose company information, especially financial data, to the employees (Barbot-Grizzo, 2013). The owner may also be concerned that selling to the employees will result in a lower price than selling to a third party.

For employees, lack of preparation, change of status and purchase of capital can constitute impediments. 'Paying to work in the enterprise' is not an easy sell. This implies that securing the commitment of all employees to invest collectively in the project is critical. The fear, the lack of motivation of certain actors, a centralised management style and a bad social climate are also potential obstacles which need to be overcome. The cooperative transfer also means the employees will have to accept the risks inherent in any entrepreneurial project—a new concept for some, foreign to their way of thinking about labour relations (Barbot-Grizzo, 2013).

All these obstacles are made more daunting when the company is experiencing liquidity issues, and even more so if it becomes subject to legal bankruptcy procedure, adding to the stress of employees and making a recovery more problematic. Legal actors, foreign to the company and its business, are making decisions impacting the future of the enterprise, leaving the leader with only an advisory role, without any executive power. In such an environment, deadlines are dictated by the company circumstances, not by the stakeholders. The recovery alternatives considered, their timing and the change of the actors imposed by the judicial process greatly increase the difficulties and risks, making business turnaround less likely. For these reasons, the transfer of a financially distressed business to its employees motivated mainly by the desire to safeguard the company and its jobs should not be systematically encouraged by built-in incentives in the legal/regulatory framework, as is often the case, especially in Italy (Di Stephano, 2018), where companies experiencing difficulties exceed healthy ones.

Conclusion

Business transfer to employees through the creation of a worker cooperative is an attractive solution to overcome the numerous difficulties often encountered in transferring small or medium businesses to a new owner, and frequently the only solution to avoid their liquidation. But it is not a panacea, and indeed can be particularly challenging in the case of a business facing severe liquidity issues. However, for financially healthy companies, these transfers potentially bring many benefits for the stakeholders, particularly the employees, and better business survival prospects. Skilful planning and process management, paramount to all successful business transfers, is even more so when using the employee cooperative alternative. The transition from 'employee' to 'co-operator' status involves learning. A clear definition and shared understanding of the respective roles of the key actors who have to implement the transaction and the transfer of management competences are paramount among success factors. It is demanding and time-consuming for the seller and also for the employees, whose involvement and commitment are essential in what is a long-term project that directly affects their lives.

Furthermore, although welcome, measures providing a well-defined legal framework and tax incentives, as in France, are no substitutes for the motivation, determination, and commitment of SME owners-managers and their employees. The recent media campaigns for Scop creations, as well as newly enacted legislation in favour of employees' rights aimed at promoting interest for this kind of venture, have had limited impact so far. The main obstacle is ignorance, and, to a lesser extent, the reluctance of those who know about this scheme to consider it as a sustainable option. Indeed, the existence and mode of operation of employees' cooperatives still remains little known by entrepreneurs, many other economic agents and the public at large. Professional organisations and government agencies which have been promoting Scop are very well aware of this situation and are carrying out information campaigns targeting SME owners and managers, as well as employees. Only when potential owner-sellers and employees are aware of this possibility to carry forward their common business under a cooperative framework will they consider it as an alternative worth considering.

Notes

1. For the European Commission, SMEs are defined as "enterprises that employ fewer than 250 persons and either have an annual turnover that does not exceed EUR 50 million or an annual balance sheet total not exceeding EUR 43 million".
2. Concretized in particular by five conferences and three publications in academic journals from 2008 to 2019. Several case studies of healthy SMEs transmitted in worker cooperatives were analysed. 26 semi-structured interviews were carried out with all the stakeholders (owner-sellers, employee successors, employees, advisors, and managers of the cooperative network).
3. It's a non-governmental organisation founded in 1895 that represents cooperatives worldwide.
4. ICA, 2020.
5. These different categories of cooperatives are also differentiated in France with a taxonomy taking into account the categories of associates and sectors of activity (Coop FR, 2018).
6. US Federation of Worker cooperatives (2020).
7. CECOP, cecop.coop.
8. Confédération générale des Scop.
9. Revenue for all cooperatives enterprises.
10. As in Italy and Spain, for example.
11. Cooperatives Europe, transfertocoops.eu.
12. US Federation of worker cooperatives, Worker Cooperative Definition.
13. Canadian Worker Co-op Federation (2020).

14. CECOP, cecop.coop
15. The law 'Economie sociale et solidaire' adopted in july 2014.
16. Japan Workers' Co-operative Union (2020).
17. The European Confederation of Cooperatives and worker-owned enterprises active in industries and services, June 2013.
18. In particular, according to the stakeholders interviewed.

References

Bah, T. (2009). "La transition cédant-repreneur: une approche par la théorie du deuil", *Revue Française de Gestion*, 35(194), 123–148.

Bah, T. (2011). "Vers une compréhension des freins à la transmission des PME aux salariés", in G. Lecointre (Ed.), *Le Grand Livre de l'Economie PME 2012*, 547–567, Paris: Gualino Lextenso éditions.

Barbot-Grizzo, M.C. (2012). "Gestion et anticipation de la transmission des TPE artisanales: vers une démarche pro-active du dirigeant propriétaire", *Management & Avenir*, 52, 35–56.

Barbot-Grizzo, M.C. (2013). "Opportunités et difficultés des transmissions de PME en Scop: quelles solutions?" *Entreprendre & Innover*, 17, 73–82.

Barbot-Grizzo, M.C. (2019). "Une gestion innovante du processus de transmission d'une TPE saine aux salariés sous forme de SCOP", *Recherches en Sciences de Gestion*, 132, 179–205.

Barbot-Grizzo, M.C., Huntzinger, F. and Jolivet, T. (2013). "Transmissions de PME saines en Scop: quelles spécificités", *Revue Internationale de l'économie sociale RECMA*, 330, 57–70.

BPCE. (2019, mai). *La cession- Transmission des entreprises en France*, France: Les Carnets de BPCE -L'Observatoire.

Cadieux, L. (2005). "La succession dans les PME familiales: Vers une compréhension plus spécifique de la phase de désengagement", *Journal of Small Business and Entrepreneurship*, 18(3), 343–356.

Cadieux, L. and Brouard, F. (2009). *La transmission des PME, Perspective et enjeux*, Québec: Presses de l'Université.

Canadian Worker Co-op Federation. (2020). https://canadianworker.coop/about/what-is-a-worker-co-op/, accessed 7 April 2020.

CECOP-CICOPA Europe. (2013, June). *Business transfers to employees under the form of a cooperative in Europe: opportunities and challenges*. http://www.socioeco.org/bdf_fiche-document-2110_fr.html.

Confédération générale des Scop. (2019). *Rapport d'activité CG Scop 2018*. www.les-scop-limousin.coop.

Coop FR, les entreprises coopératives. (2018). www.entreprises.coop/images/documents/outilscom/panoramacoop2018/coopfr_panorama_2018_web.pdf, accessed 5 April 2020.

Cooperatives Europe. (2020). www.transfertocoops.eu/, accessed 6 April 2020.

Davis, P.S. and Harveston, P.D. (1998). "The influence of family on the family business sucession process: a multi-generational perpsective", *Entrepreneurship Theory and Practice*, 22(3), 31–53.

Deschamps, B. (2000). *Le processus de reprise d'entreprise par les entrepreneurs personnes physiques*, PhD Thesis, University Pierre Mendès-France, Grenoble II.

Di Stephano, C. (2018). "The business transfer through the cooperative model. A comparative analysis Italy-France", *Journal of Entrepreneurship and Organizational Diversity*, 7(2), 62–86.

Donckels, R. and Lambrecht, J. (1999, June). "The re-emergence of family-based enterprises in east central Europe: what can be learned from family business research in the western world", *Family Business Review*, 12(2), 171–188.

Estève, J.M. (1997). *La gestion des ressources humaines intrapreneuriales et le succès du rachat de l'entreprise par les salariés*, PhD Thesis, University Montpellier II, Montpellier.

European Commission. (2013, June). *Entrepreneurship 2020 action plan*. http://ec.europa.eu/europe2020/pdf/ags2013_en.pdf.

European confederation of industrial and service cooperatives (CECOP). (2020). https://cecop.coop/aboutCecop, accessed 12 April 2020.

Handler, W.C. (1990). "Succession in family firms: a mutual role adjustment between entrepreneur and next-generation family members", *Entrepreneurship Theory and Practice*, 15(1), 37–51.

Handler, W.C. (1994). "Succession in family business: a review of the research", *Family Business Review*, 7(2), 133–157.

Howorth, C., Westhead, P. and Wright, M. (2004, July). "Buyouts, information asymmetry and the family management dyad", *Journal of Business Venturing*, 19(4), 509–534.

Hugron, P. (1991). *L'entreprise familiale, modèle de réussite du processus successoral*, Montréal: Institut de recherche politique et les Presses HEC.

Huntzinger, F. and Jolivet, T. (2010). "Transmissions d'entreprises PME saines en Scop au regard de la relève de la direction: une étude exploratoire de faisabilité en France", *Revue Internationale de l'économie sociale RECMA*, 316, 58–71.

International Co-operative Alliance. (2020). www.ica.coop/en/about-us/international-cooperative-alliance, accessed 16 April 2020.

International Labour Office. (2018, October 10–19). *Report III: Report of the Conference, 20th International Conference of Labour Statisticians*, Geneva: Department of Statistics. www.ilo.org/public/---stat/documents/publication/wcms_651209.

Japan Workers' Co-operative Union. (2020). https://jwcu.coop/en/2019/01/19/legislation/, accessed 22 April 2020.

Kets de Vries, M. (1996). *Family business: human dilemmas in the family firm*, Boston, MA: International Thomson Business Press.

Murphy, L., McCarthy, O. and Carroll, B. (2017). "No heir apparent? Exploring the worker co-operative model as a solution to family business continuity", *Journal of Entrepreneurship and Organizational Diversity*, 6(2), 20–39.

Picard, C. and Thévenard-Puthod, C. (2004). "La reprise de l'entreprise artisanale: spécificités du processus et conditions de sa réussite", *Revue Internationale PME*, 17(2), 93–121.

Roelants, B., Dovgan, D., Eum, H. and Terrasi, E. (2012, June). *The resilience of the cooperative model*, Brussels: CECOP-CICOPA Europe.

Sharma, P., Chrisman, J.J. and Chua, J.H. (2003, March). "Succession planning as planned behavior: some empirical results", *Family Business Review*, 16(1), 1–15.

Thévenard-Puthod, C. and Picard, C. (2006). "Confiance et défiance dans la reprise d'entreprises artisanales", *La Revue des Sciences de Gestion*, 3(219), 94–121.

US Federation of Worker Cooperatives. (2020). https://institute.coop/what-worker-cooperative, accessed 7 April 2020.

Ward, J.L. (1987). *Keeping the family business healthy: how to plan for continuing growth, profitability and family leardship*, San Francisco, CA: Josey-Bass. www.usworker.coop/wp-content/uploads/2018/02/Worker-Cooperative-Definition-2015.pdf, accessed 7 April 2020.

Part IV

External Business Transfers

Part 4 of this handbook is dedicated to external business transfers—that is, to businesses taken over by external persons (alone or in a team) with no previous link with the firm or the seller. The problematic is quite different from that presented in part 3 of this handbook because the new owner-managers in external business transfers have, in most cases, only approached the firm through the intermediary of the seller. Once they have purchased the firm, they have to learn about the firm culture, the employees and their know-how. They are the 'intruder', and yet the new deciders.

Chapter 10, **A Research Framework for External Business Transfers of SMEs,** is a literature review of some of the issues specific to external business transfers. **Bérangère Deschamps** and **Susanne Durst** propose a theoretical analysis and a research framework for the international community of researchers, especially those interested in the external business transfers of SMEs. This chapter includes topics addressing external business transfers that have been well-researched and those that have not been. The research framework is organised around the process of the external business transfer, taking a broad perspective on the concerned actors and the internal/external environments. It also takes time into account.

One of the main difficulties for external buyers consists in uniting the existing team around them as new entrants. Two chapters focus on the post-transfer phase and issues of legitimacy and socialisation. In Chapter 11, **The Legitimacy of the External Buyer: Issues and Means of Acquisition, Lyès Mazari, Sandrine Berger-Douce** and **Bérangère Deschamps** provide details on the means for acquiring legitimacy in the eyes of employees and external stakeholders. Unlike family heirs, external buyers with no close ties to the company do not benefit from traditional legitimacy. The authors insist on the psychological mechanisms underlying employees' attribution of legitimacy to an external buyer. They describe the personal and professional qualities that contribute to external buyers' legitimacy: managerial exemplarity, the ability to develop the company, relational skills and professional (technical and managerial) skills. In Chapter 12, **From Outsider to Insider: Organisational Socialisation in Takeover Situations, Sonia Boussaguet** studies organisational socialisation in external business transfers. She shows that external business transfers often fail because the incoming CEO is rejected socially. For her, socialisation, the process by which an outsider becomes an insider—in this case, meaning a part of the team—is a crucial issue. She offers facilitation conditions before and after the entry of the buyers and activation conditions for the new CEO. Both chapters are empirical and give short case studies (Chapter 10) or verbatim (Chapter 11) illustrations.

Chapter 13, **How to Effectively Support External Buyers in a Post-Business Transfer Situation,** is also dedicated to the post-transfer period. Analysing the risk of failure of the external business transfer, **Catherine Thévenard-Puthod** points to the specific features of this type of business transfer, especially during the post-transfer phase, and then proposes ways to offer appropriate support to external buyers. The extent and variety of the highlighted difficulties, as well as the diversity of the profiles of external buyers and acquired companies, argue in favour of personalised forms of support. The author shows how the tutoring process can be an efficient support for the external buyer.

10 A Research Framework for External Business Transfers of SMEs

Bérangère Deschamps and Susanne Durst

In the extant literature, business transfers are still mainly discussed in the field of family business research where the focal point lies with intergenerational business transfers (Sharma *et al.*, 2003; Le Breton-Miller *et al.*, 2004; Sharma, 2004; De Massis *et al.*, 2008; Salvato *et al.*, 2010; Ramadani *et al.*, 2017; Mustafa *et al.*, 2019) (Chapter 2, Drapeau and Tremblay, this volume). There is only a little research that has considered external business transfers as an alternative way of embarking on entrepreneurial activities (Durst and Gueldenberg, 2010; Parker and Van Praag, 2012). The underdeveloped academic interest in external business transfers of small and medium-sized enterprises (SMEs) is surprising considering the following: (1) more jobs are created by previously established firms than by new ones (Pasanen and Laukkanen, 2006); (2) at the European level, there is an increasing number of SMEs waiting to be transferred to new owners (in absolute terms, this means that every year, around 450,000 firms and over two million employees are transferred to new owners [European Commission, 2019]); (3) changing demographic trends and decreasing interest of family members is leading to a lack of successors in family firms (Durst and Sedenka, 2016); and (4) that the majority of European business transfers are non-family, meaning they are external transfers (Camerlynck *et al.*, 2005; Van Teeffelen *et al.*, 2011).

In light of the facts just outlined, limiting discussion of business transfers to a family business point of view is unsatisfactory and suggests an unbalanced understanding of the topic. Furthermore, this perspective can give the impression that intergenerational business transfers are comparable with external business transfers, which is not the case. We argue that the fields of entrepreneurship and small business management could benefit from looking more closely at external (non-family) business transfers.

The purpose of this chapter is to develop a research framework intended to support more rigorous research on the topic. The present monograph of research is focused on scientific contributions produced in francophone countries. In this environment, external business transfers are common practice (e.g., in France, family business succession is rare, thus CEOs need to look for external solutions). Therefore, to complement the findings from the francophone world, in this chapter we are interested in determining the study of external business transfers in non-francophone countries and published in English-speaking journals. Against this background, we reviewed extant research focusing on external business transfers of small, privately held firms to respond to the following research question: Which are the topics addressing external business transfers that are well researched and which are not? In this chapter, following the definition given in Chapter 1.1, an external business transfer is a process involving the transfer of an SME from a seller to an external buyer. Thus, the second party (a person or group of people) becomes the new dominant owner and manager of the firm.

Our chapter is organised as follows: in the next section, we present the scope and methodology used for studying external business transfers. Following this, we present a synthesis of the current state of knowledge regarding external business transfers. This is followed by a discussion on this knowledge base. Based on that, we propose a research framework for external SME business transfers. In the final section, the conclusion and implications of our study are outlined.

Scope and Methodology

To better understand the current body of knowledge addressing external business transfers of SMEs, we adopted the principles of a systematic review as recommended by Jesson *et al.* (2011), namely: (1) mapping the field through a scoping review, (2) comprehensive search, (3) quality assessment, (4) data extraction, (5) synthesis and (6) write-up.

We selected peer-reviewed journal articles in the English language. The papers selected focused on small and medium-sized privately held enterprises. Papers published before 1986, including 'grey literature', such as reports and non-academic research documents, and articles published in languages other than English represented exclusion criteria. The search was conducted using two major databases, EBSCO Business Source Premier and ProQuest. We looked for "business transfer, takeover, executive succession, non-family succession and ownership/leadership transfer" as keywords in the titles, keywords and abstracts. Depending on the keyword used, different numbers of hits were generated. For example, the keyword "business transfer" resulted in 72 hits with ProQuest and four hits with EBSCO, whereas the keyword "external succession" resulted in 22 hits with ProQuest and only two hits with EBSCO. We came to a final selection of 24 articles that fulfilled the criteria set and could thus serve as a basis for analysis.

The 24 papers were published in 18 different journals (see Table 10.1). Six of them can be assigned to the fields of entrepreneurship and small

Table 10.1 Information About Published and Cited Papers on External Business
Transfers

Domain	Frequency	Cited
Entrepreneurship and Small Business Management		304
Journal of Business Venturing	4	
Small Business Economics	3	
International Journal of Entrepreneurial Venturing	1	
International Journal of Entrepreneurship and Small Business	1	
Family Business Review	1	
Gestion 2000	1	
General Management		603
Irish Journal of Management	1	
Journal of Management Studies	1	
Journal of Management	1	
Administrative Quarterly	1	
Organisation Studies		725
Organisation Science	2	
Leadership Quarterly	2	
Miscellaneous		379
International Journal of Innovation Management	1	
Journal of Information and Knowledge Management Systems	1	
British Journal of Industrial Relations	1	
Regional Studies	1	
Strategic Management Journal	1	
Total	24	2011

business management, four to general management, two to organisation studies and the remaining journals address fields such as innovation, knowledge, finance and strategy. This suggests that business transfer research interests a broad audience.

Fifty authors contributed to the 24 papers. They come from seven countries, but external business transfer research appears to dominate in the Western world. Most articles came from the US (six articles representing 25% of the papers), followed by the UK (four articles), the Netherlands (three articles), Belgium (two articles), and Germany and Sweden (one article each). The field seems to be of interest primarily in the Western world. Three articles examined several countries in the same study and four articles were conceptual with no specific country.

Determining the Body of Knowledge

In the following sections, we will draw a picture of the non-francophone research on external business transfers addressing different topics.

What Is Known About Theories and Perspectives

The theories and perspectives applied in the papers reviewed are summarised in Table 10.2. Several contributions can be drawn from the entrepreneurship perspective (seven papers): background and entrepreneur typologies (Cooper and Dunkelberg, 1986), incentives (Graebner and Eisenhardt, 2004), trait approach (Mason and Harrisson, 2006), entry mode (Parker and Van Praag, 2012), strategic choice of the entrepreneur (Van Teeffelen and Uhlaner, 2010), planned behaviour (Zellweger *et al.*, 2011) and entrepreneurial exit (DeTienne, 2010). Four papers address mergers and acquisitions (Mickelson and Worley, 2003; Camerlynck *et al.*, 2005; Ooghe *et al.*, 2006; Grundström *et al.*, 2011). Agency theory appears in four papers (Robbie and Wright, 1995; Bacon *et al.*, 2004; Howorth *et al.*, 2004; Scholes *et al.*, 2007). UK authors seem to have a particular interest in agency theory. The remaining papers use game theory (one paper), trust theory (two papers), negotiation theory (one paper), threshold theory (two papers) and resource-based view (one paper). Specific issues related to human beings in the business context were addressed via human capital theory (one paper) and human resources management (two papers). The paper by Virany *et al.* (1992) studies the topic from an organisational learning point of view and Ballinger *et al.* (2009) apply leadership theory. Three papers did not specify their theoretical orientation (Donckels, 1995) or were literature reviews

Table 10.2 Theories and Perspectives in External Business Transfers

Theories and perspectives	Authors
Entrepreneurship	Cooper and Dunkelberg (1986); Graebner and Eisenhardt (2004); Mason and Harrisson (2006); Van Teeffelen and Uhlaner (2010); DeTienne (2010); Zellweger *et al.* (2011); Parker and Van Praag (2012)
M&A	Mickelson and Worley (2003); Camerlynck *et al.* (2005); Ooghe *et al.* (2006); Grundström *et al.* (2011)
Agency theory	Robbie and Wright (1995); Bacon *et al.* (2004); Howorth *et al.* (2004); Scholes *et al.* (2007)
Game theory	Scholes *et al.* (2007)
Trust theory	Howorth *et al.* (2004); Ballinger *et al.* (2009)
Negotiation theory	Howorth *et al.* (2004)
Threshold theory	DeTienne (2010); Ryan and Power (2012)
RBV theory	Durst and Gueldenberg (2010)
Human-related fields	
Human capital	Van Teeffelen *et al.* (2011)
HRM	Bacon *et al.* (2004)
Leadership	Ballinger *et al.* (2009)
Organisational learning	Virany *et al.* (1992)

(Kesner and Sebora, 1994; Giambatista *et al.*, 2005). A recent but clear direction in the extant literature is the assumption that a business transfer is a good example of the entrepreneurial process, as it involves both an entrepreneurial exit (i.e., seller-side, Wennberg *et al.*, 2010; DeTienne, 2010) and an entrepreneurial entry (i.e., buyer-side, Parker and Van Praag, 2012).

Table 10.2 also highlights that several papers adhere to more than one theory/perspective.

What Is Known About Research Methods?

Our literature review indicates that the current literature primarily consists of empirical studies. Only four of the 24 articles represented conceptual or theoretical papers. These papers were literature reviews (Kesner and Sebora, 1994; Giambatista *et al.*, 2005), discussed business transfers as an alternative entrepreneurial mode (Donckels, 1995), or addressed entrepreneurial exit settings and conditions (DeTienne, 2010).

In terms of empirical studies, quantitative papers (11 papers) dominate over qualitative (six papers) ones (see Table 10.3). This finding is different from the francophone research on external business transfers that is mainly focused on qualitative methods. Among the quantitative works, there is an emphasis on survey approaches (11 papers). Data collection through interviews dominates in the qualitative realm. Three papers are

Table 10.3 Characteristics of Conceptual and Empirical Articles

Conceptual articles	4
Descriptive	1
Literature review	2
Definition	1
Empirical articles	20
Qualitative methods	6
Quantitative methods	11
Regression	7
Descriptive statistics	1
Correlations	1
Analysis of industry-adjusted variables	2
Mixed Methods/Combination of Methods	3
Data collection	
Questionnaire	12
Interviews	8
Secondary data	5
Archival data	2
Simulation	1

based on a combination of research methods (Wasserman, 2003; Ballinger *et al.*, 2009; Durst and Gueldenberg, 2010). Longitudinal studies are rare, with the exceptions of the works by Virany *et al.* (1992) and Ballinger *et al.* (2009).

Regarding the industries, 12 papers look into a mix of industries, four papers include internet or technology-based companies and three papers have a single-sector focus (i.e., manufacturing and hospital). The average sample size is 829 for the 24 papers that were based on quantitative research. This finding was skewed by the works by Cooper and Dunkelberg (1986) and Zellweger *et al.* (2011). When these articles are excluded, the average sample size falls to 222. Papers based on qualitative research reported an average sample size of 20.

What Is Known About the Business Transfer Process and Actors Involved?

Different stages of the business transfer process are addressed. For example, Camerlynck *et al.* (2005) look into the pre-acquisition profiles of acquiring and acquired Belgian firms. Durst and Gueldenberg (2010) focus on the preparation stage of the buyer in Germany, which they define as the phase in which "the successor seeks and analyses companies of interest" (Durst and Gueldenberg, 2010, p. 112). Mickelson and Worley (2003) study the success factors for the post-acquisition integration process. Ooghe *et al.* (2006) investigate the post-acquisition performance of acquired Belgian firms. From the third year after acquisition and onward, the profitability, solvency and liquidity of the acquiring firm worsen, hinting at a higher long-term failure risk. Van Teeffelen and Uhlaner (2010) base their study in the Netherlands on the post-transfer stage. Grundström *et al.* (2011) also address the post-transfer stage by investigating how successors view and manage innovativeness once the succession is complete. Donckels (1995) describes the entire process from the buyer's perspective and gives advice for succeeding.

The articles studied suggest that two actors are primarily involved in business process transfers: the seller and the buyer. We identified papers that specifically focused on the *seller* side (e.g., Graebner and Eisenhardt, 2004; Mason and Harrisson, 2006; Ballinger *et al.*, 2009; Van Teeffelen *et al.*, 2011; Ryan and Power, 2012) and articles that emphasised the *buyer* perspective (e.g., Robbie and Wright, 1995; Durst and Gueldenberg, 2010). We also identified four papers that look into the transformation from individuals into SME owners while in the process of buying a firm (Cooper and Dunkelberg, 1986; Virany *et al.*, 1992; Wasserman, 2003). Two papers focus on both the buyer and seller sides (Mickelson and Worley, 2003; Howorth *et al.*, 2004).

Discussion About What Is Not Studied

Based on the findings reported, it can be concluded that an initial understanding of external business transfer has been developed. However, this understanding is rather fragmented. The following discussion is intended to outline those areas researchers that have published in English-speaking journals do not yet understand or where the understanding is under developed. We compare this situation with research published in French.

A Broad Range of Definitions Is Used

Different terms are used to describe business transfers: executive succession, passing the baton, CEO transition, succession, buy-in, purchase, buyout, MBO, transition, transmission, takeover, transfer and acquisition. Within those terms, we also find sub-categories like CEO succession, business succession, leadership succession or ownership transfer. In most of the papers analysed for this study, a specific term for business transfer was not defined. Even Parker and Van Praag (2012), who compare entrepreneurial entry modes, are silent on the subject.

Given the focus on publications in English-speaking journals, a broad mix of definitions used in the papers was found. For example, Wasserman (2003) uses the term CEO succession when discussing the exit of Internet start-up founders. Ballinger *et al.* (2009) apply the term leader succession when investigating the affective reaction of employees in the event of the introduction of a new group leader, and Durst and Gueldenberg (2010) define the term company succession as the simultaneous transition of property and/or management of a firm from one person to another, thus suggesting that this can mean both family and non-family succession. Kesner and Sebora (1994) use the term external business transfer when discussing succession in general, including family business succession. One argument from Chapter 1.1 is that succession equals an internal family business transfer, which in turn claims that it should not be confused with an external business transfer.

Bringing together the insights from this study and the findings from francophone research, one can conclude that there is a strong need for research aimed at establishing a generally accepted definition that could work in different countries and environments so that research findings will be easier to assess.

Theoretical and Perspective Issues

Table 10.2 has shown that the studies covered take advantage of a broad mix of theories. Many of them are established theories that are tested in the context of business transfers, which is in line with the dominance of quantitative studies observed in the papers considered. However, to develop the field further, researchers should be willing and prepared to develop new theories that are dedicated to business transfers as well. This would increase the chance of establishing the study of business transfers as an independent field of research.

Research Methods

The papers analysed revealed that external business transfer research is based on traditional research designs, i.e. surveys and case studies. Researchers may also consider other research techniques as a way to enhance our understanding of external business transfers, taking into consideration the difficulties of access to those individuals involved in business transfers. For instance, mixed-method approaches could help develop a more holistic understanding of external transfers. Durst and Gueldenberg (2010) did base their study on a sequential mixed-methods approach. Furthermore, as an external business transfer is a process rather than an event, there is a strong need for more longitudinal studies. They would help researchers better understand how the process is experienced by the individuals involved (buyer, seller, employees and other stakeholders) as well as what changes take place within the firm prior to, during and after the transfer.

Besides studying business transfers, using a multilevel lens would allow researchers to understand the context in which some practices occur. Again, the study by Durst and Gueldenberg (2010), who had German trade corporations and chambers of commerce and buyers involved in their study can be highlighted, which fits nicely with the work by Thévenard-Puthod (Chapter 13, this volume), who studied European chambers of commerce actions on external business transfers. More research with a multilevel perspective would help researchers better understand not only the relationship between the actors involved, but also the outcomes of the business transfer at the individual level.

As to the geographical scope, the papers reviewed primarily consist of single-region or single-country studies, which is understandable considering the impact of institutional and cultural dimensions on business transfers. Yet, comparative research would provide an opportunity to discuss and understand if and to what extent culture, firm characteristics, business environment and institutional dimensions affect external business transfers. This clearly calls for more research comprised of researchers from different countries on business transfers. Thus, research funded by the European Commission, such as, for example, the BTAR (Business Transfer Awareness Raising) project, which included countries such as Croatia, Finland, France, Spain and Sweden, can be viewed as important to initiate comparative studies.

The External Business Transfer Process

We follow Deschamps's proposal, dividing the external business transfer process into three phases (Chapter 1.1, this volume). Concerning the pre-transfer process, we do not know much about what business transfer planning looks like, either from the seller's or the buyer's viewpoint. How is the non-financial side of planning handled? Astrachan and Jaskiewicz (2008) argue that the total value of a business is the sum of its financial value and emotional value. How does a potential buyer perceive the issue of emotion in the context of business transfers? How do emotions influence the negotiation process between the two actors? What set of emotions do the prospective new owners bring to the table? Planning a business transfer also refers to the preparation of the firm for this event. Areas to be considered include the firm's organisational structure, its management and control systems, its business processes and operations, its culture, its staff, its other stakeholders, etc. The question of how the organisation as a whole is being prepared for the business transfer and changes likely to occur should also be explored. What kinds of changes are needed and how can they best be implemented? When do the sellers/buyers know that the firm is ready for the transition? During the joint management period where previous and new CEOs are together in the firm, what is happening: what kind of knowledge is transferred? How do the stakeholders react to this joint management period? Considering the post-transfer stage, the performance of the business transfer is an interesting area of research to be explored further to better understand the post-transfer stage. For example, how does the new owner make use of the existing firm resources? Does the new owner's knowledge influence the type of change initiatives started in the firm? If yes, in what ways and when? How can one measure post-transfer performance? Are there key factors of success in the external business process? What are the risks and causes of failure? How do we define a successful/distressed firm? A theoretical question concerns the time of the process: when does it begin and when does it end? To conclude on the process issues, there is a need for research improvement for specifying phases.

Actors

Research on entrepreneurial exits (e.g., Wennberg *et al.*, 2010; DeTienne, 2010; Strese *et al.*, 2018) has suggested that the actor's perspective provides a strong area for future research. It would be interesting to explore insights into the decision-making process, particularly the reasons for selling the company to an external buyer (instead of an internal one), assuming that there are more complex reasons than simply a missing family successor. It might also be of particular interest to study entrepreneurs who decide to sell the company at an early stage of the firm's life cycle. How does the seller anticipate his disengagement from the firm? This question has been studied in francophone research (Chapter 2, this volume, Drapeau and Tremblay). By focusing on the decision process and preparation for sale, it could be interesting to develop typologies of sellers regarding their attachment to the firm, their motivations to sell and their collaborative behaviour. Some of those questions are filled by francophone researchers (see, for instance, the typology of Bah, 2009, as cited in Chapter 1, this volume). Regarding the buyer, we need more research to explain the strategic component of external takeovers. This may help us understand why a buyer is seduced by a particular firm, even if there are negative signals about it. We also need to better understand the reasons why an individual decides to take over an existing firm instead of starting one from scratch. In other words, what is the motivation for taking over? What is the profile of the external buyer? How does the new owner adapt to changes in the firm? How do his/her actions influence strategic renewal during the post-transfer stage? What are the differences between external business transfers run by a team or by an individual? Finally, developing a typology of external business transfer buyers is a potentially rich undertaking. Some of those questions are also filled by francophone researchers (see, for instance, the typology of Géraudel *et al.*, 2009, as cited in Chapter 1, this volume). We did not identify any paper that specifically focused on the relationship between seller and buyer. Van Teeffelen *et al.* (2011) demonstrate that the familiarity between the two actors can be used as a predictor for transfer performance indicators. Howorth *et al.* (2004) underline the significance of a trusting relationship between the actors of the business transfer. How do the two parties act? What kind of communication style do they use? What are the causes of business transfer failures? This discussion draws attention to the danger of knowledge attrition possibly caused by the departing incumbent as well as other key staff members. What is/can be done by the new owner/manager to reduce this danger? What happens to old business relationships maintained by the previous owners? This area suggests promising research directions as well. Other stakeholders relevant to the business transfer process have not yet been studied in-depth, even though it is acknowledged that the business transfer process can have serious consequences for them: employees, customers, suppliers. How do employees react to the new management? How prepared is the staff for the business transfer? One could assume that the less adequately the transfer is prepared, the more difficult the entire transfer process will be for both the successor and the organisation. Studying emotions should not be limited to the two main actors, but should include emotional responses by the employees as well. At what stage within the business transfer process, and how, do the employees get involved? What can the buyer do to develop trust among those employees they did not recruit? Some of those questions have been studied by francophone researchers with legitimacy and socialisation (Chapter 11, Mazari, Berger-Douce and Deschamps, this volume; and Chapter 12, Boussaguet, this volume). How does the new CEO make use of old relationships with business partners (suppliers, for example)? Concerning advisors, we would like to further explore how third parties can mediate in pre- and post-transfer stages. Although this buyer is the new owner-manager, he/she did not found the firm, did not build relationships with the different stakeholders, was not part of the firm's genesis and did not hire the employees. What does this person need to tackle this situation? What role do advisors play in the business transfer process? Some answers to these questions have been published in French, e.g., Deschamps *et al.* (2010) or Thévenard-Puthod *et al.* (2014) both cited in Chapter 1.

Environmental Issues

There is also a need for studying external business transfers and their impact on economic, political and cultural environments, and on corporate governance. For example, are there any differences between takeovers that occur in dynamic business environments and those that occur in more stable business environments? Does the cultural environment influence SME takeovers and, if yes, how? What is the impact of corporate governance on external SME business transfers?

Research Framework for External Business Transfers

The outcome of this discussion process leads to a proposal for a research framework for external business transfers (see Figure 10.1). It is organised around the three stages of the transfer process and the primary actors involved in these stages. Even though it is not displayed in Figure 10.1, the buyer also goes through a pre-transfer stage (i.e., he/she takes the decision to take over a firm, looks out for promising firms, analyses them). In the same way, the seller will go through a post-transfer stage, which might be accompanied by mourning (Hessels *et al.*, 2018). Those events form critical aspects of transfer processes but mostly take place independently from the firm context. Additionally, Figure 10.1 displays the other important areas that need to be taken into consideration: (1) the role of other internal and external actors; (2) the potential impact of political, cultural, economic and legal environments; and (3) corporate governance. The issues presented in the following (i.e., terminology, theories and research methods) represent the necessary foundation for a rigorous theory development.

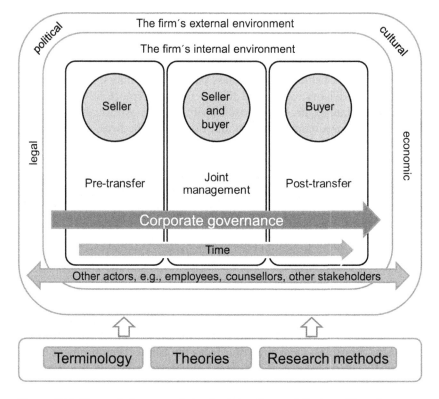

Figure 10.1 Research Framework for Studying External Business Transfers
Source: Authors created

Conclusion

Based on a literature review, our chapter seeks to shed light on what is already known about external SME business transfers and what is missing in extant research published in English-speaking journals. Overall, we argue that this type of research is not only timely but also relevant as it challenges mainstream research which: (1) still gives the impression that starting a company from scratch is the most interesting option for entrepreneurial entry and (2) underscores the notion that a business transfer within the family is the only way of transferring a business. In the domain of business transfers, it is essential to clarify what exactly is being studied and to take into consideration the differences between family business transfers and external takeovers.

The review clarifies that the study of external SME business transfers has not developed into a research field in its own right, which might be explained by the lack of a theoretical and conceptual base. To overcome this situation, we propose a framework that highlights those areas where we see the need for more intense research to establish the legitimacy of external SME business transfers as an independent research field (Figure 10.1). Without further research, particularly related to theoretical and definitional issues, the topic will not obtain the attention it deserves.

Our study is not without limitations. Total coverage of all the articles produced in the field under investigation may not have been achieved, despite the use of a wide variety of keywords. In addition, reviewing the extant literature was sometimes disconcerting, as many papers do not specify whether they are discussing SMEs or large firms. Thirdly, this chapter proposes some research directions which are not exhaustive but represent initial stages. Finally, by emphasising articles published in English, we only present a limited picture of the field of external business transfers. Research activities reported in languages other than English are not included, but would expand our understanding of the field. The present monograph of research addresses this situation by providing research insights in French.

References

Astrachan, J.H. and Jaskiewicz, P. (2008). "Emotional returns and emotional costs in privately held family businesses: advancing traditional business valuation", *Family Business Review*, 21(2), 139–149.

Bacon, N., Wright, M. and Demina, N. (2004). "Management buyouts and human resource management", *British Journal of Industrial Relations*, 42, 325–347.

Bah, T. (2009), "La transition cédant-repreneur: une approche par la théorie du deuil", *Revue Française de Gestion*, 35(194), 123–148.

Ballinger, G.A., Schoorman, F.D. and Lehman, D.W. (2009). "Will you trust your new boss? The role of affective reactions to leadership succession", *The Leadership Quarterly*, 20, 219–232.

Camerlynck, J., Ooghe, H. and De Langhe, T. (2005). "Pre-acquisition profile of privately held companies involved in take-overs: an empirical study", *Small Business Economics*, 24, 169–186.

Cooper, A.C. and Dunkelberg, W.C. (1986). "Entrepreneurship and paths to business ownership", *Strategic Management Journal*, 7(1), 53–68.

De Massis, A., Chua, J.H. and Chrisman, J.J. (2008). "Factors preventing intra-family succession", *Family Business Review*, 21, 183–199.

Deschamps, B., Geindre, S. and Fatien, P. (2010, mai–juin). "Accompagner le repreneur d'entreprise: conduire, escorter mais aussi guider", *Gestion 2000*, 3, 77–88.

DeTienne, D.R. (2010). "Entrepreneurial exit as a critical component of the entrepreneurial process: theoretical development", *Journal of Business Venturing*, 25, 203–215.

Donckels, R. (1995). "Taking over a company: an exciting carrier alternative . . . but not for adventurers", *Gestion 2000*, 6, 143–160.

Durst, S. and Gueldenberg, S. (2010). "What makes SMEs attractive to external successors?" *VINE: The Journal of Information and Knowledge Management Systems*, 40(2), 108–135.

Durst, S. and Sedenka, J. (2016). *Entrepreneurial intentions and behaviour of students attending Swedish universities global university entrepreneurial spirit students' survey 2016 — national report Sweden*. www.guesssurvey.org/resources/nat_2016/GUESSS_Report_2016_Sweden-m.pdf.

European Commission. (2019). *Transfer of businesses*. https://ec.europa.eu/growth/smes/promoting-entrepreneurship/advice-opportunities/transfer-business_en, accessed 18 September 2019.

Géraudel, M., Jaouen, A., Missonier, A. and Salvetat D. (2009). "Qui sont les repreneurs potentiels d'entreprises? Proposition de typologie en fonction de l'état de santé de la firme", *Revue Internationale PME*, in *Le repreneuriat: une pratique entrepreneuriale de plus en plus reconnue!* Numéro coordonné par L. Cadieux et B. Deschamps, 22(3–4), 13–31.

Giambatista, R.C., Rowe, W.G. and Riaz, S. (2005). "Nothing succeeds like succession: a critical review of leader succession literature since 1994", *The Leadership Quarterly*, 16, 963–991.

Graebner, M. and Eisenhardt, K.M. (2004). "The seller's side of the story: acquisition as courtship and governance as syndicate in entrepreneurial firms", *Administrative Quarterly*, 49, 366–403.

Grundström, C., Öberg, C. and Öhrwall Rönnbäck, A. (2011). "View and management of innovativeness upon succession in family-owned SMEs", *International Journal of Innovation Management*, 15(3), 617–640.

Hessels, J., Rietveld, C.A., Thurik, A.R. and Van der Zwan, P. (2018). "Depression and entrepreneurial exit", *Academy of Management Perspectives*, 32, 323–339.

Howorth, C., Westhead, P. and Wright, M. (2004). "Buyout, information asymmetry and the family management dyad", *Journal of Business Venturing*, 19, 509–534.

Jesson, J.K., Matheson, L. and Lacey, F.M. (2011). *Doing your literature review: traditional and systematic techniques*, Los Angeles: Sage Publications.

Kesner, I.F. and Sebora, T.C. (1994). "Executive succession: past, present & future", *Journal of Management*, 20(2), 327–372.

Le Breton-Miller, I., Miller, D. and Steier, L.P. (2004). "Toward an integrative model of effective FOB succession", *Entrepreneurship Theory and Practice*, 28, 305–328.

Mason, C.M. and Harrisson, R.T. (2006). "After the exit: acquisitions, entrepreneurial recycling and regional economic development", *Regional Studies*, 40(1), 55–73.

Mickelson, R.E. and Worley, C. (2003). "Acquiring a family firm: a case study", *Family Business Review*, 16(4), 251–268.

Mustafa, M., Elliott, C. and Zhou, L. (2019). "Succession in Chinese family-SMEs: a gendered analysis of successor learning and development", *Human Resource Development International*, 22(5), 504–525.

Ooghe, H, Van Laere, E. and De Langhe, T. (2006). "Are acquisitions worthwhile? An empirical study of the post-acquisition performance of privately held Belgian companies", *Small Business Economics*, 27(2–3), 223–243.

Parker, S.C. and Van Praag, C.M. (2012). "The entrepreneur's mode of entry: business takeover or new venture start?" *Journal of Business Venturing*, 27(1), 31–46.

Paranen, M. and Laukkanen, T. (2006). "Team-managed growing SMEs: a distinct species?" *Management Research News*, 29(11), 684–700.

Ramadani, V., Dana, L.P., Sadiku-Dushi, N., Ratten, V. and Welsh, D.H.B. (2017). "Decision-making challenges of women entrepreneurship in family business succession process", *Journal of Enterprising Culture*, 25(4), 411–439.

Robbie, K. and Wright, M. (1995). "Managerial and ownership succession and corporate restructuring: the case of management buy-ins", *Journal of Management Studies*, 32(4), 527–549.

Ryan, G. and Power, B. (2012). "Small business transfer decisions: what really matters? Evidence from Ireland and Scotland", *Irish Journal of Management*, 31(2), 99–125.

Salvato, C., Chirico, F. and Sharma, P. (2010). "Understanding exit from the founder's business in family firms", in A. Stewart, T. Lumpkin and J. Katz (Eds.), *Entrepreneurship and family business. Advances in entrepreneurship, firm emergence and growth*, 31–85, Greenwich, CT: Emerald Group Publishing, Chapter 12.

Scholes, L., Wright, M., Westhead, P., Burrows, A. and Bruining, H. (2007). "Information sharing, price negotiation and management buy-outs of private family-owned firms", *Small Business Economics*, 29, 329–349.

Sharma, P. (2004). "An overview of the field of family business studies: current status and directions for the future", *Family Business Review*, 17(1), 1–36.

Sharma, P., Chrisman, J.J. and Chua, J.H. (2003). "Predictors of satisfaction with the succession process in family firms", *Journal of Business Venturing*, 18, 667–687.

Strese, S., Gebhard, P., Feierabend, D. and Brettel, M. (2018). "Entrepreneurs' perceived exit performance: conceptualization and scale development", *Journal of Business Venturing*, 33(3), 351–370.

Thévenard-Puthod, C., Picard, C. and Chollet, B. (2014). "Pertinence du tutorat comme dispositif d'accompagnement du repreneur individuel après la reprise. Une étude empirique à l'échelle européenne", *Management International*, 18(4), 80–96.

Van Teeffelen, L. and Uhlaner, L. (2010. "Strategic renewal after ownership transfers in SMEs: do successors' actions pay off?" *International Journal of Entrepreneurial Venturing*, 2(3/4), 347–365.

Van Teeffelen, L., Uhlaner, L. and Driessen, M. (2011). "The importance of specific human capital, planning and familiarity in Dutch small firm ownership transfers: a seller's perspective", *International Journal of Entrepreneurship and Small Business*, 14(1), 127–148.

Virany, B., Tushman, M.L. and Romanelli, E. (1992). "Executive succession and organization outcomes in turbulent environments: an organization learning approach", *Organization Science*, 3(1), 72–91.

Wasserman, N. (2003). "Founder-CEO succession and the paradox of entrepreneurial success", *Organization Science*, 14(2), 149–172.

Wennberg, K., Wiklund, J., DeTienne, D.R. and Cardon, M.S. (2010). "Reconceptualizing entrepreneurial exit: divergent exit routes and their drivers", *Journal of Business Venturing*, 25, 361–375.

Zellweger, T., Sieger, P. and Halter, F. (2011). "Should I stay or should I go? Career choice intentions of students with family business background", *Journal of Business Venturing*, 26(5), 521–536.

11 The Legitimacy of the External Buyer

Issues and Means of Acquisitions

Lyès Mazari, Sandrine Berger-Douce and Bérangère Deschamps

As recognised in the literature, the 'human' factor is important in the successful transfer of business operations, especially when an external buyer takes over a firm (Boussaguet, 2012; Mazari *et al.*, 2019). In such cases, the leadership and ownership of the company is transferred from the predecessor to an external person. To effectively perform their new role and make changes in what is, in fact, a new entity (Deschamps, 2003), the external buyer must establish themselves as a new leader by gaining legitimacy in the eyes of employees. Legitimacy ensures the right managerial conditions in which a new leader can effectively perform their role; in particular, it enables them to be recognised as the leader and gives them the support of employees for their vision (Mazari *et al.*, 2019). In turn, Boussaguet and Bah (2008) stress that external buyers' perceived lack of legitimacy is one reason for higher failure rates in external business transfers as compared with family successions.

This chapter seeks to shed light on the psychological mechanisms underlining employees' attribution of legitimacy to an external buyer. To do this, we will first define the concept of legitimacy and outline its impact on the external takeover of a firm. We will then focus on the different dimensions of an external buyer's legitimacy and the ways in which it can be acquired. Finally, we will identify and describe the personal and professional qualities that contribute to an external buyer's legitimacy.

Legitimacy as a Form of Power

Legitimacy is traditionally linked to the notion of power, and it concerns one of the most political and foundational dimensions of a company—namely, the right to govern it and to be recognised as its leader by corporate stakeholders (Petit and Mari, 2009).

Defining the Concept of Legitimacy

The word 'legitimacy' comes from the Latin term *lex* or *legis*, which is the root of words such as 'legal' and 'legitimate', as well as 'loyal' (Buisson,

2008). Etymologically, therefore, legitimacy describes something that is founded in law and/or justice (Laufer and Burlaud, 1980); it is based on the question 'what right do I have to act?', and to 'be legitimate' is to provide a satisfactory answer to this interrogation (Demaret and Meric, 2013). As such, legitimacy forms the basis of power and the justification for obedience (Bastid, 2000). From an academic perspective, these proposed definitions share one common theme: the recognition that legitimacy leverages obedience and subordinates' adherence to the leader (Tost, 2011). In this sense, Weber (1971) defines legitimacy as "the chance for orders to be obeyed by a specified group of individuals" (p. 289). Tyler (1997) explains it as "the belief that the authorities have the right to be obeyed" (p. 323). More recently, Petit (2013) has proposed that a leader's legitimacy is the

> recognition (formal/informal; explicit/implicit) by internal and external stakeholders of their moral right to govern the enterprise: this recognition is based on these stakeholders' belief in the validity of the leader's power in relation to shared values and standards of corporate governance and results in behaviours ranging from formal obedience to full personal adherence.
>
> (p. 83)

Legitimacy is thus a means of ensuring that a leader's power is recognised. Indeed, it refers to power that is recognised, accepted and justified by subordinates (Accardo and Corocuff, 1986). Here, 'recognised' means that the individual has a place, a role and a clear function accepted by all; 'accepted' refers to the idea that both the individual and their power are accepted by the members of the group; 'justified' refers to the fact that the leader will, from time to time, have to test their beliefs and individual way of thinking against current norms. In other words, they will have to argue for and prove the accuracy and relevance of what they propose over what already exists (Angot and Meier, 1998). In this sense, Bourdieu (1984) describes legitimacy as "an institution, action or practice which is dominant and not known as such, that is, [it is] tacitly recognized as legitimate" (p. 110). According to this concept, those who are dominated accept their position because they internalise the interests and justifications of the person in power (Hatzfeld, 2014).

The Importance of Legitimacy for External Buyers

Succession by a person with no prior connection to the company is defined as "a process, which through a buyout transaction, leads to the continuation of the life of a company, in difficulty or not, and of all that it contains (structures, human resources, financial resources, etc.)" (Deschamps, 2000, p. 145) (also see Chapter 1, Deschamps, this volume).

At the end of this process, the external successor officially becomes the new head of the company and takes control of it (Boussaguet, 2005). To effectively perform their new role and make changes in what is, in fact, a new entity (Deschamps, 2003), the external buyer must have sufficient space to act. Their level of capacity results directly from their power within the company (Petit, 2013). However, the official transfer of ownership and management from a predecessor to an external buyer does not guarantee that the decisions and choices of the new owner-manager will be accepted and/or that the employees will support their strategic project (Lamarque and Story, 2008). As such, the main challenge for the external buyer is to legitimise their power in the eyes of their employees (Boussaguet, 2005; Cullière, 2009; Boussaguet, 2012; Mazari *et al.*, 2019). Indeed, a leader who is recognised as legitimate by their employees does not need to systematically justify their choices and decisions, nor do they need to resort to incentives or controls to ensure that employees do as they are asked (Mazari *et al.*, 2019). Legitimacy thus represents a form of influence accepted by employees and has many positive effects in the context of an external business transfers (see Figure 11.1), for example the acceptance of the external buyers and their decisions by employees (Cullière, 2009; Mazari, 2018). Legitimacy also seems to help mobilise employees and gain their support for the new leader's strategic project(s) (Boussaguet, 2008; Mazari, 2018). Finally, legitimacy allows the external buyers to implement their project in an optimal way, and thus effectively assume their new leadership role (Grazzini *et al.*, 2009).

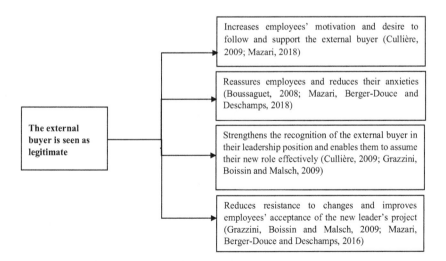

Figure 11.1 The Effects of an External Buyer's Legitimacy in Their New Role
Source: Authors created

In light of these observations, it is clearly not sufficient to simply acquire power in order to effectively run a company; it is also necessary to ensure that this power is legitimised (Petit, 2013). The legitimacy of an external buyer is thus a key condition for the effective exercise of their new leadership. Therefore, we will now look more closely at the various dimensions of an external buyer's legitimacy.

The Legitimacy of the External Buyer

As a result of its crucial role in the success of external takeovers, the legitimacy of new leaders has been of renewed interest to francophone researchers in recent years (Boussaguet, 2005, 2008; Boussaguet and Bah, 2008; Cullière, 2009; Mazari, 2018; De Freyman *et al.*, 2019). On the basis of both this literature and research material collected through multiple case studies (see Box 11.1 and Table 11.1), we propose to explain the dimensions and origins of an external buyer's legitimacy.

Box 11.1 The Research Material

The research material used in this chapter consists of interview and survey data from questionnaires, based on a research project funded by the Auvergne-Rhône-Alpes region. The objective of this project was to explore the origins of an external buyer's legitimacy. It is based on multiple case studies conducted between March 2014 and September 2015. During this period, 46 semi-structured interviews were conducted with the external buyers of nine small and medium-sized enterprises (SMEs) and 22 of their employees. The average duration of the interviews with the external buyers was two hours, and those with the employees lasted 40 minutes on average. The only criteria used to select the employees were that they had also worked with the previous CEO and had experienced the transfer of operations. Summary information about these companies is provided in Table 11.1.

The Dimensions of the External Buyer's Legitimacy

Referring to Weber's theory of legitimacy, Mazari (2018) and Mazari *et al.* (2019) identified three dimensions of the external buyer's legitimacy: traditional legitimacy; rational—legal legitimacy; and charismatic legitimacy. We will now take a closer look at how each of these three dimensions is characterised.

Table 11.1 Characteristics of SMEs in Our Sample

SME	Year of creation	Year of transfer	Total number of current employees	Number of employees interviewed	Company's turnover (millions, EUR)	Business activity
1	1958	2015	7	7	1.5	Design and production of furniture
2	1952	2009	9	2	2	Manufacture and maintenance of heat pumps and air conditioners
3	1980	2010	17	3	1	Landscape gardening
4	1915	2012	6	2	0.7	Electricity, heating, plumbing
5	1978	2012	11	2	0.6	Landscape gardening
6	1916	2013	50	1	9	Industrial wood packaging
7	1927	2009	8	1	0.9	Electricity, heating, plumbing
8	1956	2014	17	2	2.7	Carpentry
9	1994	2015	30	2	5.8	Label manufacturing

Traditional Legitimacy

Traditional legitimacy refers to a form of power that is legitimised by the sanctity of tradition or custom. Individuals obey their rulers because of the individual honour conferred on the leader by tradition. In particular, this form of legitimacy is granted to a leader as a result of their connections with the predecessors and the history of the organisation in question. Upon their appointment as head of the company, therefore, an external buyer often suffers from a significant lack of legitimacy (Mazari, 2018). According to these authors, it is the absence of a prior link with the acquired company that exacerbates the new leader's lack of legitimacy. Indeed, the arrival of a new leader about whom they know little can lead to anxieties and fears among employees; they might wonder, for example, whether their own skills will align with any functional or managerial changes initiated by the new manager. Employees may also question the competencies of the external buyer and how they will manage the company in the future (Bastié *et al.*, 2010). As such, it is not possible for an external buyer with no prior link to the company to benefit from traditional legitimacy. On the contrary, they may be considered an 'intruder' and rejected by employees. In this context, Boussaguet and Bah (2008) argue that the family heir is perceived as more legitimate and will feel less uncertain about taking up their duties, compared with an external buyer with no close ties to the company. Such proximity to the company is a decisive factor in the perceived legitimacy of a new leader, in that it establishes a hierarchy in the right to succession (Cullière, 2009). Thus, a family heir taking over a business founded by their parent would appear more legitimate than a person from outside the history of the company and its members. Consequently, the external buyer cannot rely on this form of legitimacy; indeed, the absence of a prior link with the company undermines their legitimacy (Mazari, 2018; Mazari *et al.*, 2019).

Rational—Legal Legitimacy

Rational—legal legitimacy refers to the formal aspect of power. It is linked to the status and not the professional and/or personal qualities of a leader. This form of power refers to what Mintzberg (2003) calls authority, that is, the ability to get things done by others as a result of their hierarchical position. In this context, the ability of the external buyer to gain the obedience of their collaborators is based on the power associated with their position; for example, the new leader might reward employees who adhere to their project, or punish those who do not comply with their expectations (Mazari, 2018). With their status as a 'new' owner-manager, the external successor benefits from the rational—legal legitimacy endowed to them as they assume office (Mazari *et al.*, 2019). However, this form of legitimacy is not sufficient to effectively exercise their new leadership role or to obtain the support of the employees (Mazari, 2018). The employees may not necessarily adhere to the external buyer's project and ideas, and will only comply with the buyer's expectations under coercion. In the words of one external buyer interviewed for the present study, "when you write a cheque", you of course acquire the company and everything it contains; but as soon as you "step through the door" of the company, you are no longer at home but "at the employees' home". This example highlights the significant efforts an external buyer has to make to establish themselves as the new leader of the company and to be recognised as such by their employees.

> **Box 11.2   The Need to Go Beyond Rational—Legal Legitimacy to Establish Leadership**
>
> After 20 years first as a sales representative and then as a marketing and communications manager in a chemical industry company, Marc, aged 45, took over a company of 17 employees in the landscaping industry in 2010. When asked about the origins of his legitimacy, Marc stated that an external buyer will not gain legitimacy by relying on power to reward or punish employees. On the contrary, he felt the need to prove himself to his employees and demonstrate the value he added to the company.
>
> > When I took over the company, the employees looked at me with huge eyes and said to themselves: Will he be able to manage the company? Will he be the right man for the job? After five years, the projects I initiated have been successful, the company is still making money and we continue to have customers. All these things have helped me to build my legitimacy.

Charismatic Legitimacy

According to Mazari *et al.* (2019), the legitimacy of an external buyer is acquired mainly through their charisma. Charisma is defined as a "certain quality of an individual personality, by virtue of which he is set apart from ordinary men and treated as endowed with supernatural, superhuman, or at least specifically exceptional powers or qualities" (Weber, 1971, p. 239). In this particular case, employees obey the external buyer as a result of their personal and professional qualities (Mazari, 2018). This form of legitimacy is necessary for employees' support of their leader's project. The latter does not need to systematically justify their choices and decisions, nor do they need to resort to incentives or controls to ensure that employees do as they are asked. The new leader can therefore focus on the strategic management of the company (Tyler, 1997).

The qualities of an external buyer that contribute to their legitimisation in the eyes of employees can be classified into two main categories: (1) instrumental qualities, according to which a leader's legitimacy is based on their ability to promote the material interests of the employees; and (2) relational qualities, according to which individuals evaluate their leader in terms of the quality of the relationship they have with them, rather than on the basis of what they earn or lose through their interactions (Mazari, 2018; Mazari *et al.*, 2019). According to Mazari *et al.* (2019), however, these two categories do not have the same effect on an external buyer's legitimacy. Indeed, in assessing the legitimacy of an external buyer, employees give central importance to their relational qualities, such as their efforts to improve employees' well-being and to involve them in the decision-making process. Above all, therefore, the external buyer gains their legitimacy from the kind of relationship they build with employees.

Necessary Qualities to Gain Legitimacy

Four main qualities are needed to enhance the legitimacy of a buyer in the eyes of their employees: their managerial exemplarity, their ability to develop the company, their relational skills and their professional (technical and managerial) skills.

Demonstrating Managerial Exemplarity

An external buyer's legitimacy is built, above all, on their managerial exemplarity. This competency is based on an alignment between what a leader says and what they do, but also on the demonstration of commitment, integrity and involvement in the company's life (Mazari, 2018; Mazari *et al.*, 2019). In this context, legitimacy is acquired through simple actions, such as arriving first in the morning and leaving last in the evening, being physically present 'on the field' and moving around on-site. It is thus not on a technical level that the external buyer will demonstrate their added value, but through their involvement in the company's projects and their willingness to move things forward. This more relational approach is favoured for the simple reason that external buyers often take over companies in sectors outside their own specialisation, and not many buyers undergo technical training related to their new company's activities (Mazari, 2018).

Managerial exemplarity enhances the external buyers' legitimacy by reassuring employees about their intentions. They may no longer be seen as an 'opportunistic' leader intending to capitalise on their previous career path, but rather as a dedicated leader concerned about the fate of their new employees (Mazari, 2018).

Box 11.3

The importance of setting an example According to Pascal, a former commercial director who took over a small company with eight employees in 2009, legitimacy is acquired through a 'flawless' application of the company's core values and operating rules. He states that

> when you ask your staff to arrive on time, I think the least you can do is to arrive on time. So, in order to be able to ask others to arrive on time, I have to arrive before everyone else in the morning. But if I don't arrive on time, it's going to be difficult to do it because I'm not going to be legitimate.

The importance of managerial exemplarity as a source of the external buyer's legitimacy is also reflected by Julie, the accountant in SME 9,

> We did a big clean-up, and he was there from morning to night to clean up with us. He was involved like everyone else. That is reassuring for us and motivates us to follow him and support his project.

Developing the Company

From this perspective, the innovation and initiation of new ideas enables the external buyer to be recognised as a leader of a new company vision that they must explain, lead, master and execute successfully. As such, they can assert their leadership and establish their legitimacy. Bringing new ideas and developing a new mind-set is therefore key to obtaining legitimacy in the eyes of their employees (Deschamps and Paturel, 2009; Cadieux and Brouard, 2009), in addition to the external buyer's efforts to promote the company and expand its customer portfolio. Such achievements enhance the buyer's instrumental legitimacy by contributing to the dynamism of the company. Indeed, for employees, a 'good' leader is one who looks for more work and new customers (Mazari *et al.*, 2019). The challenge for the external buyer is therefore to both show employees what they can gain from supporting their project and to ensure that employees perceive the project as necessary for the development of the company (Deschamps, 2003; Boussaguet, 2005).

Demonstrating Relational Skills

The relational skills of the external buyer are assessed in three ways. First, their kindness and interest in employees' needs. Here, the physical proximity between the external buyer and their employees, direct and regular contact, and their capacity to meet employees' expectations all contribute to the perception of the external buyer as legitimate (Boussaguet, 2005; Mazari, 2018).

Second, the external buyer's relational skills are considered through their efforts to involve employees in the decision-making process (Boussaguet, 2008; Mazari, 2018). This kind of involvement increases an external buyer's legitimacy because it gives employees a feeling of control over management decisions that affect them (Mazari *et al.*, 2019).

Finally, the relational qualities of an external buyer are reflected in their efforts to implement a just and fair distribution of benefits. Relational qualities thus promote the external buyer's instrumental legitimacy as they protect the economic interests of employees.

Displaying Professional Skills

The professional skills of the external buyer include knowledge of the company's business, technical competence and management skills (Lamarque and Story, 2008). As a new leader, the external buyer has to demonstrate their ability to lead others and to develop the company. This particular quality appears to be an essential element of their legitimacy (Mazari, 2018). In contrast, the external buyer's technical expertise, although important in acquiring legitimacy, is not sufficient in itself. Indeed, the study of Mazari (2018) shows that a lack of technical legitimacy is mitigated by the relational skills of the external buyer. As such, external buyers who value, listen to and empower their employees will be recognised in their leadership position despite any technical shortcomings.

Box 11.4   Human and Relational Aspects as a Means of Overcoming a Lack of Technical Legitimacy

In 2009, after 20 years' experience in a range of sectors, including retail distribution, construction and transport, Pascal (49) decided to take over a company operating in a sector outside his sphere of experience, namely heating, ventilation and air conditioning. Despite his technical shortcomings, Pascal was able to gain the acceptance of his employees thanks to his interpersonal skills (listening to, empowering and valuing employees). Furthermore, by communicating the benefits of working as a team, and as a result of their complementary skills, he managed to unite his new employees around his project. To establish his legitimacy with his employees, he states that he had to say to them:

> I'm not a technician, I don't know anything about this; you're going to help me and I'm going to learn. I need you, but I know how to do this.' It was important for him to be honest about his

strengths and weaknesses, and to tell them that 'my weaknesses are your qualities, so we have to work as a team.' He goes on to say that 'this team spirit was a definite advantage in the beginning of our relationship.

Fred, a technician within this company, confirms Pascal's comments, specifying that

he used to ask our opinion, he questioned us, he asked us how things have to be done, and we were very happy to advise him. He had no knowledge on the technical aspects, [but] we were happy to share our experience with him and it went very well.

The combination of these four qualities helps the external buyer to be recognised as the new leader of the company. This recognition in turn increases their chances of being accepted by employees, and gaining their respect and their support of the buyer's project. We propose a model of the relationship between these four qualities and the external buyer's legitimacy among employees in Figure 11.2.

Conclusion

The purpose of this chapter was to understand how an external buyer can gain legitimacy in the eyes of their employees. From this perspective, we have shown that, unlike a family heir, an external buyer with no close ties to the company does not benefit from traditional legitimacy. On the other hand, it has been pointed out that through the acquisition of ownership and control of the company, the external buyer benefits from rational—legal legitimacy (Mazari *et al.*, 2019). The source of this form of legitimacy is impersonal; it is afforded to the external buyer because of their new status. However, acquisition alone does not guarantee them the managerial conditions necessary to effectively exercise their new leadership power, nor the support of the employees (Mazari, 2018). To gain this, the external buyer must prove themselves to employees and demonstrate the value they add to the company. Indeed, in the case of external takeovers, the legitimacy of the new leader is acquired mainly through what Weber (1971) describes as charismatic legitimacy, that is, through their personal and professional qualities. These four qualities are managerial exemplarity, the ability to develop the company, relational skills and professional (technical and managerial) skills.

Our study presents a number of limitations that open up opportunities for future research. From a methodological point of view, our field of

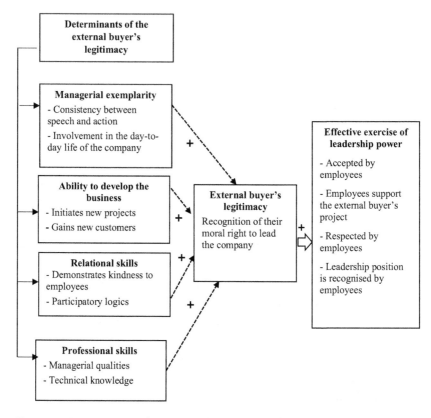

Figure 11.2 Legitimacy of an External Buyer
Source: Authors created

investigation is mostly limited to SMEs with fewer than 20 employees, so our results should be generalised with caution. It would thus be valuable to replicate this research with more companies to obtain results that are more representative of the SME population. In terms of conceptual limitations, a longitudinal approach would also significantly improve our understanding of how an external buyer gains legitimacy.

References

Accardo, A. and Corcouff, P. (1986). *La sociologie de Bourdieu*, Bordeaux: Le Mascaret.

Angot, J. and Meier, O. (1998, May 27–29). "Les problèmes de légitimités au sein d'un mode d'organisation non hiérarchique: le cas d'une 'reprise en main'", *7ᵉ conférence internationale de management stratégique*, Louvain La Neuve, Belgique.

Bastid, P. (2000). "Légitimité", in *Dictionnaire de philosophie, encyclopædia universalis*, Paris: Albin Michel.

Bastié, F., Cieply, S. and Cussy, P. (2010). "Impact de la forme de la reprise sur les réactions des stakeholders", *Revue d'Economie Industrielle* (132), 9–30.

Bourdieu, P. (1984). *Ce que parler veut dire. questions de sociologie*, Paris: Editions de minuit.

Boussaguet, S. (2005). *L'entrée dans l'entreprise du repreneur: un processus de socialisation repreneuriale*, PhD Thesis, University Montpellier I, Montpellier.

Boussaguet, S. (2008). "Prise de fonction d'un repreneur de pme: repérage de conditions de facilitation et d'activation", *Revue de l'entrepreneuriat*, 7(1), 39–61.

Boussaguet, S. (2012). "L'épreuve de la cession/reprise, rupture de vie pour le duo d'acteurs?" *Entreprendre & Innover*, 2(15), 20–29.

Boussaguet, S. and Bah, T. (2008, November 9–12). "La psychologie de la transmission de PME", *19ᵉ congrès de l'AGRH*, Dakar, Sénégal.

Buisson, M.L. (2008). "Légitimité et sciences de gestion: état des lieux et perspectives", *Humanisme et entreprise* (4), 29–57.

Cadieux, L. and Brouard, F. (2009). *La transmission des PME: perspectives et enjeux*, Québec: Presses de l'Université du Québec.

Cullière, O. (2009). "La légitimité du repreneur d'entreprise: proposition d'une grille d'analyse", *Marketing et management entre Eros et Polemos: principes de liaison et déliaison en entreprise. actes du colloque scientifique du 8 décembre 2009, organisé par l'ecole supérieure de commerce et marketing "istec-paris"*, Paris, France.

De Freyman, J., Cullière, O. and Boussaguet, S. (2019, juin 3–5). "Accompagner le repreneur dans la construction de sa légitimité", *11ᵉ congrès de l'AEI*, Montpellier, France.

Demaret, J. and Meric, J. (2013, mai 31–juin 1). "La constitution de la légitimité des contrôleurs de gestion: une étude exploratoire", *34ᵉ congrès des AFC*, Montréal.

Deschamps, B. (2000). *Le processus de reprise d'entreprise par les entrepreneurs personnes physiques*, PhD Thesis, University of Grenoble II, Grenoble.

Deschamps, B. (2003). "Reprise d'entreprise par les personnes physiques: conduite du changement et réactions des salariés", *Revue de Gestion des Ressources Humaines* (48), 49–60.

Deschamps, B. and Paturel, R. (2009). *Reprendre une entreprise, de l'intention à l'intégration*, 3rd ed., Paris: Dunod, Collection Entrepreneurs.

Grazzini, F., Boissin, J.P. and Malsch, B. (2009). "Le rôle du repreneur dans le processus de formation de la stratégie de l'entreprise acquise", *Revue Internationale PME*, 22(3–4), 139–164.

Hatzfeld, H. (2014). "Au nom de quoi? Les revendications de légitimité, expressions de mutations sociales et politiques", *Vie sociale* (4), 25–36.

Lamarque, T. and Story, M. (2008). *Reprendre une entreprise*, Paris: Editions Maxima.

Laufer, R. and Burlaud, A. (1980). *Management public: gestion et légitimité*. Eds. Dalloz Gestion, Paris: Collection systèmes et stratégies.

Mazari, L. (2018). *Effets de la RSE sur le management de la reprise des PME: une analyse par la légitimité du repreneur externe vis-à-vis de ses salariés*, PhD Thesis, University Jean Monnet, Saint-Etienne.

Mazari, L., Berger-Douce, S. and Deschamps, B. (2019). "Analyse du potentiel de la RSE sur la légitimité du repreneur externe d'une PME", *Revue Internationale PME*, *32*(2), 151–180.

Mintzberg, H. (2003). *Le pouvoir dans les organisations*, Paris: Editions d'Organisation.

Petit, V.C. (2013). *Leadership: l'art et la science de la direction d'entreprise*, Montreuil, France: Pearson Education.

Petit, V.C. and Mari, I. (2009). "La légitimité des équipes dirigeantes: une dimension négligée de la gouvernance d'entreprise", Documents en ligne. cahier de recherche d'edhec business school, Roubaix, France. récupéré le 23 mars 2017 du site d'edhec business school. www.edhec.edu/fr/publications/la-legitimite-des-equipes-dirigeantes-une-dimension-negligee-de-la-gouvernance.

Tost, L.P. (2011). "An integrative model of legitimacy judgments", *Academy of Management Review*, *36*(4), 686–710.

Tyler, T.R. (1997). "The psychology of legitimacy: a relational perspective on voluntary deference to authorities", *Personality and Social Psychology Review*, *1*(4), 323–345.

Weber, M. (1971). *Economie et société: les catégories de la sociologie*, Paris: Plon.

12 From Outsider to Insider

Organisational Socialisation in Takeover Situations

Sonia Boussaguet

This chapter aims to improve understanding of the entry phase by reviewing seminal work on organisational socialisation in takeover situations. The concept of organisational socialisation originated in the field of human resources management. Research on recruitment used organisational socialisation to describe the process by which newcomers make the transition from organisational outsiders to insiders (Bauer *et al.*, 1998). Organisational socialisation is mainly associated with integrating new employees to help them contribute effectively to the organisation (Feldman, 1976).

Initially, definitions of organisational socialisation focused on the organisation, but they have gradually come to recognise the proactive role of the newcomer. Thus, organisational socialisation occurs via the organisation's efforts, identifiable in defined procedures and those of the new recruits, which combine different individual integration tactics. The success or failure of socialisation can be assessed through the newcomer's level of adjustment (Bauer *et al.*, 2007). Lacaze and Bauer (2014) consider that this adjustment comprises role clarification, self-efficacy, cultural fit and social acceptance.

However, can we compare the external buyer's situation to that of a new recruit? Do socialisation practices exist for future owners? Are they effective, and to what extent? This chapter explores these questions based on eight case studies in which I contrast certain socialisation practices with their observable effects.

Each case covers a period when newcomers arrive after a takeover and concerns healthy French SMEs (between 20 and 50 employees). I conducted 39 interviews, with both external buyers (8) and existing staff answering to the future owner (31). I divide the employees into subpopulations of executives (12) and non-executives (19). I analyse the content of the empirical material using the methods recommended by Huberman and Miles (1994) and mainly illustrate my results with 'words of the actors' (Wacheux, 1996). This study on organisational socialisation in takeover situations[1] not only contributes to theory but also has practical implications.

From a theoretical viewpoint, 'entry in the enterprise' is the last stage of the external business transfer process (Deschamps, 2000). Academic research has paid insufficient attention to this entry phase, despite it being the period when the takeover finally becomes reality: buyers become the new owner-leaders. However, even if their status is formally absolute, they arrive physically in an enterprise that they cannot know, and have to deal with members of staff who are used to the previous owner's way of working (Deschamps and Paturel, 2009). In these circumstances, they are naturally unable to exercise their power effectively. At this stage of the takeover, the new owner can find it difficult to adapt, and may even be incapable of integrating satisfactorily (Boussaguet, 2005; Rollin, 2006).

From a practical perspective, this research demonstrates the importance of the entry period for a successful takeover. Too often, buyers do not pay enough attention to post-acquisition dangers. They make mistakes that can ruin all their previous efforts. Those with little experience of the sector, or of small companies, are the most threatened by such managerial problems. Unsurprisingly, takeovers often fail because the new leader is rejected socially (Boussaguet and Defreyman, 2018).

I have divided the chapter into three sections. First, I study organisational socialisation practices, and I deduce from empirical observation a number of 'facilitation conditions' favouring buyer integration. Second, I analyse individual socialisation tactics, and I infer from empirical observation a number of 'activation conditions' implemented by buyers themselves. In conclusion, I discuss how a new leader-owner can effectively take up his/her position by listing the 'facilitation and activation conditions' observed in the situations studies.

Organisational Socialisation Practices as Takeover 'Facilitation Conditions'

In early studies, socialisation covered the activities implemented by organisations to welcome and integrate new recruits (Schein, 1968; Feldman, 1976; Van Maanen and Schein, 1979). Similarly, most organisational socialisation practices occur after the arrival of the new owner. This deferred action has many drawbacks, which I will describe here, showing the importance of acting both before and after the organisational entry.

Preparation (Before Organisational Entry)

The organisation pays little attention to the pre-entry period (Wanous, 1992). In external business transfer situations, the main reasons for the lack of preparation are that the buyer and seller focus on negotiating and that a level of confidentiality is required until the deal has been signed. In my view, preparing the future owner and the existing staff (subordinates) before the takeover appears essential.

Communication With the Candidate: The Future Owner

Organisations generally communicate with the candidate by defining the vacant position, a traditional recruitment practice. In takeover situations, sellers may prepare a detailed file on the business to help buyers imagine what to expect from their new organisational context. My observations show that this happens very rarely, either through neglect or for fear of giving too many details or of criticism of the previous action. This period feeds the imagination of prospective buyers (sometimes unreasonably so), creating the danger of a 'reality shock' (Wanous, 1992) with all its surprises and disillusions (Louis, 1980):

> When you take over an enterprise, you base your action on a number of disclosed elements; with regard to what is not disclosed, if people lie to you or if they lie by omission, well, you can be fooled. You don't hold all the cards.
>
> (buyer)

Very often, I observed that access to the enterprise was very limited, sometimes impossible, and contact with the staff ('key men') practically inexistent before the takeover: "I carried out audits, but had no contact with the enterprise until I took over" (buyer). "I had visited the enterprise, but not met the employees. My predecessor had said 'I will introduce you to the technical director' and a scenario was staged in which I was introduced as a client" (buyer).

In almost all the cases studied, the buyers lacked knowledge about the business: "I didn't have all the information concerning the business. When I arrived in the enterprise, there were still many unanswered questions, figures don't tell you everything" (buyer). This can generate 'role ambiguity'[2] for buyers, making it difficult for them to know how to act (Jablin and Miller, 1991):

> At the beginning, I actually wondered what I was doing. It was a new job. You were left to yourself, whereas in a big company when you arrive, there are other people. Here, I thought at first that everything depended on me. But, at the end of the day, I wondered what my role actually was. When you are a site manager, you arrive and you're the site manager. Here, I had to rely on myself, and it was rather destabilizing. There was nobody to give advice.
>
> (buyer)

It has become compulsory for potential buyers to sign a letter of confidentiality in which they commit themselves not to disclose any information released:

> [The seller] was reluctant to let me visit the company, and as I asked for more precise information, I felt he was unwilling to give it to me. Therefore, by mutual agreement, we decided to draw up a letter of confidentiality. After this, he instantly became less reluctant.
>
> (buyer)

Communication With Existing Staff: The Subordinates

Studies show the importance of concentrating on communication to existing members of staff (Van Maanen and Schein, 1979). In most cases, I observed that sellers only very rarely informed staff of their intentions. They did not wish to arouse suspicion and worry them. This fear may appear well founded, but must be put into perspective, as such a reaction can paradoxically generate incomprehension and anxiety:

> At first, it's true, it was a shock, we wondered who we were going to have, we had all sorts of questions and especially, about what kind of person were we going to find. We imagined all sorts of things. Some of us, who have left since then, took things really badly; they were shocked not to have been warned beforehand.
>
> (executive)

In addition, rumours often spread: "Rumours are very damaging; they are very destabilizing!" (executive). Beyond legal obligations, announcing the change and explaining the situation should become standard practice. Employees are particularly sensitive to this: "I had the feeling we were being sold off to the buyer, a bit like the factory machines. We knew absolutely nothing! It all happened very quickly. It was unacceptable for us!" (non-executive).

Control (After Organisational Entry)

Here, 'control' refers to the moment when the individual encounters reality (Fisher, 1986). Unlike traditional recruitment procedures, there are no programmes for buyers. However, in such cases, I list several formal or informal practices to help the buyer take his first steps as the new leader.

Formal Practices: "Mentoring" by the Seller

My observations reveal that once the deal is clinched, both an official presentation of the new owner and a mentoring during the transition period are necessary.³ Usually, the buyer is introduced at a welcoming event, which creates a warmer atmosphere with the existing staff: "We assembled everybody for a party; it introduced some humanity and a different first contact with people" (buyer). In my view, it is also important because it acts as a true 'transition rite' to establish or consolidate the new leader's role: "The seller introduced me briefly; he played his role perfectly by saying that I didn't know the sector very well but that I had the potential to develop the company. It helped my integration with the employees" (buyer).

This introduction of the new owner often coincided with his/her physical arrival at the enterprise. It appeared important to choose the buyer's office carefully. Ideally, the new owner will share the previous owner's office: "When I arrived, nothing was ready, I didn't have an office, he offered to share his office. Looking back, I did well to accept, as it enabled me to observe him" (buyer).

A transition period provides a perfect opportunity to train the buyer in his/her new management function. The buyer can thus be initiated by a peer (Comer, 1991), that is, a role model (Van Maanen and Schein, 1979), before the seller leaves the enterprise.

> It was a good thing, we needed to keep him [the seller] because everybody considered him a pillar of the enterprise, he represented the enterprise, he was the founder. . . . This shows that the information was transmitted, it wasn't just a matter of "I'll sell the enterprise and then I'll go". Because the question was: will someone who has just arrived and who has no experience, who doesn't know the products, who knows nothing, be able to run this enterprise? Thus, I think that the fact that the seller stayed on, put an end to the controversy.
>
> (executive)

Mentoring proves essential to buyer socialisation:

> I personally expected efforts to teach me the job, give me advice and train me in this type of job. As they were people who knew the job very well, they did it a bit too quickly, that was the only drawback, otherwise the sellers played the game well.
>
> (buyer)

I observed another, more informal type of socialisation practice often used to complement the practices described in this section.

Informal Practices: 'Organisational Support' by the Subordinates

'Organisational support' generally refers to any kind of organisational help with the integration process via interpersonal relationships (Ostroff and

Kozlowski, 1992). Colleagues and hierarchical superiors often help with in the integration of new recruits (Settoon and Adkins, 1997); subordinates occasionally (Louis *et al.*, 1983). In external business transfer situations, subordinates are more useful because they know the enterprise perfectly, having worked there for such a long time, and they possess key know-how and precious information that the new owner needs (Boussaguet and Grima, 2015).

From the start, the buyer must use people he/she considers influential (Jablin, 1984) or experienced (Morrison, 1993): "If you are new in a company, have nobody to confide in and don't know the work, I believe you have to go and see the people who are likely to give you the information you need" (buyer). Failing that, the buyer should ask them directly for help: "When I have a decision to make, I automatically ask my technical manager's advice. I trust him fully. It reassures me" (buyer).

> He will ask for advice. Often, it's just between the two of us, because I'm the only one in the firm that knows the sector. But, on the other hand, the final decision is up to him, but he often goes in the direction I have suggested. He listens to what I say.
>
> (executive)

As I have suggested, new leaders must realise that they have a role to play in their own socialisation. I will discuss this in more detail in the following section.

Individual Socialisation Tactics as Takeover 'Activation Conditions'

More recent research focuses on the active role of new recruits (Bauer *et al.*, 1998). A newcomer's proactive behaviour refers to individual-driven or informal means of 'self-socialising' (Ashford and Black, 1996). The takeover situation encourages new owners to be proactive rather than submit passively to the organisation's influence.

Newcomers' Behaviour: New Leader Proactivity

The literature recognises information-seeking as the main activity of new recruits (Jablin and Miller, 1991; Morrison, 1993; Ostroff and Kozlowski, 1992). This is also the case in the situations I analysed. However, the new leader also has to produce information, which immediately translates into action (Ashford and Black, 1996).

Information-Seeking Behaviour

Deliberately and purposefully seeking out information is necessary to reduce the uncertainty associated with arriving in a new organisation

(Morrison, 1993). It helps newcomers to understand, predict and control their new organisational environment. My field research confirmed this feeling that they often 'lack information' (Jablin, 1984): "I wanted confirmation of my analysis, to confirm how the enterprise operated. I wanted a clear image of the enterprise; of each person's responsibility" (buyer*)*. ". . . It's my role to be curious; you have to be extremely curious: to know everything, quickly open the cupboards to find possible skeletons, question people . . ." (buyer).

Traditionally, the organisational socialisation literature discusses two types of information sources. The first type is impersonal sources (Ostroff and Kozlowski, 1992), such as official internal documents, easily accessible to the new leader and often used in a takeover context: "He took initiatives concerning documentation. . . . He learnt from the documents" (executive). "He watched us work in order to learn. He took notes about what was really happening in the enterprise to become integrated. . . . An SME leader does everything, sees everything; it's his role, his work" (executive).

The second type are interpersonal sources. The literature refers to these as 'socialising agents' (Van Maanen and Schein, 1979). When taking over an enterprise, useful information sources include the seller, and then the staff, questioned directly or indirectly. However, such information-seeking can create significant problems. It can create additional work for those involved: "He asked a lot of questions, and answering the questions and explaining things in situ, why we did this or that disrupted our work; it delayed the progress of the worksite" (non-executive). "As for me, I found myself with a substantial workload, a lot of things to do, and a boss who needed a lot of information and explanation. We worked hard at first, which was to be expected" (executive).

It can be difficult to ask subordinates for information: "This is where it is more complicated, because you arrive in a position where you are supposed to manage people, and it's not always easy to go and ask the people you are going to manage to train you" (buyer).

Asking questions can affect the buyer's image, making him/her susceptible to judgment by the person questioned (Morrison, 1993). However, such employees feel respected and valued: "We had to help the buyer who was supposed to be the head of the firm, we felt valued" (non-executive).

Information-Production Behaviour

The newcomer not only collects but also produces information (Ashford and Black, 1996). If they are not introduced by the sellers, the new leaders start by aiming to win the trust of the staff: "He has to win people's trust because we don't know him at all, especially when he is anonymous; he has no references, no past, he has never worked in the sector" (executive). "They say 'you aren't one of us', so you need to convince them" (buyer).

Next, they present the takeover project. All the buyers I studied explained the situation openly, clearly formulating their intentions for the business:

> They are afraid of the future; so you must get them together and explain where the firm stands, as well as its projects. It's a good thing for them. As soon as I came in, I explained what I was going to do, how I proposed to do it. I told them about my ideas. A firm is a living entity, it's a challenge.
>
> (buyer)

However, during this first meeting, most buyers recommended a neutral attitude: "You avoid criticizing the past and committing yourself for the future" (buyer).

New leaders can then organise individual interviews with the different members of the organisation. This seems to depend on the urgency of the situation. Some of them made sure that they talked to each of their employees, insofar as it was possible, to develop a personal relationship and assess each person's situation: "His first action was to meet people individually. Meeting people helped him put things into perspective, identify whether there were problems of competence, work or with people, and this brought us into closer contact with him" (executive).

More precisely, depending on individual feelings, individual interviews provide an opportunity to get to know each other better, and to answer the employees' questions:

> There was an individual interview with each employee, he met us to know what our job was, what we did in the firm, how long we had been there, what we expected from him, from the future, if we had questions.
>
> (non-executive)

In my experience, what I call 'progress interviews' should become routine. In the recruitment context, individual interviews are indeed an integral part of induction programmes, and an increasingly common employee integration practice. At the same time, more than half the new leaders studied also said that they practiced an 'open-door policy' to demonstrate that the employees would always be listened to when they felt the need: "I told them that my door would always be open; that they could come and talk to me; unknowingly, I noticed it made a very positive impact on them" (buyer).

Finally, the interviews showed the need to organise regular meetings to give employees information about the state of the firm and achievement of its objectives, particularly during the years following the takeover, as recommended by the following buyer: "If you want it to work, you need to give a lot of information in the two or three years following the take-over" (buyer).

Through their questions and reactions to the responses, the apprentice leaders had to show their openness and determination to deal with difficult situations; this undeniably helped their pursuit of legitimacy. Indeed, one can well understand that this reassured the employees and gave them a sense of security. This brings me to the final point in this section: it appeared clearly in every case analysed that the new owner's attitude communicates very strongly (alongside verbal communication) how they intend to deal with the complexity of their new function.

The New Leader's Attitude Towards Existing Staff

Psychological capital is likely to render newcomers' proactive behaviour more efficient and successful (Lacaze and Bauer, 2014). In every case encountered, a good attitude towards the staff includes humility, respect for what is already in place and the ability to listen.

Humility and Respect for the Existing Situation

If they want to make a successful start in their new organisation, buyers cannot immediately revolutionise everything, just because they are the new leader. Such an attitude is often perceived as arrogance, and just a desire to show they are the boss:

> Change, novelty . . . in all cases, it must be done in good conditions and not be imposed. But if the boss wants to show off, and act like that because he's the boss; then he's got no chance!
>
> (non-executive)

"Things are going to change, because I'm new, so I'm going to show you how I work without bothering to look at how things are done; I think that's not a good thing" (non-executive).

Thus, the buyer must settle in before upsetting the company's operating methods too much, or at least must make gradual changes that respect the organisation's values:

> Every firm has a past and a culture. To say that a firm doesn't have a culture is untrue, totally untrue. Anyway, in a first stage, you must apply the sponge theory. You must absorb, and then digest, so as to keep the essential moral code. Take your time! You have arrived in a firm that has experience, a past, that has created a history,

whether good or bad, but it's there. And so, you must immerse yourself in it.

(buyer)

Employees really appreciate this as a sign of respect for their experience: "That's why he's very well integrated, because he has adopted the company's system. He hasn't obliterated the company's past. There hasn't been a break with the past" (non-executive).

Humility seems essential for the successful integration of a new owner: "I think that when someone takes over a firm, and the firm is doing well, the right strategy is to be humble and not act as if he were on conquered ground" (executive).

Active Listening

Listening seems to be a vital quality when taking office, particularly in an SME: "You need to be available, willing to listen. It is very important, but it's not only part of management; it's the everyday reality of an SME" (buyer). "He listened to us for many things; he understands, he has a sharp eye; that's proof he respects us" (non-executive). Ultimately, this attitude gives the new leader credibility: "You have to listen; I believe it's very important to give people time and be available when they explain what they do, you try to understand, and, after a while, your credibility grows" (buyer). Employees feel that respect for the past, humility and the ability to listen are undeniable assets. Without them, the leader will be at a considerable disadvantage:

He needs to work harder at human relations. He does not really care much about the employees, but I think that will come. In the future, he will be more attentive. At least I hope so; otherwise it will be more difficult for him. Really more difficult, I'm sure of that.

(executive)

Conclusion

This chapter discussed the socialisation practices observed when a newcomer takes over an SME. Despite his 'right of entry' (to take possession of his/her property), the buyer cannot afford to make an unsuccessful entry in this unfamiliar organisational setting. To manage this entry phase, I have identified from empirical observation a number of 'facilitation and activation conditions' likely to favour his/her integration. I have summarised these socialisation conditions in the table that follows (Table 12.1).

Table 12.1 Conditions for Successful Integration in Takeover Situations

FACILITATION CONDITIONS *(created by the organisation)*

Preparation (before organisational entry)	❶ **Seller prepares the buyer** provided the seller has started to accept the idea of losing his enterprise	Diffusion of accurate information Facilitate access to the enterprise and contact with the 'key men' ✍ Signature of a confidentiality agreement and preparation of an information file for the buyer 💣 Risk of 'role ambiguity' and 'reality shock'
	❷ **Seller prepares the staff** provided the seller has anticipated his departure	Takeover announcement: – Explanation of reasons for management change (separation = source of resentment) – Notification of/consultation with workers' council (if applicable = legal obligation) 💣 Risk of rumour, incomprehension, fear . . .
Regulation (after organisational entry)	❸ **Seller supports buyer** unless the takeover requires a transition period provided the seller's mind is clear about his future and that of his employees; provided that the buyer is really determined to learn	Welcoming event = 'rite of passage' Formal presentation by the seller to consolidate the buyer's position 'Physical' installation in an office shared with the seller 💣 Risk of confused situation for all actors; resistance = difficult position for the buyer (unwelcome) Mentoring = power transfer ✍ Formal transition process (clarification of operating methods: roles, responsibility, duration) ⌛ Six months maximum; three months if buyer has experience of the sector 💣 Risk of leadership rivalry and ambiguous situation for employees . . .
	❹ **Staff support buyer**	'Organisational support': ideally, the seller asks the staff to actively help the buyer; otherwise, the new owner must ask them directly for their cooperation ✍ Insertion of a non-competition clause in key-staff work contracts 💣 Risk of loss of expertise (know-how) which could have serious consequences for the buyer

ACTIVATION CONDITIONS *(created by newcomer)*

❶ **Buyer's proactive behaviour** Provided he/she shows positive intentions towards the enterprise	Information search (documentation, observation, experimentation) Presentation of project (display clear vision without disclosing too much) Scheduling of individual interviews

(Continued)

Table 12.1 (Continued)

ACTIVATION CONDITIONS *(created by newcomer)*	
	'Open-door policy' (provided the 'rules of the game' are shared and complied with)
	Organisation of regular meetings
	☙ Risk of anxiety and insecurity, preventing remobilisation and reassurance . . .
❷ Buyer's attitude to employees	Show respect for what is in place, humility, active listening
	☙ Risk of discontent, questioning of authority, loss of trust . . .

Beyond this need for socialisation, takeovers generate much more difficult situations than 'normal' recruitment does. Most current work on takeovers confirms some aspects of this (Bah, 2009; Cadieux and Deschamps, 2011; Mahé de Boislandelle and Estève, 2015). For example:

- The sellers' ambivalence: they hold all the keys for a successful integration, but their own departure can prove a wrench, especially if they founded the enterprise.
- The employees' wait-and-see policy: buyers should not underestimate their new employees. Since they know the firm and have access to key knowledge, buyers must listen to them and recognise their crucial role. Meanwhile, the staff must accept this role; some may have close ties with the seller and find it difficult to accept the new leader.
- The buyers' potential impatience: they may want to assert themselves immediately rather than rely on the existing setup to achieve better integration and mobilise people.

A successful integration also depends on the organisational context. Clearly, the circumstances will be harsher if the external business transfer requires substantial reorganisation rather than the continuation of a successful business. Overall, without appropriate socialisation, taking over will be fraught with danger: unfortunately, the new owner often seeks refuge in solitude and loneliness (Gumpert and Boyd, 1984).

Notes

1. For more information, see previous work by Boussaguet on 'repreneurial socialisation' (Boussaguet, 2005, 2007, 2008; Boussaguet and Grima, 2015).
2. Role ambiguity is defined as a lack of clear information about job responsibilities and expectations, preventing someone from working effectively in an organisation (Jablin and Miller, 1991).

3. Of course, this practice cannot apply when the takeover occurs after the sudden death of the previous owner.

References

Ashford, S.J. and Black, S.J. (1996). "Proactivity during organizational entry: the role of desire for control", *Journal of Applied Psychology* (81), 199–214

Bah, T. (2009). "La transition cédant-repreneur: une approche par la théorie du deuil", *Revue Française de Gestion* (194), 123–148.

Bauer, T.N., Bodner, T., Erdogan, B., Truxillo, D. and Tucker, J.S. (2007). "Newcomer adjustment during organizational socialization: a meta-analytic review of antecedents, outcomes, and methods", *Journal of Applied Psychology* (92), 707–723.

Bauer, T.N., Morrison, E.W. and Callister, R.R. (1998). "Organizational socialization: a review and directions for future research", *Research in Personnel and Human Resources Management*, 16, 149–214.

Boussaguet, S. (2005). *L'entrée du repreneur dans l'entreprise: un processus de socialisation repreneuriale*, PhD Thesis, University Montpellier I, Montpellier.

Boussaguet, S. (2007). "Réussir son entrée dans l'entreprise: le processus de socialisation du nouveau dirigeant", *Revue Economie et Société*, 16, 145–165.

Boussaguet, S. (2008). "La prise de fonction d'un repreneur de PME: repérage de conditions de facilitation et d'activation", *Revue de l'Entrepreneuriat*, 7(1), 39–61.

Boussaguet, S. and Defreyman, J. (2018). "Les voies d'entrée en défaillance des reprises externes de PME", *Revue Internationale PME*, 31(3–4), 67–95.

Boussaguet, S. and Grima, F. (2015). "L'intégration d'un repreneur-dirigeant de PME: le rôle socialisateur des subordonnés?" *Management International*, 20(1), 26–37.

Cadieux, L. and Deschamps, B. (2011). *Le duo cédant/repreneur: pour une approche intégrée du processus de transmission/reprise des PME*, Québec: Presses Universitaires du Québec.

Comer, D.R. (1991). "Organizational newcomers' acquisition of information from peers", *Management Communication Quarterly*, 5(1), 64–89.

Deschamps, B. (2000). *Le processus de reprise d'entreprise par les entrepreneurs personnes physiques*, Thèse de doctorat en sciences de gestion, Université de Grenoble.

Deschamps, B. and Paturel, R. (2009). *Reprendre une entreprise . . . de l'intention à l'intégration du repreneur*, Paris: Dunod, Collection Entrepreneurs.

Feldman, D.C. (1976). "A contingency theory of socialization", *Administrative Science Quarterly*, 21, 433–437.

Fisher, C.D. (1986). "Organizational socialization: an integrative review", *Research in Personnel and Human Resources Management*, 4, 101–145.

Gumpert, D. and Boyd, D. (1984, November–December). "The loneliness of the small-business owner", *Harvard Business Review*, 18–23.

Huberman, A.M. and Miles, M.B. (1994). *Qualitative data analysis. An expanded sourcebook*, 2nd ed., Beverly Hills, CA: Sage Publications.

Jablin, F.M. (1984). "Assimiling new members into organization", in R. Bostrom (Ed.), *Communication Yearbook*, Vol. 8, 594–626. Beverly Hills, CA: Sage Publications.

Jablin, F.M. and Miller, V.D. (1991). "Information seeking during organizational entry: influences, tactics and a model of the process", *Academy of Management Review*, 6(1), 92–120.

Lacaze, D. and Bauer, T.N. (2014). "A positive motivational perspective on organizational socialization", *Revue Interdisciplinaire Management, Homme & Entreprise*, 5(14), 58–75.

Louis, M.R. (1980). "Surprise and sense making: what newcomers experience in entering unfamiliar organizational settings", *Administrative Science Quaterly*, 25, 226–251.

Louis, M.R., Posner, B.Z. and Powell, G.N. (1983). "The availability and helpfulness of socialization practices", *Personnel Psychology*, 36, 857–866.

Mahé de Boislandelle, M. and Estève, J.M. (2015). *Conduire une transmission en PME*, Cormelles-Le-Royal: Editions EMS.

Morrison, E.W. (1993). "Newcomer information seeking: exploring types, modes, sources and outcomes", *Academy of Management Journal*, 36(3), 557–589.

Ostroff, C. and Kozlowski, S.W.J. (1992). "Organizational socialization as a learning process: the role of information acquisition", *Personnel Psychology*, 45, 849–874.

Rollin, M. (2006). *Reprise/rachat d'entreprise: les 100 premiers jours. Comment les réussir?* Paris: Maxima.

Schein, E.H. (1988). "Organization socialization and the profession of management", *Sloan Management Review*, 53–65, 1st ed. 1968.

Settoon, R.P. and Adkins, C.L. (1997). "Newcomers socialization: the role of supervisors, coworkers, friends and family members", *Journal of Business & Psychology*, 11, 507–516.

Van Maanen, J. and Schein, E.H. (1979). "Toward a theory of organizational socialization", *Research in Organization Behavior*, 1, 209–264.

Wacheux, F. (1996). *Méthodes qualitatives et recherche en gestion*, Paris: Economica.

Wanous, J.P. (1992). *Organizational entry: recruitment, selection, orientation and socialization of newcomers*, 1ére ed., 1980, Reading, MA: Addison Wesley.

13 How to Effectively Support External Buyers in a Post-Business Transfer Situation

Catherine Thévenard-Puthod

Business transfers are extremely challenging for companies (Calabrò *et al.*, 2018), as ownership and management discontinuities disrupt work routines, generate employee insecurity and may hinder organisational performance (DeTienne, 2010; Haveman and Khaire, 2004; Wasserman, 2003). However, among the different types of transfers, external transfers appear to be both the most dangerous and the least studied. The business transfer literature tends to focus on family succession (e.g., Le Breton-Miller *et al.*, 2004; De Massis *et al.*, 2008), even though there has been a decline in this type of transfer in several countries over the past several years (Transrégio, 2006; Durst and Sabbado, 2012; Kamei and Dana, 2012; Wiklund *et al.*, 2013). In France, for example, in 2017, family transfers accounted for only 10% of transactions, while external transfers accounted for 63% of company transfers (CRA, 2018). The literature on family succession is inadequate in understanding the challenges of external transfers, as an external buyer is in a very different situation from that of an heir (Bughin *et al.*, 2010). Family successors generally have the advantage of at least partial familiarity with the structure being taken over, along with its business and geographical environment, and can benefit from a certain 'blood' legitimacy in the eyes of the various stakeholders (Cadieux, 2007). Heirs are generally integrated into the company gradually, well before they take over the reins, which gives them time to train (Cabrera-Suárez *et al.*, 2001; De Massis *et al.*, 2008). Even though heirs may encounter some difficulties in the process, these difficulties are much more severe in the context of an external transfer. Studies indicate that given an average business transfer failure rate of 100, this rate drops to 27 in family transfers but increases to 126 when the takeover is carried out by a third party outside the acquired company (OSEO BDPME, 2005).

In view of the proportion and increase in the number of transfers to external buyers, the aim of this chapter is to take stock of the specific features of external business transfers, especially during the post-transfer phase, in order to propose appropriate support to external buyers.

This chapter includes two sections. The first one focuses on the challenges associated with the tricky post-transfer phase for external buyers. The second provides an overview of the existing forms of support provided to external buyers during this phase and highlights the effectiveness of individualised and external tutoring.

Post-Business Transfer: A Step Fraught With Pitfalls

The pioneering studies on business transfers focus on family succession and present it as a complex and iterative process (Cabrera-Suárez *et al.*, 2001; Calabrò *et al.*, 2018) composed of three to seven phases leading to the transfer of ownership and management of the company (Le Breton-Miller *et al.*, 2004; Lambrecht, 2005; Cadieux, 2007). However, the transfer process cannot be carried out in the same way in the context of an external transfer, with a buyer who has not been gradually integrated into the structure (Fiegener *et al.*, 1994). Picard and Thévenard-Puthod (2004) were among the first to conceptualise a process that is more specific to external transfers. This process starts before the signing of the deed of sale and ends several months after the signing of the deed. It is composed of four stages (see Figure 13.1): (1) preparation of the protagonists, (2) negotiation and agreement, (3) transition between seller and buyer, and (4) post-transfer management phase.

Based on ten case studies, Picard and Thévenard-Puthod (2004) showed that the two 'upstream' phases of the process (preparation and agreement), which have long been the focus of support systems and academic work (Deschamps, 2002; Scholes *et al.*, 2007; Grundström *et al.*, 2011),

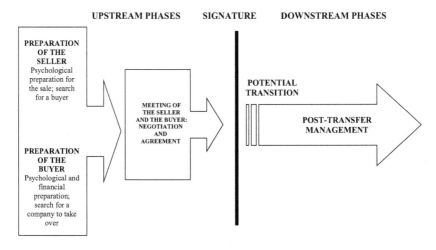

Figure 13.1 External Business Transfer Process

Source: Authors created

are not the ones that pose the greatest problems to external buyers. On the contrary, the post-transfer management phase raises particular difficulties that can affect the survival of the transferred company and require specific support. There are many types of difficulties in this situation, and they are often interrelated, making it difficult for buyers to resolve them. However, in order to provide the appropriate support to buyers, it is necessary to better identify those difficulties.

Managing a SME with few employees involves utilising day-to-day operational skills (being able to understand both accounting and financial documents to monitor the company's profitability and the legal and fiscal framework of the business). However, for buyers with a technical background, these daily management tasks can be problematic. In small organisations, information systems are often limited (Fallery, 1983) and founders or predecessors are often the sole and central repository of all information about the company, such as informal agreements with certain customers or suppliers, pricing, deadlines, stock levels, and the age of machines and equipment (Wasserman, 2003). When the predecessor leaves, it may become difficult for a buyer with no personal link with the seller to have the necessary overview for the day-to-day operation of the firm.

In the same line, in activities where technical expertise is predominant (such as crafts), a buyer with only a management background may have difficulty acquiring the essential knowledge, vocabulary and tricks for production, as well as difficulty building client and supplier relationships (Picard and Thévenard-Puthod, 2004).

As buyers often do not have sufficient funds to finance the buyout (OSEO BDPME, 2005), they are usually forced to take on significant debt and then may manage relatively tight financial arrangements. Cashflow difficulties can thus arise as early as the first or second year following the buyout, strongly constraining future development projects.

At the managerial level, buyers may encounter relational difficulties with the various stakeholders of the acquired organisation, with whom they must build legitimacy (Nordqvist, Wennberg, Bau and Hellerstedt, 2013). Internally, one of the challenges is to obtain employee support (Boussaguet, 2008). The departure of the former manager and the arrival of an external buyer can be traumatic for the employees of a company. Levinson (1970) uses the analogy of the formation of a new family through remarriage—children have to cope with both the grief caused by the departure of one of their parents and the uncertainty associated with the change in lifestyle, and they may react poorly to the authority exercised by the new person. As Larsson (1989) points out, staff resistance can be actively expressed (anger, rejection, sabotage) or passive, with employees outwardly resigned to the situation but showing no goodwill, which can also result in increased absenteeism and even staff turnover. However, the departure of employees following a business transfer can have destructive effects on a small structure, especially when employees have important know-how that is not codified (but only anchored in individual memory) and are in frequent contact with customers. This amounts to a loss of invisible but strategic assets (Thévenard-Puthod, 2009), which can have harmful consequences on the overall performance of the company (loss of know-how and skills). Most research on business transfers refers to buyers' 'organisational socialisation' difficulties in the firm they have purchased (Boussaguet, 2008). Thévenard-Puthod and Picard (2006) show that nearly a quarter of the buyers in their study encountered major difficulties with staff after the transfer. As long as buyers have not managed to gain acceptance from the employees of the taken-over organisation, it is particularly difficult for them to reorganise the company, instigate change or launch new development projects. In some cases, as in the craft industry, buyers must prove their legitimacy at the head of the company by demonstrating their mastery of the technical aspect of the trade (Thévenard-Puthod and Picard, 2006). In others, it is managerial skills and leadership ability that take precedence (Barach *et al.*, 1988), i.e., their ability to lead a team (recognising and rewarding the contribution of each employee, looking after their well-being, being able to identify missing skills, etc.) and retain employees with key skills.

An external takeover can also lead to negative reactions from stakeholders in the company environment. Lack of knowledge of industry practices, lack of technical or managerial skills, or lack of ability to manage a business network may make it difficult for buyers to maintain links with their key partners (customers, suppliers, bankers; Van Teeffelen *et al.*, 2011). Indeed, some commercial relationships are based on proximity relationships that have developed between customers and suppliers (Thévenard-Puthod and Picard, 2006). A change in management may call into question supply conditions or lead to suspicion among customers, who may wonder whether the product or service delivered will maintain the same level of quality. This can lead to commercial difficulties in the broadest sense (loss of turnover, lower margins, supply difficulties, etc.). The representations of these actors are influenced by their previous interactions with the predecessor (Bornard and Thévenard-Puthod, 2009). In some cases, interactions with the company involved only the staff, which facilitates the integration of the buyer and the application of a new management style. In others, where the former manager was the central contact for the external stakeholders, the evolution of representations will be more delicate. In a study by OSEO BDPME (2005), a quarter of the buyers surveyed faced the loss of a customer or supplier after the transfer.

All the difficulties mentioned here, as well as a lack of management skills, can affect the strategic acumen of the buyer (Grazzini *et al.*, 2009). The resolution of daily problems could prevent strategic reorientations from being defined: buyers may miss business opportunities or fail to identify significant threats.

Table 13.1 Main Post-Transfer Challenges

Nature of the possible difficulty	*Buyer profile characteristics that may increase the difficulty*	*Exacerbating company factors*
Lack of daily operational skills	Technical profile	–
Lack of technical know-how	Managerial profile or technical profile from another industry	Craft company
Financial difficulties due to a bad financial arrangement	Low initial financial contribution and lack of knowledge of financial resources	High cost of the acquired firm
Bad relationship with employees who are reluctant to accept the new owner	Lack of human resource management skills and/or technical know-how	Size of the workforce to be managed History of the firm and employee seniority
Difficulties in maintaining business relationships with key partners	Lack of knowledge of the industry and/or sales skills, etc.	The company's business activity and the level of customer demand Centrality of the previous owner in external relationship
Defining a new strategy	Lack of management skills Lack of industry knowledge	Complexity of the environment

However, these difficulties occur with varying degrees of severity depending on the buyer's profile in terms of initial training and skills, any previous management or takeover experience and the characteristics of the transferred company (size, industry, corporate culture more or less oriented towards change, financial health, etc.; see Table 13.1).

Finally, this variety of potential problems that may arise during the post-transfer management phase is mostly due to buyers' lack of knowledge, skills and/or legitimacy. In order to increase the chances that the transfer will succeed (and thereby ensure the sustainability of the transferred SME), it seems appropriate to consider a form of support that favours a *personalised* transfer of knowledge and skills to the buyer.

External Tutoring of Buyers: A Relevant Support to Reduce the Difficulties of the Post-Transfer Management Phase

It is now recognised in the entrepreneurship literature dedicated to business start-up that, depending on the entrepreneur's profile, objectives and context, it is preferable to opt for different support methods (Chabaud *et al.*, 2010; Messeghem *et al.*, 2013). However, specific support for buyers remains a subject that is not very well covered in the literature, in particular outside of family successions (Turner Foster, 1995; Boyd *et al.*, 1999; Deschamps *et al.*, 2010; Toumani-Uk, 2011; Salvato and Corbetta, 2013; Thévenard-Puthod *et al.*, 2014). Figure 13.2 summarises the few existing works, based on two dimensions of the support: (1) either it is internal (it comes from inside the firm) or external (coming from outside the firm) and (2) individual and personalised versus collective support.

In the context of craft business transfers, some authors have stressed the important role of the seller (Picard and Thévenard-Puthod, 2004; Thévenard-Puthod and Picard, 2006). Indeed, passing on a craft business is not only about selling premises and equipment (in other words, physical resources or material assets), but also about delivering intangible elements, tacit knowledge and skills on the practice of the craft (e.g., know-how, tricks of the trade, market and/or operational knowledge) (Cabrera-Suárez *et al.*, 2001; Scholes *et al.*, 2007; Van Teeffelen *et al.*, 2011; Nordqvist *et al.*, 2013). Several studies have shown that the transmission of tacit knowledge requires repeated interactions and many physical meetings between the protagonists (Nonaka and Takeuchi, 2007). For that reason, the support from the seller to the buyer during the transition phase is particularly relevant. Beyond this necessary transfer of know-how and tacit knowledge, which is essential in technical professions such as crafts, the transition phase seems all the more important, as it limits other post-transfer difficulties by giving the buyer a certain legitimacy in the eyes of the various internal and external stakeholders. A well-run transition and good chemistry between the predecessor and successor can facilitate the acceptance of the successor by employees, customers, suppliers, bankers and other key partners.

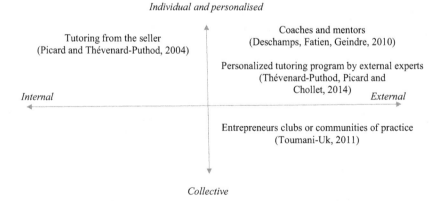

Figure 13.2 The Different Forms of Support for the External Buyer in the Literature
Source: Author created

However, there are two limitations to the support received from the seller. The first is that it does not occur systematically, as some sellers do not wish to invest in this relationship after the sale. The OSEO BDPME survey (2005), which concerns French business transfers, shows that the link between new and former managers is totally severed in 39% of cases. One would have thought that this figure would decrease with the tutoring agreement[1] introduced by the 2005 Economic Modernisation Act, but no figures are available on the success of this system, which has been amended several times. Moreover, the successful completion of this knowledge and skills transfer phase requires establishing a relationship of trust between predecessor and successor, which is not necessarily self-evident (Thévenard-Puthod and Picard, 2006; Bornard and Thévenard-Puthod, 2009).

The second limitation lies in the very content of this form of support. Indeed, according to Sammut (2003), the role of entrepreneurial support is to give entrepreneur the autonomy and skills to build their own projects. People providing guidance to entrepreneurs need to build their reasoning abilities. While the predecessor may be useful in ensuring continuity with the past, it will be difficult for them to help successors gain new momentum. In addition, the presence of predecessors sometimes hinders buyers from taking full control of the organisation and can act as a barrier between companies (its employees, customers, etc.) and their buyers. This can also catalyse employee resistance to change. For these reasons, it would then seem preferable for this support to be provided by a third party external to the company.

Toumani-Uk (2011) has focused on collective external forms of support, in particular, clubs or communities of practice where buyers can meet and confer with other company managers or buyers. Her work attributes two main limitations to those collective forms of support: the difficulty for buyers, who are very busy with post-transfer daily operations issues, to free up time to attend group meetings or training sessions; and their reluctance to express themselves in public or share their experience, especially if their competitors belong to the same group. More individualised and flexible support systems that fit buyers' schedules, specific situations and personalities (Audet and Couteret, 2005) would then be preferable.

Finally, a third type of support exists: individual support provided by an external party, like an expert, coach, trainer or mentor (Deschamps *et al.*, 2010). In the context of business foundation (Audet and Couteret, 2005; St-Jean and Audet, 2012), the effectiveness of these forms of personalised support has been examined. The results suggest that it allows three types of cognitive learning for entrepreneurs (Cope and Watts, 2000): knowledge development and access to key information, technical and management skills and enhanced managerial skills (Gravells, 2006; Valéau, 2006; Ozgen and Baron, 2007; St-Jean and Audet, 2012). On the contrary, in the context of business transfer, there are very few studies that have tested the effectiveness of this type of support. Only Thévenard-Puthod *et al.* (2014) have assessed a post-transfer tutoring program for buyers, that is to say an on-site transfer of knowledge and practical know-how, by a former entrepreneur or a more specialised expert. Their results, based on a Europe-wide experiment conducted on a sample of 889 buyers, show that this type of individualised support is effective in reducing the difficulties experienced by external buyers after a transfer.

This test project consisted in providing ten days of free tutoring to 889 new business owners of firms with fewer than 50 employees in 18 European countries. Of these 889 buyers, 62.2% were external buyers. The tutoring came in three phases. First, a diagnosis was made to review the difficulties encountered by the buyer after the transfer in order to establish a personalised support program, in terms of both content and practical arrangements (dates and spacing of sessions should be in line with the availability of the buyers and the timing of the transfer process). The second phase involved the implementation of the tutoring itself: several different tutors could work with the buyer for one to 19 half-days, depending on the needs of the buyer. It allowed an adjustment to the specific difficulties of the buyer (Gravells, 2006), which were closely linked to the profile of this new owner and the type of company acquired. In the last phase, buyers were asked to evaluate their satisfaction with the support they received.

The results show that the diagnosis in the first step forced the external buyers to classify and prioritise their difficulties. This made it easier for them to step back and sometimes better separate each problem from the others. The tutors, thanks to their expertise, then proposed ways to solve the issues identified (McGregor and Tweed, 2002) and encouraged buyers to take action. The knowledge transferred via tutoring was contextualised: tutors delivered their tailor-made knowledge and skills to the transferred company (McGregor and Tweed, 2002), based on the problems actually encountered by buyers. They took into consideration the complexity of the system formed by the different interacting components inherent in the buyer and the acquired company (Toutain and Fayolle, 2008). A proposed solution, even partial and/or temporary, allowed buyers to move forward and deal with the next problem.

Like some individualised support for entrepreneurs who founded companies (Cope and Watts, 2000; St-Jean and Audet, 2012), tutoring led to cognitive learning (Deakins *et al.*, 1998; Chrisman and McMullan, 2000, 2004), especially when an effort was made to vary the tutors to access different skills. As Cadieux and Brouard (2009) pointed out, nobody can claim to have all the necessary skills to intervene throughout the context of a business transfer. The possibility of selecting several types of tutors allowed easy access to different types of knowledge. Moreover, the multidisciplinary approach adopted in their experiment, involving several types of tutors with complementary approaches and skills, made it possible to avoid creating dependence between the buyers and a tutor. The tutors managed to make a real transfer of skills without becoming too highly involved or indispensable within the company (Bassot *et al.*, 2002). This post-transfer support was therefore widely appreciated by the external buyers who benefited from it.

However, the effectiveness of this knowledge transfer varied from one area to another. For example, Thévenard-Puthod *et al.* (2014) indicated that day-to-day operations (accounting and financial management, sales and marketing management, and human resources management) and financing were the areas where help was most appreciated (see Table 13.2). The effectiveness of individualised support in these operational areas had already been noted in other entrepreneurial contexts (Gravells, 2006; Bassot *et al.*, 2002). However, Thévenard-Puthod *et al.* (2014) noted that buyers showed the most satisfaction with areas where it is easier to 'measure' visible and concrete results in the very short term. In other words, buyers valued the contributions of knowledge and skills transfers that could be immediately used most highly. But beyond the technical aspects, one of the positive aspects of mentoring is to help external buyers acquire the legitimacy that is often lacking when they take over the purchased company. The tutors guiding the external buyers could thus not only provide useful information on how the industry operates and transfer the skills necessary to take over a company in an unfamiliar sector, but also help to legitimise their actions with all the stakeholders. Strategic know-how was, on the contrary, more difficult to transfer, absorb and implement in a short period of time. Similarly, technical know-how was difficult for buyers to acquire for two reasons. First, it was not always possible, depending on the industry, to find competent tutors. Secondly, some craft skills take a long time to acquire and require several years of training.

Table 13.2 Differences in Effectiveness According to External Tutoring Fields

Nature of the difficulty	Effectiveness of tutoring
Lack of daily management skills	++
Lack of technical know-how	+
Financial difficulties due to a bad financial arrangement	++
Bad relationship with employees who are reluctant to accept the new owner	++
Difficulties in maintaining business relationships with key partners	++
Defining a new strategy	+

Conclusion

The objective of this chapter was to take stock of the specific difficulties encountered by external buyers after a transfer and to propose relevant support measures. External buyers may lack the most knowledge about their new company's industry and generally have the shortest skills transfer process with the predecessor (Cadieux, 2007). Unlike heirs and employees, they do not benefit from prior knowledge of the purchased company thanks to a long period of cohabitation with the predecessor, and do not enjoy an apprenticeship as managers. It is also more difficult for them to find help within the family that originally owned the business or within the existing staff (Bughin *et al.*, 2010). In addition, they tend to have the most difficulty in gaining legitimacy from the various external and internal stakeholders of the transferred company (Boussaguet, 2008). The extent and variety of the highlighted difficulties, as well as the diversity of profiles of external buyers and acquired companies, argue in favour of personalised forms of support. Among them, a tutoring process, made by external experts and corresponding to the buyer's needs in terms of both content and timing, appears relevant. It not only provides the useful information and skills necessary to take over a company in an unfamiliar industry and manage day-to-day operations, but also helps buyers legitimise their actions with internal and external stakeholders.

However, considering the various forms of individualised support for buyers and the limited research on this topic, we invite researchers to pursue research in this little-explored field. First, as mentioned in this chapter, there are no quantitative studies that measure the effectiveness of the tutoring provided by the predecessor. Such a study would help to evaluate their positive versus negative effects. Further research could also assess the effectiveness of other forms of individualised support than tutoring (coaching, mentoring), or even compare them with each other. Concerning tutoring, the effectiveness of this support was only assessed in the short term, based on the satisfaction of the buyers who received this support. A longer post-tutoring follow-up could thus be useful and complement the research of Thévenard-Puthod *et al.* (2014). These authors did not measure buyers' actual acquisition of skills, but only their perceptions of their skills. Longitudinal monitoring of buyers could be very complementary to this ex-post measure of support to better understand how these skills develop. An experimental system could also measure the development of real skills before and after tutoring. Finally, the psychological contribution of individualised support (Valéau, 2006) was not taken into account, since the authors focused on cognitive learning. In line with Salvato and Corbetta's work (2013) on family succession, future research could measure the emotional or conative learning of the buyers linked to the development of their interpersonal skills or behaviour in a more qualitative way.

Note

1. In France, the law of 02/08/2005 (extended in July 2009) aims to promote the transfer of professional experience between a predecessor and a buyer. The predecessor may conclude an agreement with the company's buyer to provide a temporary mentoring service for a period of between two months and a maximum of one year. The predecessor benefits from a combination of employment and retirement benefits for the duration of the tutoring (accumulation of remuneration) and protection against accidents at work.

References

Audet, J. and Couteret, P. (2005). "Le coaching entrepreneurial: spécificités et facteurs de succès", *Journal of Small Business and Entrepreneurship*, 18(4), 471–489.

Barach, J.A., Gantisky, J., Ourson, J.A. and Doochin, B.A. (1988). "Entry of the next generation: strategic challenge for family business", *Journal of Small Business Management*, 3, 49–56.

Bassot, P., Hersscher, S., Postel-Vinay, G., Jacob-Duvernet, L., Lebaube, A., Braun, A. and Durand, T. (2002). "Figures du conseil", *Revue Française de Gestion*, 28(137), 119–134.

Bornard, F. and Thévenard-Puthod, C. (2009). "Mieux comprendre les difficultés d'une reprise externe grâce à l'approche des représentations sociales", *Revue Internationale PME*, 22(3–4), 83–108.

Boussaguet, S. (2008). "Prise de fonction d'un repreneur de PME: Repérage de conditions de facilitation et d'activation", *Revue de l'Entrepreneuriat*, 7(1), 39–61.

Boyd, J., Upton, N. and Wircenski, M. (1999). "Mentoring in family firms: a reflective analysis of senior executives' perceptions", *Family Business Review*, 12, 299–309.

Bughin, C., Colot, O. and Finet, A. (2010). "Entreprises familiales et gouvernance cognitive: quelle transmission?" *Management Avenir* (7), 14–33.

Cabrera-Suárez, K., De Saá-Pérez, P. and García-Almeida, D. (2001). "The succession process from a resource- and knowledge-based view of the family firm", *Family Business Review*, 14(1), 37–48.

Cadieux, L. (2007). "Succession in small and medium-sized family businesses: toward a typology of predecessor roles during and after instatement of the successor", *Family Business Review*, 20(2), 95–109.

Cadieux, L. and Brouard, F. (2009). *Transmission des PME: perspectives et enjeux (Entrepreneuriat and PME)*. Québec: Presses de l'Universite du Quebec.

Calabrò, A., Minichilli, A., Amore, M.D. and Brogi, M. (2018). "The courage to choose! Primogeniture and leadership succession in family firms", *Strategic Management Journal*, 39(7), 2014–2035.

Chabaud, D., Messeghem, K. and Sammut, S. (2010). "Vers de nouvelles formes d'accompagnement?" *Revue de l'Entrepreneuriat*, 9(2), 1–5.

Chrisman, J.J. and McMullan, W.E. (2000). "A preliminary assessment of outsider assistance as a knowledge resource: the longer-term impact of new venture counseling", *Entrepreneurship Theory and Practice*, 24(3), 37–53.

Chrisman, J.J. and McMullan, W.E. (2004). "Outsider assistance as a knowledge resource for new venture survival", *Journal of Small Business Management*, 42(3), 229–244.

Cope, J. and Watts, G. (2000). "Learning by doing—an exploration of experience, critical incidents and reflection in entrepreneurial learning", *International Journal of Entrepreneurial Behavior and Research*, 6(3), 104–124.

CRA (Cédant et Repreneur d'Affaires). (2018). *L'observatoire national CRA de la Transmission des TPE/PME*. www.transmettre-reprendre.fr.

De Massis, A., Chua, J.H. and Chrisman, J.J. (2008). "Factors preventing intrafamily succession", *Family Business Review*, 21(2), 183–199.

Deakins, D., Graham, L., Sullivan, R. and Whittam, G. (1998). "New venture support: an analysis of mentoring support for new and early stage entrepreneurs", *Journal of Small Business and Enterprise Development*, 5(2), 151–161.

Deschamps, B. (2002). "Les spécificités du processus repreneurial", *Revue Française de Gestion* (138), 175–188.

Deschamps, B., Fatien, P. and Geindre, S. (2010). "Accompagner le repreneur d'entreprise: conduire, escorter mais aussi guider", *Gestion 2000*, 27(3), 77–90.

DeTienne, D.R. (2010). "Entrepreneurial exit as a critical component of the entrepreneurial process: theoretical development", *Journal of Business Venturing* (25), 203–215.

Durst, S. and Sabbado, L. (2012). "Non-family succession in German SMEs: concerns about transparency and information", *Entreprendre and Innover* (2), 86–96.

Fallery, B. (1983). "Un système d'information pour les PME", *Revue Française de Gestion* (43), 70–76.

Fiegener, M.K., Brown, B.M., Prine, R.A. and File, K.M. (1994). "A comparison of successor development in family and non-family business", *Family Business Review*, 7(4), 313–329.

Gravells, J. (2006). "Mentoring start-up entrepreneurs in the East Midlands—troubleshooters and trusted friends", *The International Journal of Mentoring and Coaching*, 4(2), 3–23.

Grazzini, F., Boissin, J.P. and Malsch, B. (2009). "Le rôle du repreneur dans le processus de formation de la stratégie de l'entreprise acquise", *Revue Internationale PME*, 22(3–4), 139–164.

Grundström, C., Öberg, C. and Öhrwall Rönnbäck, A. (2011). "View and management of innovativeness upon succession in family-owned SME", *International Journal of Innovation Management*, 15(3), 617–640.

Haveman, H.A. and Khaire, M.V. (2004). "Survival beyond succession? The contingent impact of founder succession on organizational failure", *Journal of Business Venturing*, 19(3), 437–63.

Kamei, K. and Dana, L.P. (2012). "Examining the impact of new policy facilitating SME succession in Japan: from a viewpoint of risk management in family business", *International Journal of Entrepreneurship and Small Business*, 16(1), 60–70.

Lambrecht, J. (2005). "Multigenerational transition in family businesses: a new explanatory model", *Family Business Review*, 18(4), 267–282.

Larsson, R. (1989). *Organizational integration of mergers and acquisitions: a case survey of realization of synergy potentials*, Lund: Lund University Press.

Le Breton-Miller, I.L., Miller, D. and Steier, L.P. (2004). "Toward an integrative model of effective FOB succession", *Entrepreneurship Theory and Practice*, *28*(4), 305–328.

Levinson, H. (1970). "A psychologist diagnoses merger failures", *Harvard Business Review*, *48*(2), 139.

McGregor, J. and Tweed, D. (2002). "Profiling a new generation of female small business owners in New Zealand: networking, mentoring and growth", *Gender, Work and Organization*, *9*(4), 420–438.

Messeghem, K., Sammut, S., Chabaud, D., Carrier, C. and Thurik, R. (2013). "L'accompagnement entrepreneurial, une industrie en quête de leviers de performance?" *Management international*, *17*(3), 65–71.

Nonaka, I. and Takeuchi, H. (2007). "The knowledge-creating company", *Harvard Business Review*, *85*(7/8), 162.

Nordqvist, M., Wennberg, K., Bau, M. and Hellerstedt, K. (2013). "Succession in private firms as an entrepreneurial process", *Small Business Economics*, *40*, 1087–1122.

OSEO BDPME. (2005, June). *La transmission des petites et moyennes entreprises*; *l'expérience d'Oséo* BDPME, 6203.02. www.oseo.fr/IMG/pdf/Oseo_transmission.pdf.

Ozgen, E. and Baron, R.A. (2007). "Social sources of information in opportunity recognition: effects of mentors, industry networks, and professional forums", *Journal of Business Venturing*, *22*(2), 174–192.

Picard, C. and Thévenard-Puthod, C. (2004). "La reprise de l'entreprise artisanale: spécificités du processus et conditions de sa réussite", *Revue internationale PME Économie et gestion de la petite et moyenne entreprise*, *17*(2), 93–121.

Salvato, C. and Corbetta, G. (2013). "Transitional leadership of advisors as a facilitator of successors' leadership construction", *Family Business Review*, *26*(3), 235–255.

Sammut, S. (2003). "L'accompagnement de la jeune entreprise", *Revue Française de Gestion* (3), 153–164.

Scholes, M.L., Wright, M., Westhead, P., Burrows, A. and Bruining, H. (2007). "Information sharing, price negotiation and management buy-outs of private family-owned firms", *Small Business Economics*, *29*(3), 329–349.

St-Jean, E. and Audet, J. (2012). "The role of mentoring in the learning development of the novice entrepreneur", *International Entrepreneurship and Management Journal*, *8*(1), 119–140.

Thévenard-Puthod, C. (2009). "Transmission d'entreprises: pour une plus grande attention portée aux repreneurs externes et aux phases aval du processus", in B. Pras (Ed.), *Management: tensions d'aujourd'hui*, 93–104, Paris: Vuibert.

Thévenard-Puthod, C. and Picard, C. (2006). "Confiance et défiance dans la reprise d'entreprises artisanales", *La Revue des Sciences de Gestion* (3), 99–113.

Thévenard-Puthod, C., Picard, C. and Chollet, B. (2014). "Pertinence du tutorat comme dispositif d'accompagnement du repreneur individuel après la reprise. Une étude empirique à l'échelle européenne", *Management International*, *18*(4), 80–96.

Toumani-Uk, N. (2011). *La communauté de pratiques comme outil d'accompagnement en entrepreneuriat: le cas de la reprise d'entreprise*, PhD Thesis, University Nancy II, Nancy.

Toutain, O. and Fayolle, A. (2008). "Compétences entrepreneuriales et pratiques d'accompagnement: approche exploratoire et modélisation", in. G. Kizaba (Ed.), *Entrepreneuriat et accompagnement*, 31–72, Paris: l'Harmattan.

Transrégio. (2006). *Enquête sur la transmission d'entreprise dans sept pays européens*. Cambridge, MA: Harvard University Press.

Turner Foster, A. (1995). "Developing leadership in the successor generation", *Family Business Review*, *8*, 201–209.

Valéau, P. (2006). "L'accompagnement des entrepreneurs durant les périodes de doute", *Revue de l'Entrepreneuriat*, *5*(1), 31–57.

Van Teeffelen, L., Uhlaner, L. and Driessen, M. (2011). "The importance of specific human capital, planning and familiarity in Dutch small firm ownership transfers: a seller's perspective", *International Journal of Entrepreneurship and Small Business*, *14*(1), 127–148.

Wasserman, N. (2003). "Founder-CEO succession and the paradox of entrepreneurial success", *Organization Science*, *14*(2), 149–172.

Wiklund, J., Nordqvist, M., Hellerstedt, K. and Bird, M. (2013). "Internal versus external ownership transition in family firms: an embeddedness perspective", *Entrepreneurship Theory and Practice*, *37*(6), 1319–1340.

Part V

Women in Business Transfers

This last part is devoted to a very important subject: women! Although the percentage of business transfers by women has risen in the last ten years, it nevertheless remains low. It is therefore essential to increase the proportion of women involved in these transfers. Yet in order to do so, several issues need to be addressed: the obstacles that prevent women from taking over a business and the specific difficulties that they must overcome to succeed. The purpose of Part V is to alert readers to these issues and to open new paths for research on women in business transfer.

To lead off (Chapter 14), **Paulette Robic**, in her chapter entitled **Family as an Institution to Investigate the Role of Women in the Transfer of Family Businesses**, explores the processes behind the decision of some women (daughters, sisters, cousins) to take over the family business and of those who refuse to do so. This chapter looks at the factors that govern women's involvement in the families of family businesses, how these businesses are managed and particularly how succession occurs.

Chapter 15, **Gender and Succession in the Family Business**, presents state of the art French-speaking research into the succession process with regard to gender dynamics. **Christina Constantinidis** offers original contributions and reflects a rich and diverse reality anchored in various geographical and cultural contexts. The chapter starts with the study of how gendered legal, familial and societal environments influence family business transfers. The author then highlights the gendering of succession from the perspective of the various family business actors. To conclude, the author highlights the importance of developing systemic and longitudinal approaches to research on gender and family business transfers, and proposes directions for future research.

In Chapter 16, **Daughters: Invisible Heroes of Family Businesses?**, focuses on daughters in family business transfers. **Audrey Missonier, Annabelle Jaouen** and **Béatrice Albert** notably invite us to look at father-daughter transmission from a relational perspective. Based on research taking an interpretative phenomenological approach (IPA) with five daughters and four fathers, this chapter emphasises the importance of the father-daughter dynamics in transfer success. The results show that father-daughter relationships evolve: from a father-daughter relationship, to an adult-adult relationship, and finally to a successor and business owner relationship. Yet, to arrive at this point, fathers and daughters need to achieve a certain detachment and reconstruct their identities.

The last chapter of this book (Chapter 17), **Female External Successors: Difficulties During the Business Transfer Process and Types of Support Required**, explores a topic too often overlooked: external women successors. From six case studies, **Bérangère Deschamps** and **Catherine Thévenard-Puthod** explore the difficulties encountered by women buyers during the external business transfer process and how they can overcome them. The authors highlight a specific variety of gender-related difficulties for women, both before signing (for example, convincing the seller that you, as a woman, are a relevant buyer) and after the signing (for example, balancing your personal-professional life). The authors then emphasise the importance of different forms of support for external women successors (fathers, husbands, etc.). These results are important contributions to research on business transfers.

14 Family as an Institution to Investigate the Role of Women in the Transfer of Family Businesses

Paulette Robic

What is the influence of the family, as an institution, on the role women play in running family businesses (FBs)? Campopiano *et al.* (2017) suggest that the visible and invisible role of women should be investigated. This is what this chapter does. We develop a conceptual approach which we test using a typology published elsewhere (Robic, 2017). Our research question will be to understand to what extent women consent to take over a FB as a result of their own free will, or at the demand of the family, an institution which we consider a social construct.

In order to answer this question, we will use different frameworks. First, the literature on gender as a social construct in FBs (Nelson and Constantinidis, 2017) will help us investigate how this social construct impacts role inequalities between men and women in the management of FBs. We will thus follow the recommendations of Jaskiewicz and Dyer (2017) to take into account the discrimination of women, gender inequality, and the exploitation of family members within the family and the FB. Our second framework will be family businesses as complex systems (Tagiuri and Davis, 1992) in which the FB and the family are intertwined. The family is considered by Durkheim (1922) as the place where primary socialisation takes place. This feeds our interest for the family in the family business context, as FBs are considered a place for the secondary socialisation of family members (Lubinski, 2011). In order to conduct our analysis, we refer to institutions as a concept developed by neo-institutionalist sociology (NIS) (Meyer and Rowan, 1977; Di Maggio and Powell, 1983, 1991), which is our third framework.

In the first section of this chapter, we will define the family as an institution in the NIS sense of the term. In the second section, we will analyse what the family does to women through the prism of neo-institutionalism and gender.

A Neo-Institutionalist Approach to the Family Institution

NIS sees the actors within organisations as the product of their environment, while at the same time granting them some degree of freedom to act on the institutions.

The Family as an Institution

According to Berger and Luckman (1967), institutionalisation is a process of legitimising thoughts and practices. It occurs in three steps: first, externalisation when institutions do not exist; then objectification when institutions are present; and, finally, internalisation when institutions are not only present but taken for granted.

An institution relies on three forms of power which depend on its degree of institutionalisation. During the externalisation phase, power, described as episodic, is interpersonal. In order to exercise it, actors rely on their resources and on the social networks (Granovetter, 1985) in which they are embedded, but also on their ability to control uncertainty. There is no control by the institution since it does not exist. During the objectification phase, the so-called power of domination is exercised only by so-called dominant actors over dominated ones. The dominant actors shape the institution to their advantage in order to exercise and maintain their power. On their side, the dominated actors agree to submit to the rules. Finally, in the internalisation phase, power qualified as control belongs entirely to the institution. The dominant actors are still in place, but they no longer have the capacity to think about institutions; they seem natural to them. Institutions assign a status (Rancière, 1995).

Currently, there is no consensus on the definition of what a family is (Quéniart and Hurtubise, 2002). We refer to the three main family forms (Roussel, 1992): patrimonial, matrimonial and 'uncertain'. We adopt Segalen's (1993) assumption that kinship constitutes the family and that the matrimonial form is only one possible element of it.

The family is a place where social order is produced and reproduced, as well as transmitted between generations. The practice of accumulation and transmission of economic and social wealth within the family is therefore a reality that is perceived as entirely legitimate.

The family is the main locus of reproductive strategies where decisions are often collective and where its members are often required to act in a 'good spirit' as parts of a 'whole' united around the 'house', (Bourdieu, 1993) defined in particular as a set of material goods. The individual members of the group have to find a balance between their selfish individual interests and the collective interests of the family entity—in this case, the preservation of its material assets. But the family institution has its limits, as a world in which male domination (Bourdieu, 1998), or differential valence of genders (Héritier, 1996), unfolds.

Given the strong historicity of the family, which is considered natural, we can admit, with reference to NIS, that its degree of institutionalisation oscillates between objectification and internalisation.

The Family as a Place of Power

How are the powers of domination and control articulated within the family institution? In accordance with Bourdieu, for whom the family is an output of a dialectic between unity and adversity among its members, we choose the concept of social relationship (Pfefferkorn and Pereira, 2013) to understand how power is enacted within it. We must keep in mind that when business transfer occurs over several generations, we can assume that the FB family is an institution whose historicity is no longer in question. Consequently, it is an objective but also coercive reality in the sense of Berger and Luckmann (1967).

More generally, power within the family, both in the distribution of tasks and in the transmission of economic assets, is in favour of men and is played out around gender relations, but not solely—kinship also plays a role in weaving social relations between its members. This reflects Segalen's (1993) assumption that kinship is a more essential element of the family than matrimonial status is.

It turns out that the internalisation of family norms is such that its members, dominant/men and dominated/women, no longer have, or have very little, reflexive capacity with regards to the institution. They submit themselves to its power of control, which assigns each of its members a given status. Lawrence (2008) and Huault et Leca (2009) defend the idea that if actors can decide by themselves and for themselves, they are essentially doing so for the institution, so that it will survive.

The strong historicity of the family means that its members, whether men or women, must make efforts to extract themselves from its influence, especially since compliance with the role assigned to them as an agent is 'highly appreciated'. The family institution is thus a system for defining and assigning roles (Rancière, 1995). The actions of each member are guided by the family itself. The family thus shapes, identifies and assigns a status to both its dominant and dominated members. Family law is one of the instruments by which the family institution is a social construct. So are civil registers which materialise the presence of government in family affairs (Bourdieu, 1993).

Analysing What the Family Does to Women in the FB Family Through the Double Prims of NIS and Gender

We will now transpose our analytical framework of the family as an institution to the study of the influence of the FB's family on the role of women in these families in running these businesses. To do so, we will rely on a typology of the trajectories and roles of FB women published elsewhere (Robic, 2017). It is based on the study of more than 15 French FBs of the SME and intermediate types. We will use it as tool for our analysis. The heuristic dimension of our typology will help us understand whether women in FBs accept the helm of a FB as a result of their free will or as submission to family demands. More generally, we will analyse the influence of the family institution on the roles of women in running FBs.

With reference to the three types of families that we identified, we consider that the FB family belongs to the patrimonial type. It is both a place of reproduction, like any family, but also a place of production since the firm is attached to it (Chua *et al.*, 1999). The transfer of the FB over at least three generations gives it a dynastic character (Daumas, 2015).

The companies we analysed to build our typology have all reached at least the third generation. The families to which they are attached are not only of the patrimonial type, but also have a dynastic character. We identified more precisely how the FB family is organised (division of tasks and transmission of wealth) in order to highlight its influence on the roles of women and, in particular, on their involvement in running the FB.

A Highly Gendered and Unequal Distribution of Tasks and Assets

We find gender relations (Kergoat, 1982) are exacerbated in the FB's family, both through the separation of men and women and through the hierarchical principle that men's work is worth more than women's work. Indeed, this is what our previous research shows (Robic, 2017, 2018). It has guided the construction of our typology. We will first look at the distribution of tasks and then at the distribution of assets.

Women Moving Back and Forth Between the Visible and the Invisible

Four roles have been identified, marking the evolution of women between invisible and visible roles.

Within the family sphere, the first role is the one of steward, as the woman keeps the accounts of the FB, possibly manages the employees and makes appointments while staying at home. Her role is quite operational but invisible. We qualified the second role as the one of a governess, because the woman takes part in defining major long-term orientations for the company, but without receiving a pay and within the family sphere only. The woman therefore has a strategic but invisible role. She influences or even decides on the successor at the head of the FB, and keeps the company's networks active and connected to those of the family.

Within the FB sphere we have also identified two female roles, which are formal and visible. The first one is the role of manager, who does not take part in defining the company's strategy but has an operational role, such as keeping the accounts. This is a paid and visible operational role. Women in this role contribute to the preservation of family assets.

The second role, which we described as the one of an executive, is very much involved in the company's strategy. It is a strategic and visible role. The woman runs or takes part in running the company by being on the management committee, if there is one, or in a governance position as a member of the supervisory board, if there is one.

These roles differ according to family relationships and gender, and not according to the proven skills of the individual, within the couple or the siblings. Widows are very much a part of the company's strategy either as governesses or executives. Wives, on the other hand, can play three roles: steward, governess and leader in a non-linear way. They are mostly stewards and governors, as they are mostly invisible and do not appear as managers. The privileged place of girls and sisters, especially since the 1970s and 1980s, is that of manager. This allows them to make their entry into the FB. As for men, either as husbands or sons, they create and run the company and take care of technical aspects. Women, most of the time as wives, and more rarely as daughters and/or sisters, keep the accounts and take care of commercial aspects.

Moreover, the roles played by FB women in the family are not set (see Chapter 15, Constantinidis, this volume; Chapter 16, Missonier, Jaouen and Albert, this volume; and Chapter 17, Deschamps and Thévenard-Puthod, this volume). Indeed, the four roles we have identified evolve over time. There are real back-and-forth movements between visible and invisible roles within the FB according to the hazards of life: premature death of the spouse, absence of sons. Their visibility is sometimes over the long-term, but it is most often temporary and by no means linear. These women play the role of 'conveyors' to guarantee the survival of the FB, by taking over the business as long as it takes and keeping it within the hands of the family.

The separation and/or hierarchy of roles between men and women in FB families is therefore significant. The life paths of these women, of their families and of the FB are interwoven. Moreover, gender is very present in the process followed by these women when enter the FB and becoming leaders. This is in line with the research of Dumas (1998), Salganicoff (1990), Curimbaba (2002), Ginalski (2015), and Nelson and Constantinidis (2017). Although women from the FB families play an increasingly visible role in running these businesses (Crutzen *et al.*, 2012; Rodríguez-Modroño *et al.*, 2015) (see Chapter 15, Constantinidis, this volume; and Chapter 16, Missonier, Jaouen and Albert, this volume), this visibility, is still very low compared to that of men.

The Persistence of Inequality in Business Transfers, in Favour of Men

Our previous research concludes that there is inequality in the transfer of economic wealth between siblings, to the detriment of the youngest ones, *a fortiori* girls, as highlighted by Bessière and Gollac (2007). When there are mixed siblings, the daughters either inherit less than their brothers, or inherit land (see Chapter 5, Robic, Barbelivien and Antheaume, this volume), which keeps them out of the business, at least formally. The eldest male sibling, regardless of his place in the family, often buys out his siblings' shares as soon as he can, on the grounds that he does not want to disperse the family wealth. Nevertheless, we did not encounter any situation in which the opposite was true: none of the daughters we met reported unequal transfers in their favour.

Jacques-Jouvenot and Schepens (2007) also see the successor as a *Homo Memor*, the guardian of family history. It is also in this capacity that they see the successor more as a custodian than an owner. His role is therefore to ensure that the family's economic heritage, the FB, survives and thrives through the generations.

The Importance of the Transmission of Assets in Institutionalisation

In a first subsection, we will highlight how the FB family proceeds in terms of institutionalisation, in order to achieve such an unequal distribution of roles and assets related to the family business. In a second subsection, we will decipher the underlying logic behind this seemingly natural situation.

Marriage as a Vector of Transmission

As with any family, FB families use various founding acts and rites (Bourdieu, 1993) that facilitate the socialisation of their members but also maintain them over a long period of time, since we are dealing with dynastic families.

The maintenance of marriage as a privileged form of alliance is a first element that characterises the FB family and is significant with regard to the evolution of society (Théry, 1996, 2007). Although more and more marriages break down, in the circle of FB leaders (Bessière and Gollac, 2014; Jacques-Jouvenot and Droz, 2015), marriage remains very present in FB families (Hirigoyen and Villéger, 2017; Ginalski, 2015). Among the FB families that we studied, we did not meet any women who were not married, except for those who had become widows.

Marriage plays an important role for the members of the FB family because it assigns a role to each of the spouses: visibility (public sphere, paid work) for the husband, often a father; on the contrary invisibility (private sphere, domestic, unpaid informal work), for the wife, also a mother. Marriage can also reflect marital strategies. Let us mention an example. The founder of a company, wanting to develop his business while he is just starting in life as a herbalist, has technical and managerial knowledge, and a good network, but he does not have enough economic capital for his project, so he marries a relatively well-endowed woman who brings it to him. This case highlights the importance of matrimonial strategies in the trajectory of a business, by strengthening its social and economic capital and that of the family.

The House as a Vector of Socialisation

The family house is also a vehicle for the institutionalisation of the family. It also serves as a head office for the FB, at least during the first and second generations. The integration with the company helps to strengthen the sense of belonging of the family members, both to the family and the business. This promotes the historicity of the family house, and also contributes to the 'normality' and invisibility of the work 'at home' carried out by the steward and the governess. By playing an active role in maintaining and running networks, the governess is one of the key players in activating family spirit. This type of woman acts as a liaison agent in the sense of Rosenthal (1985)—a vector of family normalisation (Bourdieu, 1993, 1998). The steward is not to be outdone on this point. She 'only' keeps track of family wealth by keeping the accounts in the background (Labardin and Robic, 2008). We might even think that her invisible role in the service of the business, in the domestic rather than the professional perimeter, preserves family values and thus the family as an institution. Among the companies we studied, we met several cases where the family house is the place where professional documents are 'archived': accounting documents, human resources related documents, press reviews, but also photographs and even old machines that, although often scattered, are visited whenever a company anniversary is to be commemorated (Robic, 2014). The family house is then a place of remembrance for the family and the family business.

An Underlying Anthropological Logic

Due to the porosity between the family and entrepreneurial spheres, the FB family socialises its members (Lubinski, 2011) at the primary and secondary levels. The acquisition of business-related skills is facilitated. What we notice is that the women in our typology were indeed familiar with, and even trained in, business skills. They are sometimes encouraged to join the FB, but for tasks which are perceived as typically feminine. Based on our typology, those women who become managers have the potential to take the leadership of the FB, when allowed by life's circumstances. Sometimes they switch back to the role of manager or governess. This is the case of one of the sisters, among a large group of siblings, whose brother-in-law and brothers made it clear that she no longer had a place as a co-leader. Her sister became a governess herself. Her husband (son-in-law of the former head) took over the FB. Although there are FB families in which women are explicitly encouraged to take on responsibilities (Dumas, 1998), the prior example highlights the strong influence of patriarchy on the involvement of women in running the FB. It is also in line with the literature (Jimenez, 2009; Fattoum and Byrne, 2017) according to which girls and women are socialised with a view of keeping them out of the company.

The underlying logic of this unequal institutionalisation is the perpetuation of the family itself through the perpetuation of links between generations as vectors of its history. Links must therefore be forged between the different members of the family. For this, family reproduction strategies are necessary (Bourdieu, 1994), including the distribution of roles and assets between direct descendants and extended kinship, if necessary, with the understanding that assets are also links (Gotman, 1988). Thus, a status is assigned to each family member, such as the one of successor at the head of the FB. The latter is often attributed to the elder. Women are more often assigned the role of liaison agents (Rosenthal, 1985).

Tensions Between a Duty of Obedience and an Ability to Go Beyond It

How much freedom do women then have to choose one of these four roles and, in particular, the one of leader? Are these women totally subject to the power of domination of men in the family or more broadly to the power of control of the family, or do they have a degree of freedom?

Accepting the role of steward stems from the power of domination exercised by men over their wives. The same is true for the role of governess. Although she has an expanded role and takes part in the company's strategic choices, she is nonetheless invisible. Acceptance of such situations reflects submission to the men in the family, especially to the husband. The family has reached a sufficiently strong level of institutionalisation for the situation to become routine. It is then 'normal' for these women, whether they are wives or widows, to agree to play one of these two roles. It is natural, for example, to give up one's position as a widowed leader to one of your sons when he is 'ready' to replace you. By agreeing to relinquish their place, these widowed leaders are made invisible by becoming governesses. While women heirs-managers have prepared themselves to take over the management of the company by acquiring knowledge and experience, but also a certain legitimacy by completing a fairly advanced education and by holding a management position for a few years, they sometimes agree to give up their place to a brother-in-law, for example. Indeed, it is not uncommon for the son-in-law to be preferred to the daughter as a successor (Fonrouge, 2012). We find the idea developed by Rancière (1995), according to which the institution assigns a status to its members based on gender. The memory of the family to which the FB is linked is associated to men in a visible and valued way, as successors (Fonrouge, 2012), and to women in an invisible and well-valued way as liaison agents. We see this as the materialisation of the *Homo Memor* concept. In the name of family reproduction (Bourdieu, 1994), by accepting these roles, women are subject to men's power of domination, which is part of the family's power of control over both men as leaders and women as stewards, governesses and managers.

When women accept leadership roles, can this be considered a decision of their own or as obedience to the family as an institution? A first level of analysis suggests that these women are motivated by the desire to pass on a heritage (and an inheritance) to their heirs, deliberately becoming conveyors and key in the business transfer when it is faced with a crisis of governance. The power of these women in moments of FB governance crisis is very important. To use the expression of Jacques-Jouvenot and Droz (2015), they can make and break the family business in particular by accepting, or not, to take over the business. This configuration makes these women major actors of the strategic management of the FB when a governance crisis occurs and no men are ready and able to run the FB.

A second level of analysis shows there is tension between a duty of obedience to an institution and the ability to overcome gender stereotypes. In taking power, perhaps for the family but also for themselves, they become paradoxical leaders/governesses echoing Scott's Paradoxical Citizen (1998). The power that these women exercise, whether formally or informally, deliberately or not, is essentially in the name of the family.

There are reasons to think that the level of institutionalisation of the FB family is such that it has reached the stage of internalisation (Berger and Luckmann, 1967). This would mean that women are, in reality, not subject to men, but to the family itself as an institution, with men playing a dominant role which they exercise not deliberately, but as a response to the demands of family norms. We are faced with a power of control that does not belong to its actors but to the family as an institution, supported by family law, where the fabrication of consent (Burawoy, 1979) influences the different members of the family. Practically, this translates into the acceptance of male heirs, if there are suitable men in the family, to take over the FB when the previous generation hands it over, and otherwise, by default, the heiresses and/or wives. Women are thus subject to the power of men who themselves are subject to the power of the family institution. This recoups some of Lawrence's (2008) and also Huault and Leca's (2009) thinking. These authors argue that if the actors can eventually decide by and for themselves, they do so essentially for the institution so that it will survive and thrive. From this perspective, the members of the FB family are assigned a mission to preserve the existing status quo and the family wealth, i.e., the FB, so that in remains in the family control. Thus, when a woman in the family takes over the reins of the FB, it is to keep it within and to perpetuate the family. If she does so, it is less through her power of action or out of free will than by submission to an established order.

Conclusion

The family, and more specifically the patrimonial family, like other institutions (Di Maggio and Powell, 1983, 1991), creates stability in the life of the FB because it submits its members to its control, especially through the process of the factory of consent (Burawoy, 1979), implying the domination of men over women.

A woman who takes over the management of the FB, or at least who agrees to formally take part in it, does so to ensure endogenous transmission: she plays the role of a conveyor of the family wealth. If some researchers, such as Nelson and Constantinidis (2017), interpret it as sign of the growing power of women within the FB, we see it as a reinforcement of gender stereotypes. By agreeing to take an active part in the FB transfer when male members are not available to do so, they guarantee stability both for the family and the business.

Through the prism of NSI, we have highlighted how intertwined the family and the FB are. As an avenue for future research, we would like to investigate FBs and families in other countries so as to refine our typology.

References

Berger, P.L. and Luckmann, T. (1967). *The social construction of reality: a treatise in the sociology of knowledge*, New York: Anchor.
Bessière, C. and Gollac, S. (2007). "Le silence des pratiques. La question des rapports de genre dans les familles d' indépendants", *Sociétés Représentations*, 24(2), 43–58.
Bessière, C. and Gollac, S. (2014). "Des exploitations agricoles au travers de l'épreuve du divorce, can French farms get over divorces? Class and gender in agriculture", *Sociétés contemporaines*, 96(4), 77–108.

Bourdieu, P. (1993). "À propos de la famille comme catégorie réalisée", *Actes de la Recherche en Sciences Sociales*, 100(1), 32–36.

Bourdieu, P. (1994). "Stratégies de reproduction et modes de domination", *Actes de la recherche en sciences sociales*, 105(1), 3–12.

Bourdieu, P. (1998). *La domination masculine*, Seuil: Points Essais.

Burawoy, M. (1979). *Manufacturing consent: changes in the labor process under monopoly capitalism*, Chicago: University of Chicago Press.

Campopiano, G., De Massis, A., Rinaldi, F.R. and Sciascia, S. (2017). "Women's involvement in family firms: progress and challenges for future research", *Journal of Family Business Strategy*, 8(4), 200–212.

Chua, J.H., Chrisman, J.J. and Sharma, P. (1999). "Defining the family business by behavior", *Entrepreneurship: Theory and Practice*, 23(4), 19–39.

Crutzen, N., Pirnay, F. and Aouni, Z. (2012). *La place des femmes dans les entreprises familiales belges francophones en 2012*, Liège: Ecole de Gestion-Université de Liège.

Curimbaba, F. (2002). "The dynamics of women's roles as family business managers", *Family Business Review*, 15(3), 239–252.

Daumas, J.C. (2015). "L'entreprise au risque de la famille: réflexions d'un historien sur le capitalisme familial (France, 1945–2013)", in D. Jacques-Jouvenot and Y. Droz (Eds.), *Faire et défaire les affaires en famille*, 19–42, Besançon: Presses universitaires de Franche-Comté.

Di Maggio, P.J. and Powell, W.W. (1983). "The iron cage revisited: institutional isomorphism and collective rationality in organizational fields", *American Sociological Review*, 48(3), 147–160.

Di Maggio, P.J. and Powell, W.W. (1991). *Introduction. In the new institutionalism in organizational analysis*, 1–38, Chicago: University of Chicago Press.

Dumas, C. (1998). "Women's pathways to participation and leadership in the family-owned firm", *Family Business Review*, 11(3), 219–228.

Durkheim, E. (1922). *Education et sociologie*, Paris: Presse Universitaire de France.

Fattoum, S. and Byrne, J. (2017). "L'influence du genre dans le choix du successeur en entreprise familiale", *Revue de l'Entrepreneuriat*, 16(3), 229–254.

Fonrouge, C. (2012). "Le recours à un gendre en période de crise: innovation ou forclusion organisationnelle? Jean Barennes chez Bardinet S.A entre 1912 et 1934", *Entreprises et Histoire*, 4(69), 38–48.

Ginalski, S. (2015). *Du capitalisme familial au capitalisme financier?* Neuchatel: Presses universitaires suisses.

Gotman, A. (1988). *Hériter*, Paris: PUF.

Granovetter, M. (1985). "Economic action and social structure: the problem of embeddedness", *American Journal of Sociology*, 91(3), 481–510.

Héritier, F. (1996). *Masculin/féminin: la pensée de la différence*, Paris: Odile Jacob.

Hirigoyen, G. and Villéger, A. (2017). "Le pouvoir dans l'entreprise copreneuriale: Implications théoriques et managériales", *Gestion 2000*, 34(5), 227–248.

Huault, I. and Leca, B. (2009). "Pouvoir: une analyse par les institutions", *Revue française de gestion*, 35(193), 133–149.

Jacques-Jouvenot, D. and Droz, Y. (2015). *Faire et défaire des affaires en famille*, Besançon: Presses universitaires de Franche-Comté.

Jacques-Jouvenot, D. and Schepens, F. (2007). "Transmettre et reprendre une entreprise: de l'Homo? Economicus à l'Homo memor", *Revue du MAUSS*, *29*(1), 377–391.

Jaskiewicz, P. and Dyer, W.G. (2017). "Addressing the elephant in the room: disentangling family heterogeneity to advance family business research", *Family Business Review*, *30*(2), 111–118.

Jimenez, R.M. (2009). "Research on women in family firms current status and future directions", *Family Business Review*, *22*(1), 53–64.

Kergoat, D. (1982). *Les ouvrières*, Paris: Éditions Le Sycomore.

Labardin, P. and Robic, P. (2008). "Épouses et petites entreprises", *Revue française de gestion*, *8*(188–189), 97–117.

Lawrence, T.B. (2008). "Power, Institutions and Organizations", in R. Greenwood, C. Oliver, R. Suddaby and K. Sahlin-Andersson (Eds.), *The Sage handbook of organizational institutionalism*, 170–198, Thousand Oaks, CA: Sage Publications.

Lubinski, C. (2011). "Succession in multi-generational family firms. An exploratory study into the period of anticipatory socialization", *Electronic Journal of Family Business Studies (EJFBS)*, *5*(1–2), 4–25.

Meyer, J.W. and Rowan, B. (1977). "Institutionalized organizations: formal structure as myth and ceremony", *American Journal of Sociology*, *83*(2), 340–363.

Nelson, T. and Constantinidis, C. (2017). "Sex and gender in family business succession research: a review and forward agenda from a social construction perspective", *Family Business Review*, *30*(3), 219–241.

Pfefferkorn, R. and Pereira, I. (2013). "Des rapports de domination aux luttes d'émancipation. Entretien avec Roland Pfefferkom. Propos recueillis par Irène Pereira", *Raison présente*, *185*(1), 17–26.

Quéniart, A. and Hurtubise, R. (2002). "Nouvelles familles, nouveaux défis pour la sociologie de la famille", *Sociologie et sociétés*, *30*(1), 133–143.

Rancière, J. (1995). *La mésentente, Politique et Philosophie*, Paris: Galilée.

Robic, P. (2014). "Fêter son anniversaire—une manière, pour l'entreprise familiale, de voir et donner à voir son temps comme une ressource", *In 23ème Conférence Internationale de Management Stratégique—AIMS*, Rennes.

Robic, P. (2017). *Le management stratégique des PME et ETI familiales Une histoire de trajectoires individuelles et collectives entre rupture et continuité*, Université Nantes: Note de synthèse des activités de recherche en vue du diplôme d'Habilitation à Diriger des Recherches.

Robic, P. (2018). "Rôle des femmes à la direction des entreprises familiales: Va-et-vient entre le visible et l'invisible", in B. Michon and N. Dufournaud (Eds.), *Femmes et négoce dans les ports européens Fin du Moyen-Age—XIXe siècle*, 231–248, Brussels: Pour une histoire nouvelle de l'Europe: PERTERLANG.

Rodríguez-Modroño, P., Gálvez-Muñoz, L. and Agenjo-Calderón, A. (2015). "The hidden role of women in family firms. In working papers", *History & Economic Institutions, H&EI 15*(1), 2–23.

Rosenthal, C.J. (1985). "Kinkeeping in the familial division of labor", *Journal of Marriage and the Family*, *47*(4), 965–974.

Roussel, L. (1992). "La famille en Europe occidentale: divergences et convergences", *Population (French Edition)*, *47*(1), 133–152.

Salganicoff, M. (1990). "Women in family businesses: challenges and opportunities", *Family Business Review*, *3*(2), 125–137.

Scott, J.W. (1998). *La citoyenne paradoxale*, Paris: Albin Michel.

Segalen, M. (1993). *Sociologie de la famille*, Paris: Armand Colin.

Tagiuri, R. and Davis, J.A. (1992). "On the goals of successful family companies", *Family Business Review*, 5(1), 4362.

Théry, I. (1996). "Différence des sexes et différence des générations: L'institution familiale en déshérence", *Esprit (1940)*, 227(12), 65–90.

Théry, I. (2007). *Transformations de la famille et "solidarités familiales": questions sur un concept*, Paris: Presses Universitaires de France.

15 Gender and Succession in the Family Business

Christina Constantinidis

This chapter aims to highlight the research work developed for over 20 years in the French-speaking world around topics pertaining to gender and succession in the family business setting. Based on the observation of a certain impenetrability between research communities, we propose state-of-the-art French-speaking research with regard to gender dynamics, which are at the heart of many difficulties and challenges faced during the succession process. This work contains original contributions reflecting a rich and diverse reality anchored in various geographical and cultural contexts, including France and Quebec, but also other regions of the world such as Belgium, Switzerland, Tunisia, Senegal or Cameroun. Findings provide theoretical frameworks and empirical insights on a variety of topics related to gender and succession in family businesses (Missonier and Gundolf, 2017). Through this chapter, we wish to highlight the rich and complex thought that has been developed in the French-speaking world, with the aim to present the most comprehensive portrait possible of research at the intersection of gender studies and family business succession, and to advance the global agenda. In the first section, we reveal the influence of gendered legal, familial and societal environments on family business succession. In the second section, we highlight the gendering of succession from the perspective of different family business actors. Our conclusion stresses the importance for researchers to develop systemic and longitudinal views on gender and family business succession.

Gendered Environments and Family Business Succession

Legal and Regulatory Frameworks

In different parts of the world, family laws have historically treated women and men as non-equals in couples, making it impossible for married women to own, inherit or manage a commercial company. Women's legal subordination to their husband's decisions has set profound roots to spouses' roles in family businesses and to the prevalence of sex- and gender-based criteria in succession choices. The dominant patrilineal inheritance laws have reinforced this state of affairs (Cornet and Constantinidis, 2004; Robic and Antheaume, 2014; Tchékémian, 2014; Bah *et al.*, 2017; Ndami, 2017).

However, legal frameworks have been evolving over the last decades in a number of countries, and women have seen their roles transform in progressive but profound ways. In former colonial countries such as Cameroun or Senegal, for instance, the co-existence of two different legal systems has opened new paths for spouses and daughters in family businesses (Bah *et al.*, 2017; Ndami, 2017). In other contexts, such as France or Belgium, recent laws have created formal statuses for entrepreneurs' spouses, therefore increasing their weight in family businesses, including in terms of transmission choices (Bertaux-Wiame, 2004; Cornet and Constantinidis, 2004; Robic and Antheaume, 2014; Tchékémian, 2014).

The ambition here is not to describe all the laws and regulations that have been influencing family business succession, nor would it be possible to do so. We focus instead on two fascinating, historical examples from different cultural settings—France and Cameroun—to illustrate how the legal background can impact the gendered succession process.

In France, for more than a century, married women have been considered as legally incapacitated adults who could not undertake any juridical act or financial transaction without their husband's authorisation. While the Napoleon Civil Code of 1804 had given equal rights to family daughters and sons in terms of inheritance, and while the sex-based legal commercial incapacity was suppressed since 1893, these legal rights did not apply to married women until 1965. Therefore, before that time, only female widowhood allowed these women to take over the family business. Research work undertaken by Robic and colleagues (Labardin and Robic, 2008; Robic and Antheaume, 2014; Robic *et al.*, 2014) reveals the key role that widows have played over time in multi-generational French family businesses. These women managed their companies until their children were ready to take over, thereby allowing the company to stay under familial control and ensure family business unity and continuity (Robic and Antheaume, 2014).

In the Camerounese Bamiléké society, women have traditionally been fully in charge of the family farm operations and management, due to cultural customs assimilating women's fertility to earth. If women had a formal right of land use, constituting the basis of their economic autonomy, they were, however, considered a part of their husband's property, and could never own the land themselves (Ndami, 2017). During the French colonisation after World War I, large portions of lands were given to Europeans and increasing numbers of forest reserves and coffee plantations were created, reducing the portion of exploitable land available for women. In parallel, the French administration introduced new law regulations to increase control over the lands. From the 1930s, the region experienced strong protests initiated by women, who mainly acted to protect their rights to use the land autonomously. Nowadays, in order to secure their access to land, women have begun to use the French property legislation to acquire ownership of their family farms. The food surplus trade, essentially managed by them, has drastically developed and allows them to accumulate enough financial means through their savings and the organisation of female tontines (Ndami, 2017).

As illustrated by these historical examples, the legal context has a key influence, but it is not sufficient to grasp the complex gendered processes pertaining to family business succession. Changes in legal frameworks were accompanied by changes in women's position within couples and families, with a disruption in gender social relations and a restructuring of traditional family models.

Family Models and Women's Roles

The rise of the nuclear family as a model and the individualisation of societies are main drivers of transformation in terms of family business succession. In Western societies, dual-career couples have gradually become the norm, with women gaining independence with regard to enlarged family systems in which they were previously jointly in charge of multi-generational family needs. In parallel, the position women wish and can occupy in the public and economic spheres is changing too, leading to their emancipation within the couple and the family, and increasing participation in the labour market. These familial and societal trends have profoundly influenced transmission processes in family firms, in particular with regard to daughters' and spouses' roles.

The ways these influences take place, however, largely depends on the geographical locations and social groups under consideration. Studies reveal specific realities pertaining to distinct social groups, with particular meanings attached to the 'family business', where individuals' roles are imbued with the specific economic, social and cultural history of each of these microcosms. For instance, the context of family business succession in agricultural and artisanal sectors has been largely documented in the French-speaking literature, given the economic historical predominance of these sectors in France (Bessière, 2004; Cardon, 2004; Gollac, 2005, 2013; Tchékémian, 2014), Quebec (Richer and St-Cyr, 1995; Dumas *et al.*, 1996; Richer *et al.*, 2004) and other French-speaking contexts (e.g., Gillet and Jacques-Jouvenot, 2004 in Switzerland; or Ndami, 2017 in Cameroun). These sectors have encountered major legal and socio-cultural transformations, drastically reshaping rural family business models.

French agriculture, for example, was legally defined as a 'familial activity' since World War II. It was organised into small units of production called *'maisonnées'*—family groups constituted of multiple generations living together on the farm (Bessière, 2004; Tchékémian, 2014). The same type of configuration could be found in other countries (e.g., Quebec, Switzerland) and sectors (e.g., small artisanal businesses) (Dumas *et al.*, 1996; Gollac, 2005; Droz, 2017). This logic of *'maisonnée'* was characterised by geographic and emotional proximity of family members, relations based on solidarity and a common vision about the family business continuity. This enabled families to make difficult decisions regarding the division of responsibilities between family members, the successor choice or the division of assets between siblings collectively, even in cases where these decisions could be perceived as unequal between spouses or siblings (Bessière, 2004; Gollac, 2005; Tchékémian, 2014; Droz, 2017).

In the 1960s, a law defined agriculture as a 'conjugal activity' in France, marking a turning point. This initiated a progressive but steady movement towards the nuclearisation of the family model and the autonomisation of couples, mirroring urban families. Intergenerational tensions arose around key decisions and activities, such as the installation of the new-generation couple in a detached house, the organisation of activities involving different generations and the perceived engagement of young spouses in the family farm (Bessière, 2004). More women also began to work as salaried employees outside the farm, questioning traditional norms and reorganising family gender relationships (Bessière, 2004; Cardon, 2004; Gollac, 2005; Tchékémian, 2014). If women gained financial independence, their increasing autonomisation also took place in a context where family business continuity (mainly though male inheritance) was a key priority (see Chapter 16, Missonier, Jaouen and Albert, this volume). Therefore, women's emancipation can also be understood as a way to lower the financial burden for family businesses and ensure their long-term survival especially in difficult economic times (Bessière, 2004; Cardon, 2004).

Similar trends are observed in the context of artisanal businesses, where the craftsman traditionally needed his wife by his side to create and run the business. The modern view on gender social relations in couples and families, essentially carried by the young generation of women (see Chapter 17, Deschamps and Thévenard-Puthod, this volume), enters in tension with the traditional, masculine view related to the artisanal job, and forms the basis of important social changes (Bertaux-Wiame, 2004; Gollac, 2005; Tchékémian, 2014). The reality is very different in other cultural settings. Bah *et al.* (2017) investigated family business succession in Senegal, where polygamist families coexist with monogamist ones. They highlight the extreme complexity of the succession process in polygamist families due to the rivalry between spouses as well as between siblings, often threatening the survival of the business itself (Bah *et al.*, 2017).

The Gendering of Succession by Family Business Actors

The Wives' Key Roles

The spousal dimension of family business succession, which is often overlooked in the literature, is highlighted in French-speaking research and helps to render wives' hidden management visible. Indeed, women's personal journeys—as daughters, spouses, mothers, employees and/or co-managers—influence the way they conceive their children's future, in particular with regard to the latter's professional careers inside or outside the family business. Three distinct women's personal trajectories can be identified, with different dynamics in terms of gender and business transmission.

Some spouses are formally identified as employees or partners from the business creation or take over (Bertaux-Wiame, 2004; Cardon, 2004; Gillet and Jacques-Jouvenot, 2004; Tchékémian, 2014; Droz, 2017; Fattoum and Byrne, 2017). However, in practice, women's and men's choices take place in an environment where gender inequalities exist as they regard access to salaried employment. In short, men are expected to develop their career while women are seen as devoted to the family project first, narrowing their professional options. Over the years, these spouses become difficult to replace by salaried employees, and cannot leave the firm without putting the couple, family and business at risk.

Other spouses remain at home and take care of all domestic and family tasks (Bertaux-Wiame, 2004; Cardon, 2004; Tchékémian, 2014; Fattoum and Byrne, 2017). Despite this traditional gender division of work, women still participate to the family business management (i.e., accounting, administrative tasks, staff management and customer relations). This informal and flexible engagement is crucial for business survival, especially in the first years. When the business develops, these women are often excluded from the operational management, while they are also marginalised from the labour market due to the non-recognition of their professional experience.

Finally, some spouses work as employees outside the family business (Bertaux-Wiame, 2004; Cardon, 2004; Fattoum and Byrne, 2017). This situation cannot be understood in terms of women's emancipation only, as it also derives from the need for a stable revenue to sustain the family business continuity. Spouses are also often expected to take charge of the family and domestic tasks as well as to eventually help their husbands with business activities. At some point, these women might quit their jobs to develop new branches of activities within the family business. This decision takes place in the broader family business project, with the transmission to children in mind.

In all cases, entrepreneurs' spouses develop strong feelings and expectations with regard to how their children position *vis-a-vis* the family business. Women who have sacrificed their own careers to support their husband tend to push their children out of the family business in order for them to achieve a better social and professional position. Children might therefore receive contradictory injunctions, being torn between two different wishes: the desire to transmit the business to the next generation (usually expressed by the father) and the wish to see children develop professionally and socially outside the business (usually expressed by the mother). In contrast, wives who have had the opportunity to occupy a formal, recognised position, will rather be keen to transmit what they have contributed to build to the next generation. In that case, parents achieve a consensus more easily, and the transmission process is smoother and better-prepared.

Spouses finally play a key role for family business survival and continuity when their husband dies (Robic and Antheaume, 2014; Cornut, 2017). Robic and Antheaume (2014) reviewed hundreds of cases from the 17th century to show the importance of this phenomenon over the years. Their study reveals three mechanisms leading widows to take over the family business. First, through their hidden managerial position as spouses, widows have acquired key business knowledge and skills, and have practiced the family business power dynamics for years. They hence appear as legitimate, 'natural' successors. Second, widows are driven by their wish to ensure family business continuity, and transmit it to the next generation as harmoniously as possible. Therefore, they play a 'link' role between generations, taking the business over temporarily to allow time for the successor to prepare and to smoothen eventual family conflicts. Third, their choice is also related to economic factors, as the family business is a way of earning their life in a position they know well (Robic and Antheaume, 2014).

Family Business Owners

Gender dynamics influence family business succession from the owners' perspective, in terms of successor choice and regarding predecessor-successor relationships. In terms of successor choice and preparation, the father, owner and manager of the family business, often has a strong wish to see his son pursue what he has built and developed for many years. Therefore, he will tend to put pressure on his son, making him understand (intentionally or not) that it is his moral duty or obligation to take over the business. Therefore, the relationships between fathers and sons—between predecessors and successors—often oscillate between collaboration and conflict. On the one hand, the father is proud of his son, gives him advice and trusts him to take on responsibilities in the business;

on the other hand, he tends to remain in command and controls his son's decisions and actions, leading to power struggles and conflicts (Fattoum and Byrne, 2017).

Gender dynamics appear to be different for male compared to female owners (Cadieux, 1999). Women entrepreneurs' journeys in a historically and culturally masculine world might be an explanation (Cadieux *et al.*, 2002). In terms of successor choice, women owners tend to favour daughters as future successors, contrary to men who have a bias towards their sons (Gollac, 2013). Other questions regarding succession from the women owners' perspective are related to: how they live with the loss of their company given their propensity to see professional and private spheres as strongly interconnected, how the mother-child relationship reflects in the predecessor-successor relationship during the different stages of succession, and how women manage family tensions and conflicts arising during succession given their tendency to preserve family harmony (Cadieux *et al.*, 2002; Koffi *et al.*, 2005).

The study of Koffi and Lorrain (2011) highlights five specific behaviours deployed by women owners in terms of succession management. Their findings are based on in-depth case studies of successful mother-son and mother-daughter succession processes in family businesses in Quebec. First, they show that women owners have an excellent relationship with their child, which they take as a basis to develop a trustworthy predecessor-successor relationship. This trust is reflected in their actions: they give responsibilities very early in the process, encourage initiatives and changes, accept mistakes, and demonstrate their respect and pride publicly. Second, women predecessors support the successor's learning process, not only in regards to technical skills, but also in terms of critical spirit and learning capacities. Third, female predecessors tend to collaborate and communicate a lot with their son or daughter along the succession process. They have a participative and collegial management style, integrating work and family. Fourth, women demonstrate an empathetic, 'maternal' leadership style; and fifth, they try to be a model and inspire their successor in order to transmit their vision (Koffi and Lorrain, 2011).

These comparisons between male and female owners' preferences in terms of gender mask a more complex reality, however. First, gender is not a binary concept, differentiating between men and women, or even between masculinity and femininity. Instead, there are multiple masculinities and femininities that can be performed by both women and men. Hegemonic masculinity is the historical, traditional masculinity, valorised in a given society, but it is only one type among many others. Therefore, in family businesses, sons who do not conform with the standards of hegemonic masculinity might be excluded from family business management, while daughters who exert those characteristics might be identified as suitable successors (Fattoum and Byrne, 2017). For example, Bah *et al.* (2017) analysed the case study of a Senegalese family business where the founder, aged 62, chose his third-born daughter to take over the business, in contrast with the dominant family and societal culture that favours sons in terms of succession in Senegal. He and his wife believed that their daughter had the necessary rigor in business management, the ability to manage teams and a strong legitimacy among employees, which are usually perceived as masculine attributes.

Next-Generation Members

A number of firm founders prefer to transmit the business to one child (often the oldest son) and to give compensation to the other siblings as a way to preserve the unity and continuity of the family business (Gollac, 2005, 2013). Supporting the international literature, sons are more likely to be identified as family business successors in France (Bayad and Barbot, 2002; Gollac, 2013; Fattoum and Byrne, 2017), Quebec (Richer and St-Cyr, 1995; Dumas *et al.*, 1996) and other geographical contexts (Gillet and Jacques-Jouvenot, 2004; Constantinidis, 2010; Bah *et al.*, 2017).

The gendered socialisation of sons and daughters has been mobilised as a key explanation of daughters' under-representation in successor roles. The family business constitutes an inequitable social structure in terms of gender, where the 'successor' role is symbolically representing the whole family group in terms of social status, and culturally perceived as masculine (Bessière, 2004; Gollac, 2013). Hence, sons are often socialised from a young age to the family business, and receive adequate support and preparation for succession. Daughters, in contrast, are not perceived as potential successors, and do not receive the same levels of socialisation and preparation with regard to family business leadership (Constantinidis, 2010; Gollac, 2013; Fattoum and Byrne, 2017). They are even depicted as in need of protection from the stress and conflicts inherent to family business management (Fattoum and Byrne, 2017).

Another explanatory factor is the prevalent patriarchal social system in family businesses, and its overarching male primogeniture practice (Dumas *et al.*, 1996; Gollac, 2013; Fattoum and Byrne, 2017). Family businesses conceived as patriarchal systems are seen as 'masculine' worlds, where the most valued characteristics are those relating to hegemonic masculinity (e.g., authority, strength, competition), at the expense of femininity and other forms of masculinity. Therefore, particularly in some sectors, sons are 'naturally' perceived as holding the necessary or adequate characteristics to take over the business (Gollac, 2013; Fattoum and Byrne, 2017). On the contrary, in this 'men's world', daughters (and sons exerting different forms of masculinities) are not expected to hold those necessary attributes, and are therefore excluded from the business successor and management roles, reproducing the existing gender inequality in terms of successor choice (Fattoum and Byrne, 2017).

Patriarchy as a gendered system is not immovable, as it is co-created by family actors through their daily interactions unfolding over time. Individuals collectively and discursively produce a gendered successor identity, which can change and evolve in the long run (Fattoum and Byrne, 2017). Daughters' and sons' individual gendered identities therefore evolve and develop in relation with the other family members and the family system. The study of Constantinidis (2010) reveals the influence of the family context on the development of daughters' gender and successor identities along the succession process, distinguishing between two cases, depending of the presence or absence of a brother.

When a brother is present, the daughter experiences no pressure to take the family business over. She might either display affective commitment (enjoying to work inside the business), calculative commitment (due to the flexibility provided by the family business), normative commitment (if she feels morally obliged to support the family) or imperative commitment (if she perceives a lack of competence to work outside the family business) (Sharma and Irving, 2005). If the brother quits, there is a turning point in the daughter's positioning *vis-à-vis* the family business: daughters who were affectively committed see that event as an opportunity (calculative commitment), whereas daughters who experienced a calculative commitment feel morally obliged to take over the company to ensure its continuity (normative commitment) (Constantinidis, 2010). When there is no brother in the family, the daughter is likely to be identified as the potential successor sooner in the process, and is therefore prepared to take over the business from an earlier age (Constantinidis, 2010; Gollac, 2013; Fattoum and Byrne, 2017). The evolution of her commitment and positioning in the family business is smoother and more 'linear' than in the first case. Daughters who have a normative or imperative commitment gradually understand the opportunities that the family business can offer (calculative commitment), and finally become more emotionally attached to it during the last succession stages (affective commitment) (Constantinidis, 2010).

Successoral Teams

Whereas most studies focus on contexts where the family business is taken over by one successor only, some authors have explored the specific dynamics of succession when multiple successors are involved (Deschamps and Cisneros, 2012; Cisneros and Deschamps, 2013; Deschamps *et al.*, 2014; Robic *et al.*, 2014; Thévenard-Puthod *et al.*, 2014).

This research work has covered different contexts: in terms of sex and gender composition, family and non-family successoral arrangements, and ownership versus management transfers.

Gender dynamics play a role in the motivations to form a successoral team in the first place. For example, in a case study explored by Thévenard-Puthod *et al.* (2014), the decision to have a mixed team of former salaried employees with the owner's daughter was driven by the owner's wife. The latter indeed wished to retire, and wanted her daughter to replace her in the family business in order to ensure family continuity. In another case, the motivation to transmit the business to the son and to one former employee was a preference of the owner's wife, who wished to give her son the possibility to reconcile his professional and private life (Thévenard-Puthod *et al.*, 2014).

In other cases, the motivation to constitute successoral teams instead of a unique successor is driven by the company size and complexity. Through the historical study of a large, fifth-generation family business, Robic *et al.* (2014) reveal that the firm development led to a growing complexity of the succession process, involving an increasing number of family members over time. In consequence, the family decided to formalise the decision-making process in order to choose the next-generation team of managers between the multiple family candidates while avoiding family tensions and conflicts. The selection criteria combined tradition—through the application of the male primogeniture rule—and competence, through a thorough selection process. Therefore, female members of the family were excluded from the process until the fifth generation. Given the socio-cultural context at that time, women were indeed seen first as spouses, mothers and daughters, and were expected to take care of the household and domestic responsibilities. The only exception was a widow of the third generation, who was included in the successoral team on a temporary basis until her sons were ready to integrate into the management team (Robic *et al.*, 2014). At the fifth generation, influenced by the more egalitarian culture and career aspirations of young generations of men and women, the family business changed the rules. The new vision was to select and prepare the best possible mixed team of male and female successors, based on their complementary competences and their interest in the family business (Robic *et al.*, 2014).

Even if families generally evolve towards more egalitarian models, it should be noted that unequal processes are still very present in family businesses. For example, whereas French law imposes equality between siblings in terms of inheritance, many families underestimate the family business assets on purpose in order to prevent their successor heir, the oldest son, to pay too much financial compensation to his female siblings (Gollac, 2017). In terms of leadership, successoral teams might also encounter difficulties related to the existing differences between team members, in terms of experiences and profiles, including in regards to gender (especially in sectors of activity traditionally perceived as masculine (Deschamps and Cisneros, 2012; Thévenard-Puthod *et al.*, 2014).

Conclusion

Research work undertaken in the French-speaking community points to the necessity to consider the temporal and spatial contexts when exploring women's and men's positions and roles in the family business succession processes. The rich descriptions and understandings provided also draw attention to the existence of multiple gender forces at play. Legal, social and family trends influence gender dynamics in family businesses, and represent the moving landscape where the succession process takes place. The strengthening of women's rights, the rise and erosion of the nuclear family as a model, the changing gender power relations in couples, the individualisation of professional careers and women's increasing participation in the labour market are some of the key trends that have changed the ways spouses and daughters have been engaging with family businesses. This literature review has also revealed the key role played by gender dynamics in terms of successor choice and preparation, family relationships during and after succession, and implementation of the different succession stages. Beyond enriching our understanding of women's and men's realities in the family business setting, it calls on researchers to adopt systemic and longitudinal perspectives to approach the succession process. We conclude this chapter by highlighting some directions for future research.

First, it appears crucial to address the systemic nature of individual decisions and actions regarding the family business succession process. Studies might focus on how women's succession choices are influenced by their embedded family and professional statuses enacted through a diverse set of roles, including consideration for more or less visible and more or less formal roles, both in the family and the business circles (e.g., as both wives, daughters, mothers, counsellors, leaders). It would be meaningful to explore the intertwining of women's individual choices with other key actors' choices (e.g., their husbands, fathers, children, managers, employees), or with regard to the family vision and business strategic directions. Investigating the impact of legal and regulatory frameworks would also offer a fruitful line of research. For instance, with regard to the French case, the 1982 and 2002 laws relating to the status of entrepreneurs' spouses guarantee their social protection but do not make their remuneration compulsory. Therefore, though formally recognising women's roles in the family business, they also paradoxically 'enclose' them in a voluntary support role. Undertaking comparative studies around these topics could be particularly valuable (e.g., comparing French laws versus German laws).

Second, we need studies adopting a longitudinal perspective to consider the evolution of women's and men's statuses and roles over time, and to reveal how their accumulated experiences influence the choices in terms of family business transmission. For example, women's positioning with regard to business transmission can hardly be studied as disconnected from their past experiences, and research might explore to what extent their choices reflect their personal life path. How their multiple identities and lived experiences—as daughters, wives, mothers, successors and co-managers—lead women to reproduce, change or break the family tradition when the transmission takes place also constitutes an interesting research question. It would also be valuable to address the ways gender forces during succession affect the sustainability of family businesses, but also the interwoven trajectories of women and men themselves. Finally, researchers might dig into historical data in order to highlight the progressive transformation of women's and men's roles in family businesses, in relation with the evolution of their regional or national contexts in terms of laws and policies, family models and functions, and societal values and practices influencing succession processes.

References

Bah, T., Boussaguet, S., de Freyman, J., Ndione, L.C. and St-Pierre, J. (2017). "La transmission des entreprises familiales au Sénégal: quelles spécificités culturelles?" *Revue Internationale PME*, 30(3–4), 127–161.

Bayad, M. and Barbot, M.C. (2002). *Proposition d'un modèle de succession dans les PME familiales: étude de cas exploratoire de la relation père-fille*, Montréal: 6ème CIFEPME.

Bertaux-Wiame, I. (2004). "Devenir indépendant, une affaire de couple", *Cahiers du Genre*, 37(2), 13–40.

Bessière, C. (2004). "Vaut mieux qu'elle travaille à l'extérieur! Enjeux du travail salarié des femmes d'agriculteurs dans les exploitations familiales", *Cahiers du Genre*, 37(2), 93–114.

Cadieux, L. (1999). *La succession en entreprise familiale: analyse du processus dans le cas de quatre entreprises manufacturières fondées par des femmes*, PhD Thesis, University of Quebec in Trois-Rivières (UQTR), Trois-Rivières.

Cadieux, L., Lorrain, J. and Hugron, P. (2002). "La succession dans les entreprises familiales dirigées par les femmes: une problématique en quête de chercheurs", *Revue Internationale PME*, 15(1), 115–130.

Cardon, P. (2004). "Histoires de femmes, histoires de fermes", *Cahiers du Genre*, 37(2), 131–153.

Cisneros, L. and Deschamps, B. (2013). "Comment transmettre l'entreprise familiale à plusieurs enfants?" *Gestion*, 38(4), 82–89.

Constantinidis, C. (2010). "Entreprise familiale et genre: Les enjeux de la succession pour les filles", *Revue Française de Gestion*, 200(1), 143–159.

Cornet, A. and Constantinidis, C. (2004). "Entreprendre au féminin: Une réalité multiple et des attentes différenciées", *Revue Française de Gestion*, *151*(4), 191–204.

Cornut, J. (2017). "Implications féminines dans l'entrepreneuriat militaire familial en Suisse romande (XVIIe-XVIIIe siècles)", *Genre & Histoire*, *19*.

Deschamps, B. and Cisneros, L. (2012). "Co-leadership en succession familiale: un partage à définir", *Entreprendre & Innover*, *14*(2), 49–57.

Deschamps, B., Cisneros, L. and Barès, F. (2014). "PME familiales québécoises: impact des parties prenantes externes à la famille dans les co-successions en fratrie", *Management International*, *18*(4), 151–163.

Droz, Y. (2017). "Amour, famille et entreprise: la transmission du patrimoine au sein de l'entreprise familiale", *Recherches Familiales*, *14*(1), 9–22.

Dumas, C., Dupuis, J.P., Richer, F., St-Cyr, L. and Fortin, A. (1996). "La relève agricole au Québec, une affaire de fils . . . et de filles", *Recherches Sociographiques*, *37*(1), 39–68.

Fattoum, S. and Byrne, J. (2017). "L'influence du genre dans le choix du successeur en entreprise familiale", *Revue de l'Entrepreneuriat*, *16*(3), 229–254.

Gillet, M. and Jacques-Jouvenot, D. (2004). "La dépendance dans l'indépendance", *Cahiers du Genre*, *37*(2), 171–190.

Gollac, S. (2005). "Faire ses partages", *Terrain: Anthropologie & Sciences humaines*, *45*, 113–124.

Gollac, S. (2013). "Les ambiguïtés de l'aînesse masculine: Transferts patrimoniaux et transmission du statut social de génération en génération", *Revue Française de Sociologie*, *54*(4), 709–740.

Gollac, S. (2017). "Le genre caché de la propriété dans la France contemporaine", *Cahiers du Genre*, *62*(1), 43–59.

Koffi, V. and Lorrain, J. (2011). "Comment des femmes à la tête de PME réussissent-elles leur succession?" *Gestion*, *36*(1), 35–40.

Koffi, V., Lorrain, J. and Raymond, L. (2005). "L'intégration du successeur dans l'équipe de gestion des entreprises familiales: le cas des femmes chefs d'entreprise", *Revue Internationale PME*, *18*(3–4), 73–92.

Labardin, P. and Robic, P. (2008). "Épouses et petites entreprises*: Permanence du XVIIIe au XXe siècle", *Revue Française de Gestion*, *34*(188–189), 97–117.

Missonier, A. and Gundolf, K. (2017). "L'entreprise familiale: état et perspectives de la recherche francophone", *Finance Contrôle Stratégie*, *20*(2).

Ndami, C. (2017). "Les agricultrices et la propriété foncière en pays bamiléké (Cameroun). Un droit foncier coutumier en tension", *Cahiers du Genre*, *62*(1), 119–139.

Richer, F. and St-Cyr, L. (1995). "La transmission des exploitations agricoles familiales: le cas des filles d'agricultrices et d'agriculteurs", *Recherches Féministes*, *8*(2), 91–105.

Richer, F., St-Cyr, L. and Lambaraa, Y. (2004). "La transmission d'entreprise au Québec: des stratégies diversifiées", *Gestion*, *29*(3), 95–102.

Robic, P. and Antheaume, N. (2014). "La veuve: une partie prenante méconnue dans la transmission des entreprises familiales", *Management International*, *18*(4), 175–190.

Robic, P., Barbelivien, D. and Antheaume, N. (2014). "La fabrique de l'entrepreneur familial. Comment des héritiers deviennent entrepreneurs et reprennent la direction d'une entreprise familiale", *Revue de l'Entrepreneuriat*, *13*(3), 25–50.

Sharma, P. and Irving, P.G. (2005). "Four bases of family business successor commitment: antecedents and consequences", *Entrepreneurship Theory & Practice*, 29(1), 13–33.

Tchékémian, A. (2014). "Être agricultrice en France au XXIe siècle: La reconnaissance du statut d'exploitante agricole", *Etudes Rurales*, 193, 61–77.

Thévenard-Puthod, C., Picard, C. and Chollet, B. (2014). "Formation et difficultés de fonctionnement des équipes successorales: une analyse fondée sur deux études de cas exploratoires et longitudinales", *Management International*, 18(4), 131–150.

16 Daughters

Invisible Heroes of Family Businesses?

*Audrey Missonier, Annabelle Jaouen
and Béatrice Albert*

Family businesses (FBs) make up a sizeable portion of the European economy, yet only 30% of these firms survive beyond the first generation (Daspit *et al.*, 2016). Previous research has shown that intergenerational successions can fail for many reasons, not just unclear succession plans, incompetent or unprepared successors and family rivalries, but also a host of emotional, affective and relational issues that may surge to the fore (Sharma *et al.*, 2003; Hytti *et al.*, 2016). In 1998, Nelton noted that the best successors in terms of firm survival and performance are daughters. The author predicts that by 2023, a third of American family businesses will be managed by women. Bernard *et al.* (2013) recall that according to the report published by Women Equity Partners, out of 40,000 French companies, companies run by women have a growth rate significantly higher than companies run by men. Over 30% of American FBs say they may have a woman successor in the future (MassMutual, 2007). Yet, most of the research on FB transmissions has been focused on transmissions from fathers to their sons. Only a few studies have investigated cases of succession by women (Smythe and Sardeshmukh, 2013) (and see Chapter 14, Robic, this volume; and Chapter 17, Deschamps and Thévenard-Puthod, this volume).

The first and foremost reason is that when a business owner is thinking of a successor, the son is the natural first choice (Dumas *et al.*, 1995; Keating and Little, 1997), as daughters have traditionally been invisible in this context (Cole, 1997; Vera and Dean, 2005; Jimenez, 2009) except in crisis situations where the founder has no other choice. Another reason is that daughters often do not feel they are legitimate successors and experience difficulties in having their managerial skills recognised within the company, thus preferring to first prove themselves elsewhere (Dumas *et al.*, 1995; Dumas, 1998). These perceptions restrict the possibilities of succession, as the daughters tend to see themselves as merely having a 'job' in the FB rather than imagining themselves someday taking over. When they do become successors, it is likely to have been a progressive process, whereas sons are more likely to have been designated from the start (Dumas, 1998).

The sustainability of a FB is based on the father's ability to hand over power, ownership, control and leadership to the next generation, and the quality of the father-daughter relationship (respect, understanding and collaborative behaviour) is a factor that can facilitate this transfer and thus the transmission (Smythe and Sardeshmukh, 2013). In 1990, Dumas noted that father-daughter succession should be observed from an emotional point of view. Yet research that explicitly examines this parameter, although increasing, is still rare (Sharma *et al.*, 2003; Smythe and Sardeshmukh, 2013; Halkias *et al.*, 2016; Hytti *et al.*, 2016).

Therefore, the main objective of this chapter is to examine the relationship between the father-predecessor and his daughter-successor during FB transfer. The research question is the following: What elements in the father-daughter relationship favour the transmission of the FB?

The Father-Daughter Relationship in FB Succession

Academic literature on women and FB succession has, for the most part, focused on women as owners or transmitters (Cole, 1997; Cadieux *et al.*, 2002), wives (Jimenez, 2009) or widows (Robic and Antheaume, 2014). Studies of them as successors were rare until the late 1990s and have been increasing since the mid-2000s. These studies have tended to focus on the legitimacy and visibility of these women in managerial positions (Keating and Little, 1997; Vera and Dean, 2005; Jimenez, 2009), the conditions of succession (Dumas, 1998), intercultural perspectives (Halkias *et al.*, 2016) and the impact of gender on their motivations (Hartung *et al.*, 2005) (see Chapter 15, Constantinidis, this volume). Few have specifically focused on the father-daughter relationship as a parameter that can influence the transmission process (Dumas, 1990, 1992; Haberman and Danes, 2007; Smythe and Sardeshmukh, 2013).

The Daughter's Self-Assertion, Legitimation and Identity Construction

Transmission can bring to the fore very powerful emotional issues, such as feelings of jealousy or rivalry, complex family relationships, the search for self-respect, etc. (Hytti *et al.*, 2016). As the father's identity is often so tied up with the business that he *is* the business (Dumas, 1992), when the daughter tries to assert herself in the business, she finds that she is also asserting herself to her father.

Assertiveness is difficult and complex for daughters (Halkias *et al.*, 2016; Hytti *et al.*, 2016), as they may become successors by default when the son refuses or renounces the succession, or following an unforeseen event (e.g., a death). Yet daughters who commit to succession out of a sense of duty or necessity following the brother's departure are likely to encounter difficulties in managing personnel and relating to the environment (Vera and Dean, 2005). In cases where there are no sons, daughters are brought into the life of the business from the outset and immediately appear as legitimate successors (Vera and Dean, 2005). The daughter's motivations here are emotional (love for the father, need for recognition, love of the job, attachment to the business, desire for continuity).

Several studies have linked the difficulty to the daughter's identity construction (Dumas, 1989; Halkias *et al.*, 2016; Hytti *et al.*, 2016). For the son, identity construction depends on autonomy and differentiation from the father, but for the daughter, it depends more on rapprochement and intimacy with the father (Lawson *et al.*, 2015) than separation. The construction of feminine identity generally involves the relationships with meaningful people (primarily parents) and the notion of interconnection, whereas masculine identity implies individuation and independence (Dumas, 1990). Working in the FB is therefore important for the daughter because it is important for a meaningful person: her father.

The Challenges of Father-Daughter Proximity and Role Confusion

A close collaborative relationship is important for knowledge transfer during the succession (Smythe and Sardeshmukh, 2013). The relationship can nevertheless be sabotaged by conflicts around the changes in the respective roles of father and daughter (Dumas, 1992). For example, the father may fail to clearly define the role he has attributed to his daughter by expecting her to behave like a businesswoman, while considering her (or even treating her) as 'Daddy's little girl' (Dumas, 1989). Such role confusion is problematic for the daughter, as she is never quite sure when she is the employee and when she is the daughter. This not only creates tension, but also makes it difficult for her to establish her identity and build self-confidence and legitimacy (Hollander and Bukowitz, 1990; Vera and Dean, 2005). In addition to her struggles, the father may also be finding it difficult to relinquish control of the FB (Vera and Dean, 2005), as it implies a loss of power (Gundolf *et al.*, 2013) and social and professional legitimacy (Chua *et al.*, 1999).

The collaboration can be successful if the daughter sees her father as a mentor, communicates well with him and/or tends to avoid conflict (Dumas, 1992). However, when taken to an extreme, the tendency to avoid conflict can be counterproductive, with the daughter avoiding crucial discussions about the transmission in order to avoid irritating her father. Hollander and Bukowitz (1990) pointed out that the tendency to 'hide' from one another has a negative impact on communication (conflict avoidance) and the transmission process as a whole.

Smythe and Sardeshmukh (2013) showed that three factors have a positive influence on the relationship between father-transmitter and daughter-successor: the daughter's early socialisation within the FB, good communication between the father and daughter, and a deep understanding of the long shadow cast by the father (founder's shadow, or the inability to let go; Gagnè *et al.*, 2011), all of which facilitate the negotiations for the business transfer. The authors also found that transmission is facilitated when the daughters use the company as a way to strengthen the bond with their fathers. Talking about business is thus a way for them to 'connect' with fathers who have had little time for anything else and who have let the business dominate their lives (Smythe and Sardeshmukh, 2013).

The daughters can also try to improve family relationships on the whole by seeking professional help (Smythe and Sardeshmukh, 2013). The authors noted that the daughters were often engaged in psychotherapy and that this affected both family life and the business. Family-work alignment is important for daughters (Brannon *et al.*, 2013). Therefore, positive emotions that can be transferred from the family to the business improve FB performance under the daughter's leadership, her satisfaction with her status and her relationships with employees (Powell and Eddleston, 2013).

Nevertheless, FB transmission to daughters is still largely under-studied today. Thus, the aim of this chapter is to understand which elements in the father-daughter relationship facilitate the successful succession of a FB.

Case Studies

This article is based on an interpretative phenomenological approach (IPA) with nine daughters and fathers (five daughters and four fathers). Cope (2005) explains that "in literal terms, phenomenology means the 'study or description of phenomena' (Pettit, 1969); where a 'phenomenon' is simply anything that appears or presents itself to someone in consciousness (Moran, 2000)" (Cope, 2005, p. 164). IPA is gaining importance within the issue of barriers to transmission of family firms (Gundolf *et al.*, 2013), but has not yet been applied to the relation between fathers and daughters during the transmission of family firms. The aim of our chapter was to develop a detailed 'phenomenological hermeneutical' conceptualisation of the lived experience of the succession by daughters and fathers, with emphasis on the relationship between them.

The sample consisted of five daughters and four fathers, as one father did not wish to be interviewed. The objective was to identify the relational factors involved in the succession, and we thus observed the successions

Table 16.1 Case Descriptions

	Case 1	Case 2	Case 3	Case 4	Case 5
Activity	Public works/ construction	Public works	Milling	Rental of event equipment	Industry
Founding date	1992	1987	Late 19th	1981	1970
No. employees	300	37	70	9	980
Turnover 2016	> 20 million €	> 4 million €	> 10 million €	> 1 million €	> 140 million €
Reasons for succession	Illness/Tax benefit	Age/Tax benefit/ Ready to retire	Economic/ Transmission to third party	Father's age/ Ready to retire	Father's age/ Need to reassure partners
Status of succession at time of interview	Successfully completed	Successfully completed	Unsuccessful	Successfully completed	Ongoing integration phase
Siblings	Mixed	All sisters	Mixed	All sisters	Mixed
Interviewees	Father Daughter	Father Daughter	Father Daughter	Father Daughter	– Daughter

at different stages. Six to eight is recommended as an appropriate number of participants for a typical IPA study. Table 16.1 details the characteristics of cases and Table 16.2 provides the profiles of the interviewees, who remain anonymous.

Results

Unconscious Preparation of the Daughter From Childhood

From a young age, the daughters were immersed in the FB. 2F explained: "When you're at home, talking with your wife, the way you act with suppliers, all that. She was soaking it up from a young age, kind of like a sponge . . .". They often worked there during the school holidays (2D, 5D), attended staff evenings (5D) and lunches (3D), or went to the FB simply to see their father (4D).

Early socialisation is all the more important and beneficial when the child is a daughter. To spend time with the father, who is often absent from the home, the daughters would go to the FB, even at a very young age. The daughters in cases 4 and 5 confirmed this, essentially indicating that the FB was the bond between them. Drawing closer to the FB is, as Dumas (1992) explained, a way to draw closer to the father and, as Smythe and Sardeshmukh (2013) observed, to connect with him. For Smythe and Sardeshmukh (2013), this early socialisation positively influences the father-transmitter and daughter-successor relationship.

Table 16.2 Daughters' Profiles and Fathers

	Daughter 1 (1D)	Daughter 2 (2D)	Daughter 3 (3D)	Daughter 4 (4D)	Daughter 5 (5D)
Time between daughter's integration and father's departure	1 yr	2 yrs	1 yr	> 10 yrs	Ongoing for last 3 yrs
Siblings	Mixed	All sisters	Mixed	All sisters	Mixed
Daughter's age at succession	32	36	32	44	47
Daughter's original profession	Special education teacher	Management controller outside FB	Specialised lawyer	Restaurant business then door-to-door sales	Accountant outside FB

	Father 1 (1F)	Father 2 (2F)	Father 3 (3F)	Father 4 (4F)	Father 5 (5F)
Father's age at succession	61	61	67	70	74

In case 5, when the daughter was only 12 years old, the father announced: "you'll be taking over the business". This remark strongly affected her and created a duty to become the successor. The daughter felt duty-bound and "constrained" to accept the family business: "My father issued a command, as if it were a crown he was placing on my head! The commitment came not from me but from him" (5D). A strong sense of predestination was planted in her mind very early on. This case confirms the results of Lambrecht and Donckels (2006), who noted that the chosen child-successors often experience the succession as inevitable.

Letting Go to Prepare the Return

In all five cases, the daughters started their professional lives outside of the FB without the intention of taking over the FB one day.

> My father let me choose my career. It wasn't till much later that he asked me to join the family business. . . . I had the time to have a lot of different experiences. It let me prove to myself what I was capable of.
> (5D)

For their fathers, these experiences enhanced their credibility as successors. "I think it's great that they worked elsewhere, that they saw what was out there. That gave them an advantage" (4F). The five daughters had freely chosen their university studies and careers. This feeling of freedom to choose their own future may have encouraged them to initially leave the world of the FB and then to ultimately return. If this is so, the freedom to trace one's own destiny is a factor for success for the future FB transmission. A one daughter expressed it: "unconsciously, taking over the family business was always there. Everything brought me to this point, as if I had to leave in order to come back with my own personality and experience" (5D). This feeling of freedom may thus be part of the preparation for transmission. It contributes to a favourable context as it reinforces the daughter's conviction that her role as successor has not been imposed but freely chosen.

The Transition From a Father-Daughter to an Adult-Adult Relationship

FB transmission from a father to a daughter is marked by trust, which is expressed notably by support, complicity and accompaniment. This trust is what drives the father-daughter relationship towards a relationship between two adults.

In cases 1, 2 and 4, the relationship was based on a filial bond characterised by discreet but deep trust. "I feel legitimate and confident and that's important. We tell each other everything and it works. . . . I've gradually taken over some things, but he's still there when I need him and that's reassuring" (1D). Trust lets the father make room for the successor and vice versa. "I know my daughter well, and that may be why transmission is interesting. She does not necessarily need someone looking over her shoulder, but she needs someone to clear things up for her, which will save her time" (2F). In agreement with Handler's (1991) research, transmission depends on mutual respect between the transmitter and successor, reflected by trust, encouragement, communication and mutual learning.

The fathers were convinced that their daughters would take care of the FB and that they had the capacity to do so. They also accepted their differences. This was not merely a *simple sign of respect*, but a guarantee built on mutual trust. For 1F, 2F and 4F, the trust they felt seemed natural: they knew their daughters well, with their qualities and shortcomings. They were ready to make room for them and then to withdraw. For 1D, 2D and 4D, being recognised as the successor was self-affirming and legitimising. They assumed that "it's the FB and it must be taken care of" (2D). They thus showed their fathers that they were trustworthy.

In case 5, the father has not yet transmitted the FB to his daughter. He announced that he would do so three years ago, but since then, nothing has been done to prepare the process. As she explained:

> I started to take the initiative, making big decisions about, for example, firing someone. At that point, things deteriorated. He eventually supported me on that one, but something was broken. For the staff party, he told me clearly: this is the CEO and me, and there's no room for you. There was nothing I could say. I was encroaching on him and he put me in my place just like when I was little.
>
> (5D)

As noted by Dumas (1989, 1992), the father expected his daughter to behave as a businesswoman, while treating her as a daughter, thus constraining the transmission process

From an Adult-Adult to a Transmitter-Successor Relationship

In cases 2 and 4, the daughters had to impose themselves when dealing with their fathers because *two bosses* was not good for the organisation of the company. The fathers' withdrawal then began. In case 1, the daughter spoke about making changes in management, communications and other aspects as a way to 'appropriate' the company. The fathers could accept that their daughters had different viewpoints because they could acknowledge that, if only because of their prior work experiences, they were different from them.

> It's very important to cut out the interference. I've always thought that two bosses aren't possible. . . . My daughter has had her own life, her own experiences, so she doesn't always think like me and I don't think I know everything.
>
> (2F)

Last, they understand that co-management was detrimental. In cases 1, 2 and 4, the fathers gradually withdrew as their daughters mastered certain aspects of the FB. They felt that their daughters were ready and management responsibility was transferred.

> Little by little, I began to understand how things worked, to have other ideas. Then I suggested them. . . . It's more an adult-adult relationship. Dad has always had a hard time letting go of the fact that I'm his daughter. . . . I think I was his favorite, I was the oldest. But in talking with him, I had to make it very clear that now he has to let me do it.
>
> (2D)

The father-daughter relationships evolved towards greater freedom for the daughters as they became business owner-managers, notably by making the fathers understand that it was time to go. The relationship became a more objective business relationship and transmission could occur. This relational dimension was present in the three cases of successful transmission and was totally absent in the two failed transmissions.

Discussing the Successful Process of FB Transfer From Father to Daughter

The relationship between father and daughter is important to transmission success along four dimensions. The father begins to prepare his daughter to replace him from childhood and accepts that she may first need to develop her own skills outside the company, which enhances his readiness to transmit to her. These two relational dimensions instil trust, closeness and the mutual desire to work together. Then, trust fosters the transition from the father-daughter to an adult-adult relationship, and the rupture of the father-FB-daughter relationship allows the transition from the adult-adult to a transmitter-successor relationship. Table 16.3 highlights some specific issues encountered by the FB when transmitting to daughters.

We also find that four relational dimensions promote transmission. Much of the success is due to the father's groundwork (preparing his daughter and letting her 'leave'). This is in line with Gagnè *et al.* (2011) and Smythe and Sardeshmukh (2013). The contribution of our chapter relies on the last two dimensions, which emphasise the importance of the dynamics of the father-daughter relationship, with each working personally to achieve a certain detachment and change of posture. First, the father has to shift to an adult role (passing from the ego state of the Parent to that of the Adult, according to transactional analysis; Berne, 1977) and second to that of transmitter. This process is marked by his

Table 16.3 Specific Success Factors of FB Transmission to Daughters

Identifying the issues	And replacing them by . . .
The daughter is the second choice	Considering daughter and son as equal
"My little girl" syndrome	Perception of "an adult woman/a manager"
Role confusion	Defined role within the firm
Mutual overprotection/Tendency to hide to protect	Clear and trusted communication
Father as the boss/controller	Father as a mentor
Dependence	Autonomy
Internal tension due to paradoxical injunctions	Self-confidence and legitimacy

distance and progressive detachment from both the FB and his 'father function' in the FB. This dissociation is fundamental to ensure the daughter's legitimation and self-affirmation. He in fact follows the four phases of disengagement described by Cadieux *et al.* (2002): liminality (finding a provisional place in the company), reorganisation of his life (taking on technical functions in the FB or spending more time with leisure activities), acceptance that the successor is the right person and that the FB is in good hands, and distancing.

The daughter has to achieve a certain detachment as well and must reconstruct her identity: she will shift successively from daughter to adult (i.e., from the ego state of the Child to that of the Adult in transactional analysis; Berne, 1977) and then from adult to successor and business owner. She therefore engages in a process of self-affirmation, individuation and appropriation-legitimation of her role as business owner-manager.

The literature indicates that the main factor that facilitates these transitions is trust, as notably recalled by Cadieux *et al.* (2002). This trust is based on the belief that the two parties have reciprocal positive intentions (benevolence, respect, sincerity), with the successor believing that the transmitter has his/her interests at heart and the transmitter believing that the successor has the skills and abilities to lead and sustain the FB. This is also due to the successor's ability to maintain what the transmitter has patiently constructed. Trust thus allows the transmitter to make room for the successor and *vice versa* and, in the father-daughter case, it allows the daughter to fully assume adult status and switch to an adult-adult relationship mode.

Another contribution of this research to academic literature on daughters in FB is the proposition of a 'symbolic patricide': two primordial confrontations between father and daughter (see Figure 16.1) are necessary to put an end to the ambiguity of the succession and thus to the joint reign. This is particularly relevant if the father-daughter relationship has been conflictual and/or the father slows down the succession because of difficulties with detaching (case 5). These confrontations are inevitable and, at a symbolic level, can be said to enact a patricide. The first confrontation occurs when the daughter is able to tell her father "I'm not your 'little girl' anymore, I am an adult and I have the skills to be your successor, recognize me as such". This confrontation effectively allows her to assert herself, which in turn is necessary for the transition to an adult status. It may result in the father's categorical refusal (he maintains his role of father) or to reflection and recognition (he assumes an adult role).

We contend that the second confrontation puts an end to the joint reign in the case of a father who is reluctant to withdraw. The daughter effectively tells the father "I am now taking over the company management; I am fully capable of doing so and you need to withdraw", though of course in a benevolent and respectful way. In case 4, the daughter had

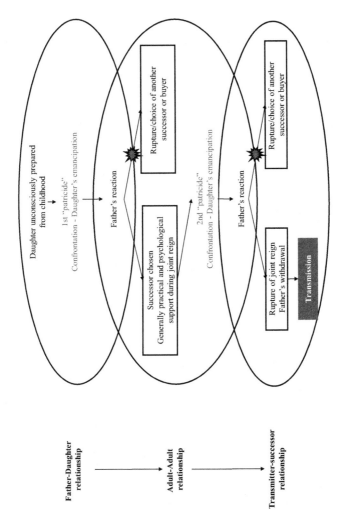

Figure 16.1 Transformation of the Father-Daughter Relationship During the Transmission Process: A Model

Source: Author created

this confrontation: "It was I who insisted: I said that in any case it was now like this and not otherwise". This second patricide made the father understand that the rupture between him and the company is necessary and that it is time to withdraw. All this can only be done after the first symbolic patricide: the daughter must 'kill' her father to become free to be a successor, owner/manager and entrepreneur. This marks her individuation and legitimation in her new function. The break must then be made by the father, signifying the end of their joint reign (which is what the three fathers did in the successful cases). The fathers thus recognise the emancipation and legitimacy of their daughters.

We might further hypothesise that the childhood relationship re-emerges during transmission and that, depending on the case, it can contaminate the transmission process. Confrontation is not easy and it requires courage. Freeing oneself from a relational history, from one's own history, requires taking a big step back and recognising one's fears of abandonment and/or loss of family relations and the FB. If the daughter cannot herself accept the transition from child to adult, the joint reign will never lead to the rupture and the father's withdrawal. The father may not give way to his daughter, instead trying to keep her dependent. The daughter, finding it difficult to emotionally detach, will then find it very difficult to seek his advice, to position herself and to assume her identity as an entrepreneur.

A future study might explore this hypothesis in greater depth by drawing on research in psychology and interviewing professionals who accompany FB transmitters. This would help to refine these theoretical propositions, validate them empirically and thus highlight the stakes of these symbolic elements that nevertheless may determine the process of transmission.

Conclusion

This chapter invites us to look at father-daughter transmission from a relational perspective. This relationship seems to be the key to the success or failure of transmission, with trust being the natural, invisible and fundamental foundation. According to Pieper (2010, p. 29), "psychological antecedents should be taken into account" in studies on FBs, and particularly on the behaviours of its stakeholders. Both actors need to be supported throughout the process. One of the solutions is to provide third-party accompaniment (e.g., psychologist, project manager in a professional union or a specialised consultant) from the daughter's pre-integration of the FB until the father's complete retirement. For the father, the accompaniment might deal with his fears about the transfer, his attachment to the company, and the construction of a conversion project. This might involve calling on theories of ambivalence and mourning to help him to gradually detach from his former power and professional and social status, to trust his successor, to make sense of his new life, and to accept his age and ultimate death. For the daughter, it is essential to work on identity construction, her bond with and dependence on her father, and the self-assertion necessary for legitimisation. She needs to dissociate the character of her father from that of the entrepreneur in her own representations, thus facilitating confrontation and symbolic patricides, key events to move her from one state to the next (child—adult—entrepreneur).

Other stakeholders could also be involved (members of the board of directors, accountants, bankers, friends), as they too can influence the transmitter and the family (Deschamps and Cisneros, 2014). These advisors can thus encourage and facilitate communication between father and daughter, defuse conflicts, clear up misunderstandings and contribute to a better understanding of each other.

References

Bernard, C., Le Moign, C. and Nicolaï, J.P. (2013). *L'entrepreneuriat féminin Document d'étape*, Centre d'Analyse Stratégique, 2013–06. file:///D:/Users/a.missonier/Dropbox/Women-Representation/Women%20representation/dt06-entreprefeminin_editing_05–04versionweb.pdf.

Berne, E. (1977). *Analyse transactionnelle et psychothérapie*, Paris: Petite Bibliothèque Payot.

Brannon, D.L., Wiklund, J. and Haynie, J.M. (2013). "The varying effects of family relationships in entrepreneurial teams", *Entrepreneurship Theory and Practice*, 37(1), 107–132.

Cadieux, L., Lorrain, J. and Hugron, P. (2002). "Succession in women owned family businesses: a case study", *Family Business Review*, 1(15), 17–30.

Chua, J.H., Sharma, P. and Chrisman, J.J. (1999). "Defining the family business by behavior", *Entrepreneurship Theory and Practice*, 23, 19–39.

Cole, P.M. (1997). "Women in family business", *Family Business Review*, 10(4), 353–371.

Cope, J. (2005). "Researching entrepreneurship through phenomenological inquiry. Philosophical and methodological issues", *International Small Business Journal*, 23(2), 163–189.

Deschamps, B. and Cisneros, L. (2014). "Les parties prenantes dans la succession des entreprises familiales: rôle, implications, enjeux", *Management International*, 18(4), 125–130.

Daspit, J.J., Holt, D.T., Chrisman, J.J. and Long, R.G. (2016). "Examining family firm succession from a social exchange perspective. A multiphase, multi-stakeholder review", *Family Business Review*, 29(1), 44–64.

Dumas, C. (1989). "Understanding of father-daughter and father-son dyads in family-owned business", *Family Business Review*, 2(1), 31–46.

Dumas, C. (1990). "Preparing the new CEO: managing the father-daughter succession process in family businesses", *Family Business Review*, 3(2), 169–181.

Dumas, C. (1992). "Integrating the daughter into family business management", *Entrepreneurship: Theory and Practice*, 16(4), 51–56.

Dumas, C. (1998). "Women's pathways to participation and leadership in the family-owned firm", *Family Business Review*, 11(3), 219–228.

Dumas, C., Dupuis, J.P., Richer, F. and St-Cyr, L. (1995). "Factors that influence the next generation's decision to take-over the family farm", *Family Business Review*, 8(2), 99–120.

Gagnè, M., Wrosch, C. and De Pontet, S.B. (2011). "Retiring from the family business: the role of goal adjustment capacities", *Family Business Review*, 24(4), 292–304.

Gundolf, K., Meier, O. and Missonier, A. (2013). "Transmission of family businesses in France", *International Journal of Entrepreneurial Behaviour and Research*, 19(1), 53–71.

Haberman, H. and Danes, S.S. (2007). "Father-daughter and father-son family business management transfer comparison: family FIRO model application", *Family Business Review*, 2, 163–184.

Halkias, D., Thurman, P.W., Smith, C. and Nason, R.S. (2016). *Father-daughter succession in family business. A cross-cultural perspective*, New York: Routledge.

Handler, W.C. (1991). "Key interpersonal relationships of next-generation family members in family firms", *Journal of Small Business Management*, 29(3), 21–39.

Hartung, P.J., Porfeli, E.J. and Vondracek, F.W. (2005). "Child vocational development: a review and reconsideration", *Journal of Vocational Behavior*, 66(3), 385–419.

Hollander, B.S. and Bukowitz, W.R. (1990). "Women, family culture, and family business", *Family Business Review*, 3(2), 139–151.

Hytti, U., Alsos, G.A., Heinonen, J. and Ljunggren, E. (2016). "Navigating the family business: a gendered analysis of identity construction of daughters", *International Small Business Journal*, 35(6), 665–686.

Jimenez, R.M. (2009). "Research on women in family firms. Current status and future directions", *Family Business Review*, 22(9), 53–64.

Keating, N.C. and Little, H.M. (1997). "Choosing the successor in New Zealand family farms", *Family Business Review*, 10(2), 157–171.

Lambrecht, J. and Donckels, R. (2006). "Towards a business family dynasty: a lifelong, continuing process", in P.Z. Poutziouris, K.X. Smyrnios and S.B. Klein (Eds.), *Handbook of research on family business*, 388–401. Cheltenham and Brookfield: Edward Elgar Publishing.

Lawson, K.M., Crouter, A.C. and McHale, S.M. (2015). "Links between family gender socialization experiences in childhood and gendered occupational attainment in young adulthood", *Journal of Vocational Behavior*, 90, 26–35.

MassMutual Financial Group/Raymond Institute. (2007). *American family business survey*. www.massmutual.com/mmfg/pdf/afbs.pdf.

Moran, D. (2000). *Introduction to phenomenology*, London: Routledge.

Nelton, S. (1998). "The rise of women in family firms: a call for research now", *Family Business Review*, 11(3), 215–218.

Pettit, P. (1969). *On the idea of phenomenology*, Dublin: Scepter Books.

Pieper, T.M. (2010). "Non solus: toward a psychology of family business", *Journal of Family Business Strategy*, 1(1), 26–39.

Powell, G.N. and Eddleston, K.A. (2013). "Linking family-to-business enrichment and support to entrepreneurial success: do female and male entrepreneurs experience different outcomes?" *Journal of Business Venturing*, *28*(2), 261–280.

Robic, P. and Antheaume, N. (2014). "La veuve: une partie prenante méconnue dans la transmission des entreprises familiales", *Management International*, *18*(4), 175–189.

Sharma, P., Chrisman, J.J. and Chua, J.H. (2003). "Predictors of satisfaction with the succession process in family firms", *Journal of Business Venturing*, *18*(5), 667–687.

Smythe, J. and Sardeshmukh, S.R. (2013). "Fathers and daughters in family business", *Small Enterprise Research*, *2*(2), 98–109.

Vera, C.F. and Dean, M.A. (2005). "An examination of the challenges daughters face in family business succession", *Family Business Review*, *18*(4), 321–345.

17 Female External Successors

Difficulties During the Business Transfer Process and Types of Support Required

Bérangère Deschamps
and Catherine Thévenard-Puthod

As with business creation, women who take over an existing business remain largely in the minority compared to men. In France, for example, only 20% of family business successions or transfers to employees, and only 5% of external business transfers, are undertaken by a woman (Cédants et Repreneurs d'Affaires Association (CRA), 2019). Within the Cédants et Repreneurs d'Affaires Association (CRA), women accounted for only 7% of external buyers and 15% of trainees (CRA, 2019). As it is essential to increase the proportion of women in the population of business owners, there is a need to understand the obstacles that prevent women from taking over a business in detail and the difficulties that they must overcome to succeed.

In the entrepreneurship literature, researchers show that gender—considered as the social representations and practices associated with femininity or masculinity (Ahl, 2006)—deeply affects the entrepreneurial process (Brush, 1992; Marlow, 2002; Neergaard *et al.*, 2005; Malach Pines *et al.*, 2010). But researchers focus on new business ventures, rather than on other entrepreneurial modes of entry, such as business transfers (Parker and Van Praag, 2012). A better understanding of the way that gender structures business transfer processes is essential: women may be competent and 'worthy' successors, yet they are often ignored, undervalued or poorly prepared for the process (Byrne *et al.*, 2018). The few available studies on business transfers to women have focused on family succession and mainly on the successor selection process (Wang, 2010). They reveal many difficulties for daughters who want to succeed their parents (see Chapter 15, Constantinidis, this volume; and Chapter 16, Missonier, Jaouen and Albert, this volume). More generally, a gender difference between the seller and the buyer (when a woman takes over a business initially run by a man) amplifies the disruptive nature of the process and, consequently, affects the business's performance (Zhang and Qu, 2016). However, existing research does not systematically explore all phases of the transfer process. In addition, there are no studies on the difficulties encountered by other types of women buyers (employees of the acquired company or external buyers). Another important limit of the previous literature is that it has not addressed the question of from whom they should seek help to cope with their difficulties.

Consequently, the objective of this chapter is to explore the impact of gender on business transfers realised by external women buyers. According to Deschamps in Chapter 1, an external business transfer is the transfer of the company's resources, skills, knowledge, ownership and management power to one or more individuals outside the company who have no strong prior connection with the transferred entity. It differs from internal transfers, which include family successions and transfers to one or more employees of the company. In this chapter, we aim to answer the following research questions: What difficulties are encountered by women buyers during external business transfers? And who could help them to bypass those difficulties?

This chapter is divided into four sections that present: (1) the external business transfer process; (2) the qualitative methodology used to understand the difficulties faced by women during this process and the types of help they need; (3) the obstacles to be overcome and support solicited by external female buyers during the first phase of the transfer process (before signing); and (4) the difficulties encountered and help received during the post-transfer phases.

External Business Transfer Process: Steps and Challenges

The literature on external business transfer considers that this type of transfer is quite a complex and iterative process, fraught with obstacles (Picard and Thévenard-Puthod, 2004). According to Picard and Thévenard-Puthod, this process involves a greater or lesser number of steps, depending on the level of detail retained. To simplify this process, we identify two main phases: the steps that lead to the signing of the sale and those that take place once the buyer becomes the new owner of the business.

During the initial stage of the process, the external buyer first has to find the motivation for and to prepare himself[1] for the purchase (Sharma *et al.*, 2001). Unlike an heir who takes over a company from his parents or an employee who takes over a company in which he has been able to work for many years, it may seem riskier for a buyer to embark on the adventure of purchasing a little-known company. For external buyers, the second challenge is the search for a business to target. Information is not always accessible (Durst and Güldenberg, 2010) because sellers do not openly communicate their intention to transfer ownership of their company for strategic reasons (for example, not scaring employees or offering opportunities to competitors). Once a company that matches the criteria of the buyer is found, they must convince sellers that they are trustworthy and capable of sustaining the transferred company. Unlike large companies, where ownership and management are separate, most VSEs/SMEs are owned by sole owner-managers (Ooghe *et al.*, 2006). As a result, there is often some confusion between the personal objectives of the owners and those of the company they manage (Westhead, 1997). Whatever the reason for the business transfer (such as retirement, illness or loss of profitability), a VSE/SME owner committed to their business will be concerned about its sustainability (Howorth *et al.*, 2004): the seller wants the company they have created or taken over to continue its development, maintain its know-how and the employment of its employees, continue to ensure relations with privileged partners (like customers and suppliers) and extend the legacy of historical work that may have lasted through several generations (Dalziel, 2008). The selection of a buyer is therefore performed very cautiously and even fastidiously (Favre-Bonté and Thévenard-Puthod, 2013), with the seller sometimes going so far as to relegate the financial aspects to the background (Graebner and Eisenhardt, 2004), or even postponing the transaction because they have not found the ideal candidate. For the same reasons, if the seller decides to sell, negotiating the sale price can sometimes lead to a fierce battle, where the motivations of the actors weigh more heavily than the objective evaluation criteria. Business transfer can also be complicated by the buyer's lack of financial resources or skills, the legal aspects of the transaction or the difficulties in implementing strategic, managerial and human audits.

When the deed of sale is signed, the two actors (the predecessor and the buyer) can coexist for a transition phase that lasts for variable amounts of time. This phase is considered essential for the proper transmission of the company's skills and knowledge, but also for the legitimacy of the buyer *vis-à-vis* the company's stakeholders (Handler, 1990; Picard and Thévenard-Puthod, 2004). Authors focus on the impact of the role transition and on the behaviour of sellers and buyers in this phase. The seller must succeed in letting go, leaving authority with the buyer and accepting any management differences (Marler *et al.*, 2017; Sharma *et al.*, 2001). The risk is that this process may act as a barrier between the company and the buyer, hindering the new owner from taking control of the organisation by catalysing employee resistance to change.

Finally, the external buyer has to succeed in the post-transfer management phase. When managing the takeover, one of the challenges is to obtain employee support (Favre-Bonté and Thévenard-Puthod, 2013). The difficulties for new managers lie in dealing with staff they have not recruited and running a company with its own history. They must therefore establish their legitimacy and identify a hard core among employees on which they can rely to lead (Boussaguet, 2011). Without legitimacy, dysfunctions can quickly appear, with instances of demotivation, immobility, refusal of obedience, non-compliance with rules, reduced productivity or quality of work, hostile reactions or even resignation of

Table 17.1 Obstacles to External Buyers, as Identified in the Literature

Initial stages (before signing)	Post-transfer stages
• Being motivated for buying • Searching for the target company • Gaining relevant information on target companies • Convincing the seller • Negotiating the price • Gathering financial resources for the deal	• Maintaining a good relationship with the predecessor in order to benefit from a transfer of knowledge and skills • Obtaining employee support • Convincing all the external stakeholders (customers, suppliers) • Integrating new leadership functions and managing the role transition

employees affecting the health of the acquired company (Picard and Thévenard-Puthod, 2004; Thévenard-Puthod *et al.*, 2014). Boussaguet (2011) explains that the emotions experienced by employees when faced with a 'break-up' with a former manager and the intrusion of a new company manager can lead them to behave in a 'deviant way'. The buyer must avoid any disruption or behaviour that opposes change, and manage some continuity between old and new projects, which requires certain managerial qualities (Deschamps, 2018). This may be a key point in their success in business transfer. The external buyer may also feel uncomfortable maintaining relations with key partners (such as customers, suppliers and banks), leading to commercial and/or financial difficulties (like loss of turnover, lower margins and supply difficulties) (Thévenard-Puthod *et al.*, 2014). Finally, at this stage, buyers may experience their own personal difficulties, relating to their commitments and their ability to assume their role as company manager.

Table 17.1 synthesises general difficulties according to the two business transfer stages.

Although the profile of the buyer is one of the factors that may nuance the difficulties encountered during the business transfer process (Thévenard-Puthod *et al.*, 2014), very few researchers have paid attention to the gender impact on their intensity. The limited available research focuses on family succession (Dumas *et al.*, 1995; Keating and Little, 1997; Byrne and Fattoum, 2015; Byrne *et al.*, 2018) and ignores external takeovers. Moreover, the literature does not systematically explore all phases of the process. It therefore seems appropriate to pay more attention to the experiences of women external buyers.

A Qualitative Methodology Based on Six Case Studies

Our work aims to provide a better understanding of the takeover process experienced by external women successors. The qualitative methodology is justified by the nature of this research question, which is rarely studied in the literature on business takeovers. Case studies are recommended by Yin (2009) to understand events, interactions and social, complex and particular situations, which is the case here, since it is a question of understanding the influence of gender, as a social construction, on the progress of the external business transfer. We adopt the multiple case study approach. There is no ideal number of cases (Yin, 2009). However, Eisenhardt (1989) suggests a number between four to ten. In this research, we selected six cases because the gradual improvement due to the addition of a new case became minimal at this point (Eisenhardt, 1989). Cases have been identified with the help of entrepreneurs and business networks. Our selection criteria were a woman who has completed an external takeover. Table 17.2 details the sample.

The majority of women successors have higher-education degrees and significant professional experience with positions of responsibility prior to the takeover. Five business transfers were solo and one takeover was made with a spouse. The transferred companies were in good financial health and have grown since the business transfer, in terms of turnover and workforce. The business transfers took place between 2000 and 2016.

Data collection was mainly based on semi-structured interviews. We met the six women successors and two spouses (one co-shareholder and one employee in the acquired firm). We developed two interview guides. The first concerned women successors and is divided into five parts: (1) the profile of the woman successor before the business transfer, (2) the characteristics of the acquired company, (3) the motivations for succession and the selection criteria for the company, (4) the experience as a woman in all phases of the succession process and the support they were looking for, and (5) a conclusion as to the status of the female successor. The second interview guide, used for the two husbands, included three themes: (1) the profile of the interviewees, (2) their place and support role alongside their wives at each step of the process, and (3) their opinion about their wife's succession process and success. The interviews lasted between 50 and 90 minutes, and were recorded and fully transcribed.

We codified and organised the collected information using matrices (Miles and Huberman, 1994) summarising the difficulties each woman faced and the support they received. We used another matrix to aggregate the results and facilitate the cross-case comparison. This method allows for the identification of common and unique elements from each business transfer story.

Gender Difficulties and Support Needs Before the Signing of the Business Transfer

At the beginning of the business transfer process, the possibility of success, both in their professional and private lives, was mentioned as a

Table 17.2 Description of the Six Cases

Case	Kate	Adelaide	Karen	Mary	Chloe	Esther
Profile before the takeover (age, number of children, education, professional experience)	44; 2 children; master's in management; commercial and marketing experience in the banking sector	38; 3 children; MBA; sales rep in the industrial sector	43; no children; telecom engineer and master's in political science; experience in several IT services companies	38; 2 children; mechanical engineer, master's degree in supply chain	41; 2 children; MBA; experience in real estate development	20; no children; two-year degree in technical and commercial; no professional experience
Date of takeover	December 2016	September 2010	January 2013	October 2015	June 2013	December 2000
Activity of the acquired company	Printing	Food industry	Cleaning	Building	Building renovation	Mirrors
Firm size at the takeover period (staff, turnover)	16 employees 2,588,400 €	2 employees 700,000 €	20 employees 500,000 €	9 employees 810,000 €	8 employees 1,600,000 €	1 employee 30,000 €
2018 firm size (staff, turnover)	16 employees 2,682,300 €	6 employees 1,113,800 €	30 employees 600,000 €	10 employees 1,077,100 €	8 employees 1,705,700 €	4 employees 650,000 €
Interviewees	Female buyer	Female buyer; spouse and shareholder (Paul)	Female buyer	Female buyer	Female buyer	Female buyer; spouse and employee of the firm (Robert)

motivation by all the women who have children (4/6: Kate, Adelaide, Mary, Chloe). The choice of the company was based on this personal criterion: "I have two children and a husband who is away four to five days a week; I was looking for a company 20 minutes from home, regardless of the sector" (Chloe). "I had children; I wanted to spend time with them. But I also wanted to have a more varied job, to take on more responsibility" (Mary). This appears to be a specificity of women buyers; as previous literature rarely mentions this criterion. Moreover, finding a company that meets these demanding objectives is not easy.

Then, taking the step to leave the reassuring status of employee to become an entrepreneur was not always easy and the women's personal environments played a very strong role in encouraging them.

Two people played an important role at this stage: husbands and fathers. Women successors considered their husbands' help as essential in succession. "This kind of entrepreneurial project doesn't work if the man doesn't help", summarised Adelaide. The spouse's support can be moral, but it can also be related to the financial security he provides for the family: "My husband supports me. His work is stable. We are a family of four, and we can live with his salary if there is a problem in my firm. It's a safety net." (Mary).

A father's support is also highly valued: "My father was very enthusiastic about the takeover. He encouraged me a lot" (Esther). "My father has always told me I would succeed. He gave me a lot of advice" (Mary).

Apart from finding the motivation to carry out the project and identifying a relevant firm to buy, the main obstacles mentioned by interviewees in the very first phase of the business transfer process concerned the norms and stereotypes in male-dominated industries. These issues resulted in difficulties convincing the predecessor to trust a woman as a successor. For example, Kate took over a firm in the printing industry. Kate's husband led the first meetings with the predecessor on his own, without mentioning that the takeover was a couple's project. Once the relationship was established, Kate became involved in the negotiations with her complementary skills. Alone, some female successors would have had more difficulties convincing the sellers and the investors. For instance, Kate told us, "Printing is a man's trade. My competencies appeared complementary with my husband's ones. Alone, sellers, bankers or CEO networks wouldn't have followed me". Both Kate and Adelaide also had difficulty raising financing for the transaction. Adelaide needed the help of her father, a former banker, to obtain a loan: even when a business was not male-dominated, it was hard to convince the banks.

In those first steps, it is also interesting to note that some traditional professional support networks (such as consular chambers and advisors) sometimes tried to dissuade the women from taking over a business in male-dominated industries. In the following case, the gender segregation was shared by the institution: "The chamber of trade said that a woman would never succeed in the building industry!" (Mary).

Unlike her five counterparts, Karen took over a business in a female gendered environment (the household). She had no trouble convincing the predecessor, who was already a woman. Her engineering profile, her past professional experience (she used to manage a 25-million-euro turnover) and the non-technical activity of the transferred business also reassured the banks.

Gender Difficulties and Support Needs During the Post-Transfer Phases

Despite those obstacles (and with the help of their families), the six women managed to complete the transactions. However, they were not at the end of their struggle. Once the firm officially transferred, some of them had difficulties with the predecessor during the transition phase (a period characterised by the presence of the two managers—one outgoing and one incoming—in the company). For Kate, who bought a firm with her husband (but was the leader of the project), it was difficult to argue with the seller:

> The seller is still in the firm, as an employee, until he retires. When my husband is not here, he acts against me because I haven't mastered the technical aspects of the business. He opposes me if I want to change something.

After the predecessor's departure, being a woman raised specific issues. Some women had to face disparaging comments and a lack of confidence from external stakeholders, particularly when the firm's activity is a traditionally 'male' one. They explained that they were systematically considered as an assistant, not as the CEO. They regularly saw the surprise on others' faces when they said that they were the CEO. In three cases, they had to face male customers who refused to work with them. "One of my customers couldn't work with a woman. He went mad, I directed him towards the work conductor, a man" (Mary). "A customer behaved very aggressively. I was scared and couldn't sleep for several days" (Mary). "The most difficult thing was being accepted in the profession as a woman. I lost customers" (Esther).

In fewer instances (Esther, Kate), they also felt a lack of legitimacy in the eyes of male employees. Some members of staff did not want to be supervised by a woman and sometimes they quit the firm. "Six months after the business transfer, an employee told me: 'I don't want to be managed by a woman, especially not one who is younger than me!' I didn't understand" (Esther). Here, again, the support of a husband can be substantial.

Esther hired Robert, her husband, as an employee. "He helped me a lot with the internal management as he previously worked in big companies which were well organised" (Esther). Her husband explained: "Esther had difficulties finding trusted people; I thought I could help her".

Most of the women interviewed recognised that they needed to work harder to be considered as a legitimate successor. "As women, we have to put in double the effort to prove our competencies" (Adelaide). Two of them even denied their gender and adopted more male behaviours: "To be accepted, I behave as a man, I think as a man, I act as a man, the same confident posture" (Esther). This approach was also used by Karen: "I don't really correspond to the stereotypical 'woman' image: I am not gentle, I can use male language, I am not afraid to fight" (Karen).

Another important difficulty faced by women is about the balance between professional and personal lives. Although women thought that taking over a firm could be a way to better achieve this balance, they realised that they underestimated this difficulty. "As a woman, the balance between my personal life and my professional life is now my main issue. . . . After the birth of my second child, I have had long periods of doubts" (Esther).

> In the first few years, I did not see my children. I came back home at 2.00 a.m., I slept for three hours per night. My children didn't understand. . . . It is very hard to combine everything. I didn't see my husband and my children. I thought "So what?"
>
> (Adelaide)

"The firm is more profitable today but I can't grow it, because I work fewer hours than the predecessor. My husband is often away, and I have to take care of my children" (Chloe). For Mary and Kate, it seems easier.

> I have found a way to spend time with my children. I have one week of holiday at each school break, I am at work at 7.00 a.m., but I leave at 5.00 p.m. Of course, I take my laptop home to work later in the evening. No customer has taken their business elsewhere because of my schedules!
>
> (Mary)

All women with children mentioned that their husband's support at home was essential.

For a woman, taking over a firm from outside involves managing an increased workload, taking on the responsibility of the new role of CEO, fighting against female stereotypes, dealing with hazards in management and facing difficulties in balancing a professional agenda with personal issues. These factors may generate health troubles. Among the interviewees, we found evidence of insomnia (Mary) and even burnout (Adelaide). Husbands play an important psychological support when facing those issues. "My husband helps me to put the everyday problems at work into perspective" (Adelaide). Professional networks also seem very useful for stepping back and finding advice (Esther, Karen). More particularly, women seem to find relevant help from other female entrepreneurs. "I've met business women whose advice was crucial for me. Meeting other women who have experienced the same difficulties makes me feel good" (Esther).

> Five CEOs have advised me. One of them was a woman. She gave me advice on my personal life, on the subject of vacations, whether or not to work on Wednesdays (when children are not at school). That kind of advice a man cannot give. . . . Men only advised me on technical and business subject matters.
>
> (Mary)

Esther is, for example, a member of a specific women's network founded by Chloe. For those two women, exchanges between women are essential.

As a response to Table 17.1, Table 17.3 synthesises difficulties experienced by external women buyers according to the two business transfer steps, along with the supports they received to face those difficulties.

Table 17.3 Specific Obstacles and Supports to External Women Buyers

	Initial stages (before signing)	*Post-transfer stages*
Difficulties as a woman buyer	• Being confident in the project and embarking on an entrepreneurial adventure • Finding a company that matches family/work balance criterion • Discouragement of some support networks • Convincing the seller that you are a relevant buyer, as a woman • Convincing the bank, as a woman	• Convincing internal and external stakeholders of a woman's legitimacy as a CEO • Bad relationships with some sellers during the transition phase • Bad relationships with some customers (customers who leave or who are violent) • Bad relationships with some employees who quit • Balancing personal and professional lives • Health troubles
Most solicited supports	• Husband • Father	• Husband • Women entrepreneur networks

Discussion and Conclusion

Our analysis, based on six case studies, highlights specific gender-related difficulties for women who take over a business, considering the whole process. Suffering from a lack of self-confidence and from a fear of failure, women sometimes find it difficult to embark on an entrepreneurial adventure, a phenomenon that has already been identified among more general women entrepreneurs (Blisson and Rana, 2001; Robb and Watson, 2012; Harrison *et al.*, 2015; Poggesi *et al.*, 2016). As soon as they have children, their selection criteria for companies to take over are based on the compatibility of work and family life, which limits the scope of possibilities in an already difficult environment (business transfer opportunities rarely correspond to the profiles of the buyers) (Bornard and Thévenard-Puthod, 2009).

However, before the signing of the transfer, the most difficult thing is to establish their legitimacy as soon as they wish to enter an industry that is considered masculine. They must therefore redouble their efforts to convince predecessors, banks and even support institutions. These credibility problems for women when dealing with banks has already been particularly noted in the literature on women entrepreneurs (Wu and Chua, 2012; Adkins *et al.*, 2013), but here we show that it concerns more potential partners (such as their predecessors and support institutions).

Once at the head of the acquired company, relations with the predecessor may be strained during the transition phase if the latter is reluctant to let a woman run a technical company. Women may also face negative gender-based reactions from key stakeholders in the company (customers or employees), as has already been observed in family successions (Dumas, 1998; Vera and Dean, 2005). Without the legitimacy of being an heiress, it can be particularly violent. Finally, the workload caused by the takeover, combined with the desire not to disengage from family life, creates significant stress for these women, which sometimes leads to health problems. The identification of these specific gender-related difficulties is therefore an important contribution to research on business transfers.

On this pathway of external takeover, which is fraught with pitfalls, women seek the support of various actors. First, while they mobilise a variety of professional support to benefit from advice focused on business takeovers, in most cases, they recognise the value of receiving support from a woman. Women who are already entrepreneurs are the only ones able to share their specific experiences (particularly the difficulties related to gender) and give them the knowledge to better deal with issues. They are also better able to give them more personal advice and tips on how to reconcile work and personal life. Second, we highlight the role of men in the family environment. The husband often plays several complementary support roles, in terms of family logistics, but also in terms of providing more managerial advice, or even operational assistance on a daily basis in the company. His psychological support is crucial for the woman. The husband also acts as a male guarantor in male-gendered sectors of activity. But the father can also play a strong role in the moral and managerial support of the women taking over, and replace or complement the actions of the spouse, especially in the first steps of the process. This is quite an interesting result given that the literature on family succession shows that fathers often do not pay attention to their daughters (Wang, 2010). In the case of external takeovers, fathers—whether they were CEOs themselves or not—are key people for the women in order for them to expand their self-confidence. While the complementarity of different forms of support for the buyer has already been highlighted in the literature (Deschamps *et al.*, 2010; Thévenard-Puthod *et al.*, 2014), our work indicates that it is more than necessary in the case of external business takeovers by women.

Note

1. The literature on external business transfer is 'gender blind' (Marlow and Martinez Dy, 2018), implicitly assuming that the buyer is a man. Consequently, we intentionally use the pronoun 'him' in the literature review.

References

Adkins, C.L., Samaras, S.A., Gilfillan, S.W. and McWee, W.E. (2013). "The relationship between owner characteristics, company size, and the work—family culture and policies of women-owned businesses", *Journal of Small Business Management*, 51(2), 196–214.

Ahl, H. (2006). "Why research on women entrepreneurs needs new directions", *Entrepreneurship Theory and Practice*, 30(5), 595–623.

Barrédy, C. (2008). "Gouvernance de la société familiale cotée", *Revue française de gestion* (5), 1–19.

Blisson, D. and Rana, B.K. (2001). "The role of entrepreneurial networks: the influence of gender and ethnicity in British SMEs", *46th ICSB World Conference*, Taipei, Taiwan.

Bornard, F. and Thévenard-Puthod, C. (2009). "Mieux comprendre les difficultés d'une reprise externe grâce à l'approche des représentations sociales", *Revue Internationale PME*, 22(3–4), 83–108.

Boussaguet, S. (2011). "La prise en compte des salariés en situation de transmission/reprise externe", in *Le Duo Cédant/Repreneur pour une compréhension intégrée du processus de transmission/reprise des PME*, 147–162, Quebec: PUQ Entrepreneuriat et PME.

Brush, C.G. (1992). "Research on women business owners: past trends, a new perspective and future directions", *Entrepreneurship Theory and Practice*, 16(4), 5–30.

Byrne, J. and Fattoum, S. (2015). "The gendered nature of family business succession: case studies from France", in *Context, Process and Gender in Entrepreneurship*, Cheltenham and Brookfield: Edward Elgar Publishing.

Byrne, J., Fattoum, S. and Thébaud, S. (2018). "A suitable boy? Gendered roles and hierarchies in family business succession", *European Management Review*, 16(3), 579–596.

CRA (Cédants et Repreneurs d'Affaires). (2019). *Observatoire de la transmission 2019*. www.cra.asso.fr/observatoire-de-la-transmission-2019/.

Dalziel, M. (2008). "The seller's perspective on acquisition success: empirical evidence from the communications equipment industry", *Journal of Engineering & Technology Management*, 25(3), 168–183.

Deschamps, B. (2018). "Evolution de la connaissance autour des pratiques de transmission—reprise réalisées par les personnes physiques: vers le concept de transfert d'entreprise", *Revue de l'entrepreneuriat*, 17(3/4), 189–213.

Deschamps, B., Fatien, P. and Geindre, S. (2010). "Supporting the business owner: driving, escorting but also guiding", *Gestion 2000*, 3, 77–90.

Dumas, C. (1998). "Women's pathway to participation and leadership in the family-owned firm", *Family Business Review*, 11(3), 219–228.

Dumas, C., Dupuis, J.P., Richer, F. and St.-Cyr, L. (1995). "Factors that influence the next generation's decision to take over the family farm", *Family Business Review*, 8(2), 99–120.

Durst, S. and Güldenberg, S. (2010). "What makes SMEs attractive to external successors?" *The Journal of Information and Knowledge Management Systems*, 40, 108–135.

Eisenhardt, K.M. (1989). "Building theories from case study research", *The Academy of Management Review*, 14(4), 532–550.

Favre-Bonté, V. and Thévenard-Puthod, C. (2013). "Resource and skill transfers in subcontractor SME acquisitions: influence on the long-term performance of acquired firms", *European Management Review*, 10(3), 117–135.

Graebner, M.E. and Eisenhardt, K.M. (2004). "The seller's side of the story: acquisition as courtship and governance as syndicate in entrepreneurial firms", *Administrative Science Quarterly*, 49(3), 366–403.

Handler, W.C. (1990). "Succession in family firms: a mutual role adjustment between entrepreneur and next-generation family members", *Entrepreneurship Theory and Practice*, 15(1), 37–51.

Harrison, R., Leitch, C. and McAdam, M. (2015). "Breaking glass: toward a gendered analysis of entrepreneurial leadership", *Journal of Small Business Management*, 53(3), 693–713.

Howorth, C., Westhead, P. and Wright, M. (2004). "Buyouts, information asymmetry and the family management dyad", *Journal of Business Venturing*, 19(4), 509–534.

Keating, N.C. and Little, H.M. (1997). "Choosing the successor in New Zealand family farms", *Family Business Review*, 10(2), 157–171.

Malach Pines, A., Lerner, M. and Schwartz, D. (2010). "Gender differences in entrepreneurship: equality, diversity and inclusion in times of global crisis", *Equality, Diversity and Inclusion: An International Journal*, 29(2), 186–198.

Marler, L.E., Botero, I.C., Massis, D. and Vittorio, A. (2017). "Succession-related role transitions in family firms: the impact of proactive personality", *Journal of Managerial Issues*, 29(1), 57–81.

Marlow, S. (2002). "Women and self-employment: a part of or apart from theoretical construct?" *The International Journal of Entrepreneurship and Innovation*, 3(2), 83–91.

Marlow, S. and Martinez Dy, A. (2018). "Annual review article: is it time to rethink the gender agenda in entrepreneurship research?" *International Small Business Journal*, 36(1), 3–22.

Miles, M.B. and Huberman, A.M. (1994). *Qualitative data analysis: an expanded sourcebook*, Thousand Oaks, CA: Sage Publications.

Neergaard, H., Shaw, E. and Carter, S. (2005). "The impact of gender, social capital and networks on business ownership: a research agenda", *International Journal of Entrepreneurial Behavior and Research*, 11(5), 338–357.

Ooghe, H., Van Laere, E. and De Langhe, T. (2006). "Are acquisitions worthwhile? An empirical study of the post-acquisition performance of privately held Belgian companies", *Small Business Economics*, 27(2–3), 223–243.

Parker, S.C. and Van Praag, C.M. (2012). "The entrepreneur's mode of entry: business takeover or new venture start?" *Journal of Business Venturing*, 27(1), 31–46.

Picard, C. and Thévenard-Puthod, C. (2004). "La reprise de l'entreprise artisanale: spécificités du processus et conditions de sa réussite", *Revue Internationale PME*, 17(2), 94–121.

Poggesi, S., Mari, M. and De Vita, L. (2016). "What's new in female entrepreneurship research? Answers from the literature", *International Entrepreneurship and Management Journal*, 12(3), 735–764.

Robb, A.M. and Watson, J. (2012). "Gender differences in firm performance: evidence from new ventures in the United States", *Journal of Business Venturing*, 27(5), 544–558.

Sharma, P., Chrisman, J.J., Pablo, A.L. and Chua, J.H. (2001). "Determinants of initial satisfaction with the succession process in family firms: a conceptual model", *Entrepreneurship Theory and Practice*, 25(3), 17–36.

Thévenard-Puthod, C., Picard, C. and Chollet, B. (2014). "Relevance of tutoring in business transfers. Results of a European study", *Management International /International Management*, 18(4), 80–96.

Vera, C.F. and Dean, M.A. (2005). "An examination of the challenges daughters face in family business succession", *Family Business Review*, 18(4), 321–345.

Wang, C. (2010). "Daughter exclusion in family business succession: a review of the literature", *Journal of Family and Economic Issues*, 31(4), 475–484.

Westhead, P. (1997). "Ambitions, 'external' environment and strategic factor differences between family and non-family companies", *Entrepreneurship and Regional Development*, 9(2), 127–157.

Wu, Z. and Chua, J.H. (2012). "Second-order gender effects: the case of US small business borrowing cost", *Entrepreneurship Theory and Practice*, 36(3), 443–463.

Yin, R.K. (2009). *Case study research: design and methods*, Thousand Oaks, CA: Sage Publications.

Zhang, Y. and Qu, H. (2016). "The impact of CEO succession with gender change on firm performance and successor early departure: evidence from China's publicly listed companies in 1997–2010", *Academy of Management Journal*, 59(5), 1845–1868.

Biographies

Béatrice ALBERT was Human Resources Director during 15 years in human resources. After, she joined the family business to take the direction of a business unit in order to recover financially. After, she become the marketing and communications director of the group, commercial director and then general manager of the wine sector. She is a shareholder and administrator of the group ALBERT.

Nicolas ANTHEAUME is Professor of Family Business and Corporate Social Responsibility at the University of Nantes' IAE—School of Economics & Management. He is a member of the University of Nantes' Research Team on Economics and Management (LEMNA).

Dominique BARBELIVIEN is a full lecturer in management sciences at the Institute of Business Administration of the University of Nantes, where she has been the dean since January 1, 2020 and head of the master's degree in management control and organizational audit (CGAO) since 2017. She is a member of the Laboratoire d'Economie et Management Nantes Atlantique (LEMNA). Her main research focuses on the governance, management and performance system of family-owned SMEs.

Marie-Christine BARBOT-GRIZZO is a lecturer in business management at Le Mans University, France. She graduated from Caen University with a doctorate degree in 1999. Her research focuses on entrepreneurship and the challenges related to the change of ownership of small and medium-size companies and businesses. Doctor Barbot-Grizzo participates in international conferences and publishes in academic reviews focusing on these research fields.

Céline BARRÉDY has a PhD in finance from the University of Bordeaux, and owns a diploma in PhD supervision from the University of Lille. She is currently Full Professor of Finance and Family Business at the University of Paris Nanterre and is a member of the CEROS research lab. She is Editor-in-Chief of the *Revue de l'Entrepreneuriat*. Her research and publications are in finance, equity capital and governance in family business, and she has an international orientation.

Sandrine BERGER-DOUCE is Professor of Management Science at École des Mines de Saint-Étienne (France). Her research works are dedicated to corporate social responsibility and digital transformation in small businesses. A member of the Coactis laboratory Lyon–St-Etienne (EA 4161), she regularly publishes academic articles on these issues.

Sonia BOUSSAGUET, Phd, is an Associate Professor in the Strategy and Entrepreneurship Department at NEOMA Business School, Reims Campus. Her
research focuses on the external business transfer, specifically the socialisation
of SME buyers. Her work has been published in several academic journals and
in numerous collective books.

Didier CHABAUD is Professor of Entrepreneurship and Strategic Management
at Sorbonne Business School (IAE Paris), University of Paris I Pantheon Sorbonne (France). He is the director of the ETI (entrepreneurship—territory—
innovation) chair. His research focuses on the processes of entrepreneurship,
social networks and family business.

Luis CISNEROS is Full Professor and Academic Director of the Entrepreneurship
and Business Families Hub at HEC Montréal (Canada). Dr. Cisneros holds a
masters in management (University of Aguascalientes), a MSc in management
control (University Paris-Dauphine) and a PhD in family business management
(Group HEC Paris).

Christina CONSTANTINIDIS is a professor in entrepreneurship at ESG UQAM
in Montreal. Her research work focuses on gender dynamics in entrepreneurship and family business, and has been published in international academic
journals, book chapters, conferences and reports. She is also a member of the
editorial board of *Revue Internationale PME* and of the review board of *Family Business Review*.

Bérangère DESCHAMPS is Professor of Entrepreneurship at Université Grenoble
Alpes and a researcher in the CERAG laboratory. She has worked on business transfers for 20 years and has published numerous papers and chapters,
as well as four books on external business transfers, sibling team succession
and support for external buyers. She is also Editor-in-Chief of the *Revue de
l'Entrepreneuriat*.

Marie-Josée DRAPEAU is Professor at the University of Quebec in Chicoutimi. Her
research interests include entrepreneurs, the entrepreneurial process, decision-
making and exit strategies, as well as teaching entrepreneurship classes.

Susanne DURST is Full Professor of Management at the Department of Business
Administration at Tallinn University of Technology (Estonia) and an associate professor at South Ural State University (Russian Federation). She is also
Head of the Organisation and Management Unit at the Department of Business Administration at Tallinn University of Technology.

Cédric FAVRE is a former independent consultant in corporate finance. He is
now a doctoral student in strategic management and entrepreneurship, as well
as a consultant for the Regional Union of SCOP.

Florence GUILIANI is currently a postdoctoral student at HEC Montréal (Canada). Dr. Guiliani holds a PhD degree in management and a master's in management from Montpellier University (France).

Mariem HANNACHI is Assistant Professor of Family Business and Strategy at
ESSCA School of Management (France). Her main research and publications lie
in family business, strategic renewal, entrepreneurship and digital marketing.

Annabelle JAOUEN is Full Professor of Entrepreneurship at Montpellier Business
School, France. Her research (articles and books) concerns types of entrepreneurs and SME strategy, alliances and networks, human resources management, and information systems in micro and small firms.

Lyès MAZARI holds a PhD in management science from Saint-Étienne University and is currently a post-doctoral researcher at IMT Atlantique Bretagne Pays de la Loire and a member of LEGO laboratory Bretagne (EA 2652). His field of expertise encompasses corporate social responsibility, business transfer and digital transition in organisations.

Audrey MISSONIER is Associate Professor in Strategy at Montpellier Business School. Her research activities focus on the topics of strategy, mergers, acquisitions and family business transmission, and on women as buyers. She regularly participates in international research congresses and her work has been published in journals such as *European Business Review*, *Strategic Change*, and *Journal of Entrepreneurial Behavior & Research*. She has coordinated many books.

Paulette ROBIC is Associate Professor in family business and gender issues, with a qualification as PhD advisor at the University of Nantes' IAE—School of Economics & Management. She is a member of the University of Nantes' Research Team on Economics and Management (LEMNA). She is the director of the University of Nantes' Observatory on the longevity of family businesses.

Soumaya SFEIR is a doctoral student in management sciences at Université Grenoble Alpes. Her thesis focuses on the influence of the composition of the boards of directors of family businesses on the behaviour of directors and on succession. She is also interested in all non-economic aspects that may explain the behaviour of family businesses in terms of succession.

Catherine THÉVENARD-PUTHOD is Professor in Strategic Management and Entrepreneurship at the University of Savoie Mont-Blanc and a member of IREGE (Institute for Research in Management and Economics). Her research focuses on three main themes: business transfer, external development strategies for VSE/SMEs and collaborative innovation. Concerning business transfer, she has, over the last 20 years, published several articles in French and English-speaking journals on external takeovers, support for the buyer, team takeovers and takeovers by women.

Maripier TREMBLAY is a professor of entrepreneurship at Université Laval and the director of the chair of educational leadership on the entrepreneurial spirit development and entrepreneurship, and also scientific director of responsible entrepreneurship at Laval University.

Hedi YEZZA is Associate Professor of Family Business & Entrepreneurship at EDC Paris Business School (France). His current research focuses on family business, dynamics of business creation and social networks. He serves as editorial assistant of *Revue de l'Entrepreneuriat*, a highly ranked French journal of entrepreneurship.

Index

Page numbers in *italics* indicate figures and in **bold** indicate tables on the corresponding pages.

activation conditions in takeovers 184–188
active listening 188
anger 43, 45–47
assertiveness in women 237–238
avoidance-style coping 56, 66

basic emotions 43–44
BeT (Business Transfer and Entrepreneurship) 1–2
business transfers: defined 1–2, 11–12; emotions in 43; employee buyouts and 117–127; external 149–161, 251–262; historical issues around 8–10; integration of actors in 9–10; legitimacy of external buyers and 165–176; main actors in 14–15, 154, 157–159; mapping modes of 12–14, *13*; process of 14–16, *16*; research on 7–8; supporting buyers after 193–202; via workers' cooperatives 132–142; *see also* family succession
buyers: in employee buyouts 117–127; external 149–161, 251–262; external tutoring of 197–201, *198*, **201**; legitimacy of external 165–176; post-completion support for 193–202
buyouts *see* employee buyouts

case studies 74–81, *76*, 103–107, *104*
charismatic legitimacy 171–172
commitment by successors 73–74, 79–81

continuity, family 90–96
continuous accumulation of pressures 71
coping strategies for stress 55–56, **59–64**, 66
corporate social responsibility 9
creation of positive events 56

daughters *see* father-daughter relationships
Decision-making process 25–29; foundational framework for 28; implications for understanding entrepreneurial exit 29–32, *30*; revisited framework in 29, *30*; strategic 27–28; succession planning 42
disengagement phase in succession process 53–54, 63–64; announcement of 71
disgust 43, 45–47

emotions in family business succession 39–49; attentiveness to 47–48; basic emotions and 43–44; coping strategies for 55–56; disgust, anger and fear 45–47; empirical study of emotions and 43–47; implications of 48–49; joy, fear and sadness 44–45; literature on 40–43; stress and anxiety 54–55
employee buyouts 117–127; advantages and disadvantages of 125, **126**; disagreements between members and possible

break-ups of buyout teams in 124–125; facilitated transition from predecessor to employee(s) in 122–123; forms of 118–119, 119; motivations of predecessors and employees in 119–121; negotiating sale price and seeking financing in 121–122; strengths and disadvantages of employees in downstream part of 122–125; strengths and pitfalls of employees in the upstream part of 119–122; successful post-transfer management phase in 123–124; suggestions for further research on 125, 127

employees 2–3; emotions in business transfers and 42; *see also* employee buyouts; worker cooperatives

entrepreneurial exit 22–23; decision-making as new lens on 25–29; entrepreneur at heart of 24–25; implications of decision-making process for 29–32, 30; stewardship strategy for 23–24

entrepreneurs, making of 70–82; case study on 70–74, 72; socialisation and commitment in 73–74, 79–81; stages and transitions in business handover process and 71–73, 72; theoretical framework for 74–81, 76; as three-stage process 81–82; *see also* successors

entrepreneurship: business transfers as 8, 15–16, 16; decision-making process in 25–29; exit and entry 14–15

entry 7–11, 155; in business transfer process 15–16, 16, 179–180; control after 182–184; points of 14–15; preparation for 180–181

exit *see* entrepreneurial exit

exploration of alternatives 71

external business transfers 149–161; broad range of definitions in 155; determining the body of knowledge on 151–154, 152, 153; environmental issues in 159; female successors in 251–262; legitimacy of external buyers and 165–176; main actors in 154, 157–159; process of 157; research framework for 159, 160; research methods

on 153, 153–154, 156; scope and methodology for research on 150–151, 151; steps and challenges in process of 252–254, 254; supporting buyers after completion of 193–202; theoretical and perspective issues in 155–156

external problems and stress 58

external tutoring of buyers 197–201, 198, 201

facilitation conditions in takeovers 180–184

family: daughters as invisible heroes in 236–248; home of, as vector of socialisation 215; influence on family business transfer and women 211–218; as institution 209–211, 217; next-generation members in 229–230; as place of power 211; spouses' roles in 226–227; women's roles in and models of 224–225

family succession 23–24, 25; attributes of successful 54; daughters in 236–248; emotions in 39–49; female external successors in 251–262; gender and 222–233; making of entrepreneurs for 70–82; patriarchy and 229–230; phases of 53–54, 59–64; stages and transitions in 71–73, 72; strategic renewal (SR) and 99–111; stress and anxiety in 54–55; successoral teams in 230–232; women in 209–218

father-daughter relationships 236–248; case studies on 239–240, 240; challenges of proximity and role confusion and 238–239; in family business succession 237–239; letting go to prepare the return in 241–242; study results on 240–244, 241; successful process of family business transfer in 244, 244–247, 246; transition from adult-adult to transmitter-successor relationship 243–244; transition to adult-adult relationship 242–243; unconscious preparation of daughter from childhood and 240–241, 241

fear 43, 44–47

female external successors 251–252; discussion and conclusions on 261–262; gender difficulties and support needs before signing of business transfer to 255–258, **256**; gender difficulties and support needs during post-transfer process and 258–260, **260**; steps and challenges in business transfer process with 252–254, **254**; *see also* women in family business
finance 121, 151, 195

gender: difficulties and support needs before signing of business transfer and 255–258, **256**; difficulties and supports needs during post-transfer phases and 258–260, **260**; of family business owners 227–229; legal and regulatory frameworks of family business and 222–224; spouses and 226–227; succession and 226–230; *see also* women in family business
governance *see* two-tier governance system

habitus 73
health outcomes with stress 55
heirs 3, 70–82; bringing out the right manager from 81–82; framework for understanding making of entrepreneurs from 70–74, **72**; theoretical framework on 74–81, **76**

identity construction, daughters' 237–238
implementation phase in succession process 53–54, **60–61**
incubation phase in succession process 53–54, **59**, 81
information-production behaviour 185–187
information-seeking behaviour 184–185
institutionalisation 214–216
institution(s) 79, 122, 156; family as 209–211, 217; legitimacy as 166; support 261
integration 3, 31; facilitation conditions for 180, 188, **190**; family house as vector of socialisation and 215; humility and 188; organisational socialisation and 179; organisational support for 183–184; progress interviews

on 186; of successors into family firm structure 102; vertical, of activities 108
internal business transfers 3; in employee buyouts 117–127; to worker cooperatives 132–142
International Co-operative Alliance (ICA) 133

joint management phase in succession process 53–54, **61–62**
joy 44–45

legitimacy 165–176; charismatic 171–172; daughters' 237–238; defining the concept of 165–166; by demonstrating relational skills 173–174; by displaying professional skills 174–175; of the external buyer 168–175, **169**; as form of power 165–168, *167*; importance of 166–168, *167*; managerial exemplarity and 172–173; necessary qualities to gain 172–175; rational-legal 170–171; suggestions for future research on 175–176, *176*; technical 174–175; through developing the company 173; traditional 169–170

making of entrepreneurs *see* entrepreneurs, making of
management buyout (MBO) 122
managerial exemplarity 172–173
mapping of business transfer modes 12–14, *13*
marriage 214–215

neo-institutionalist sociology (NIS): in approach to family business transfer and women 211–218; in approach to family institution 209–211
networks 9

patriarchal social system in family business 229–230
positive reappraisal 56
post-business transfer stage 193–202; external tutoring of buyers in 197–201, *198*, **201**; gender difficulties and support needs during 258–260, **260**; pitfalls of *194*, 194–197, **197**
power: family as place of 211; legitimacy as form of 165–168, *167*

pressures, continuous accumulation of 71
problem-focused coping 56, 66
process: business handover 71–73, 72; business transfer as 1–3; decision-making 25–29; disengagement phase in succession 53–54, 63–64, 71; implementation phase in succession 53–54, 60–61; incubation phase in succession 53–54, 59, 81; joint management phase in succession 53–54, 61–62; steps in business transfer 14–16, 16; strategic decision-making 27–28

rational-legal legitimacy 170–171
relational skills 173–174

sadness 44–45
Scop *see* worker cooperatives
selection and choosing stage 82
self-assertion, daughters' 237–238
sellers 120–121, 142, 253; ambivalence of 190, 199; communication by 181–183, 252; motivation of 157–158
shareholder theories of governance 85–87
social capital 9
socialisation 73–74, 79–81; commitment as product of 74; family house as vector of 215; gendered 229–230; in takeover situations 179–190
social representation 9
socio-emotional wealth 42
spouses 226–227
stakeholders 14–15
stewardship exit strategy 23–24
strategic decision-making process 27–28
strategic orientation 9
strategic renewal (SR) 99–111; conceptual overview of 100–102; implications of 108–110, 109; literature review on 99–102; longitudinal case study on 102–103; research methods on 102–107, 104; research results on 107–108; succession and 102
stress of family business transfer 52–67; coping mechanisms for 55–56, 59–64, 66; four main categories of 58; and main stressors linked to business family 65;

research findings on 58; research method on 56–57, 57; theoretical framework for studying 53–56
succession process: attributes of successful 54; coping strategies for 55–56, 59–64, 66; gender and 222–233; making of entrepreneurs and 70–82; phases of 53–54, 59–64; stages and transitions in 71–73, 72; strategic renewal (SR) and 102; as stressful and anxious 54–55, 58; as three-stage process 81–82; two-tier system for 90–96
successoral teams 230–232
successors: attitudes towards existing staff 187–188; commitment by 73–74; communication with 181–182; daughters as 236–248; in employee buyouts 117–127; external tutoring of 197–201, 198, 201; female external 251–262; main stressors linked to business family and 65; selection of 73; socialisation of 73–74, 79–81; stages in selection of 71–73, 72; in takeovers 179–190; way of working of 58; worker cooperatives as 132–142; *see also* entrepreneurs, making of
support: of buyers after business transfers 193–202; gender difficulties and needs for, before signing of business transfer 255–258, 256; gender difficulties and needs for, during post-transfer process and 258–260, 260; institution 261; for integration, organisational 183–184
surprise 44
sustainability, succession 90–96
symbolic patricide 245

takeovers 10, 179–190; conditions for successful integration in 188–190, 189–190; individual socialisation tactics in 184–188; organisational socialisation practices in 180–184
technical legitimacy 174–175
testing stage 81–82
Theory of Planned Behaviour 31
traditional legitimacy 169–170
transmission 10
transmission-takeover 10
trigger, succession 71

tutoring, external 197–201,
198, **201**
two-tier governance system
84–96; conclusions on 96;
contributions of shareholder
theories of governance to 85–87;
destabilising and triggering factors
in 92; explicit reasons and their
logics of association in 88, **88**;
exploratory methodology focused
on managerial experience in 87–90,
88, **90**; family, economic and
financial context of 91–92; focus
on performance and organisational
change in 91; focus on relationship
between performance and family
continuity in 91–96; governance
issues and interest of 92–96;
literature review on 85–87; origins
of 84; specificities of 85; study
of implicit reasons conducted by
seven case studies on 89–90, **90**;
succession sustainability and family
continuity with 90–96

women in family business: as daughters
236–248; as external successors
251–262; moving back and forth
between the visible and invisible in
212–213; persistence of inequality
in business transfers and 213–214;
roles of 211–218, 224–225; as
spouses 226–227; tensions between
duty of obedience and ability to go
beyond it and 216–218; transmission
of assets in institutionalism and
214–216; *see also* gender
worker cooperatives 132–142;
advantages of 141–142;
characteristics of transfers to
134–136; context and management
of transfers to 137–138; context and
specificities of 133–137; importance
of cooperative sector and 133–134;
motivation and involvement of
stakeholders in transfer to 138–140;
success factors and obstacles in
137–141; two components of
transfer process to 136–137

Printed in the United States
By Bookmasters